"The best guide I know for the inner work of mourning."
—Rabbi Zalman M. Schachter-Shalomi z"l

"Creates the potential for bringing Judaism to those in need, and if we are truly fortunate, it may bring those in need to Judaism."
—**Arnold R. Saltzman,** former CEO,
Mount Sinai Memorial Park and Mortuary, Los Angeles

When the Temple stood in the ancient city of Jerusalem, mourners walked through the gates and into the courtyard along a specially designated mourner's path.

As they walked, they came face to face with all the other members of the community, who greeted them with the ancestor of the blessing, "May God comfort you among the mourners of Zion and Jerusalem." In this way, the community embraced those suffering bereavement, yet allowed for unique experiences of grief.

In this new and expanded edition of a modern classic, Anne Brener brings us an innovative integration of Jewish tradition and modern professional resources. It gives spiritual insight and healing wisdom to those in our own time who mourn a death, to those who would help them, and to those who face a loss of any kind.

"As a rabbi who must deal on a daily basis with aspects of mourning, there are few books that I can turn to for guidance, let alone suggest to be read by those I am comforting.... I am unaware of a book that is as helpful or as complete.... Bridges the gap between Judaism and psychology.... Underscores the wisdom of the Jewish tradition and its understanding of the process of healing."
—**Rabbi Arthur Gross Schaefer**

"A splendid resource for readers of any philosophical persuasion."
—*The Millennium Whole Earth Catalog*

Other Grief Resources

When a Grandparent Dies
A Kid's Own Remembering Workbook for Dealing with Shiva and the Year Beyond
By Nechama Liss-Levinson, PhD
Offers children guided exercises to express their grief.

8 x 10, 48 pp, 2-color text, Hardcover
ISBN: 978-1-879045-44-6 $15.95

Grief in Our Seasons
A Mourner's Kaddish Companion
By Rabbi Kerry M. Olitzky
Offers strength from the Jewish tradition for the first year of mourning.

4½ x 6½, 448 pp, Quality PB Original
ISBN: 978-1-879045-55-2 $15.95

Rabbi Anne Brener, LCSW, is a psychotherapist, spiritual director, and frequent "scholar-in—residence" across the United States and internationally. Her work focuses particularly on the issues of grief, mourning, spirituality and healing, She works with congregations to help create caring communities, lectures on the therapeutic impact of Jewish ritual and practice, and leads workshops that explore the connection between spirituality and psychology. In her private psychotherapy and spiritual direction practice, she works with both individuals and groups. A founder of one of California's first shelters for victims of Domestic Violence, she has worked as a Hospice Chaplain and co-founded a training program for Jewish Spiritual Directors. Currently, she is Professor of Ritual and Spiritual Development at the Academy for Jewish Religion, California.

Anne's work is enriched by her own experiences with loss and personal growth, her belief in the healing power of ritual, and her professional skills in psychotherapy, communications, and community organization. Ordained a rabbi in 2008 by Hebrew Union College–Jewish Institute of Religion, Los Angeles, she holds graduate degrees in the fields of Communications, Social Work, Jewish Communal Service, and Hebrew Letters. Anne grew up in New Orleans and currently lives in Los Angeles.

About the Contributors

Rabbi William Cutter, PhD, is founding director of the Kalsman Institute on Judaism and Health and the Steinberg Professor of Human Relations at Hebrew Union College–Jewish Institute of Religion. He is editor of *Healing and the Jewish Imagination: Spiritual and Practical Perspectives on Judaism and Health* (Jewish Lights). He has published and lectured widely on health and healing.

Rabbi Jack Riemer is the coeditor of *So That Your Values Live On: Ethical Wills and How to Prepare Them* (Jewish Lights) and the editor of *Jewish Reflections on Death*.

Testimonials

"I gobbled this up and feel breathless! My experience has been named and connected to the texts of our tradition!"—**Debra Linesch, PhD,** Chair, Graduate Department of Marital and Family Therapy, Loyola Marymount University, Los Angeles

"It is a magnificent work and a masterful contribution to all spiritual understanding, not just to mourning and loss but to living. And personally it has been a beautiful exposure to Judaism—a secondary gain or unintended gain perhaps, but not one to be taken lightly."—**Tracey Ellis**

"[We] found your addendum profound and beautiful (whether Jewish or not). It takes the reader on a journey of sacred holiness with grace. You looked deeply at the template of grief in a radically new way to rediscover one's lost humanity at a time of mourning. And as for me, with tears of gratitude I pray I will circle to the left and now enjoy the awe of those Yehudah moments. You bring holiness and love into my world. With tears of gratitude."—**Evelyn Mandel**

For People of All Faiths, All Backgrounds
JEWISH LIGHTS Publishing

An imprint of Turner Publishing Company
Nashville, Tennessee
Tel: (615) 255-2665 Fax: (615) 255-5081

www.jewishlights.com
www.turnerpublishing.com
Find us on Facebook
Facebook is a registered trademark of Facebook, Inc.

MOURNING
& Mitzvah

Other Grief Resources from Jewish Lights

Grief in Our Seasons:
A Mourner's Kaddish Companion
(By Rabbi Kerry M. Olitzky)

Tears of Sorrow, Seeds of Hope, 2nd Ed.:
A Jewish Spiritual Companion for Infertility & Pregnancy Loss
(By Rabbi Nina Beth Cardin)

A Time to Mourn, a Time to Comfort, 2nd Ed.:
A Guide to Jewish Bereavement
(By Dr. Ron Wolfson)

When a Grandparent Dies:
A Kid's Own Remembering Workbook
for Dealing with Shiva and the Year Beyond
(By Nechama Liss-Levinson, PhD)

Guidelines for Using this Book

This book creates a contemporary mourning path which is rooted in ancient traditions. It does this through creative interpretation of the Jewish mourning rituals and practices. Some of these are literal readings of Jewish Law and some are interpretations which use an ancient concept as an opening to address the needs of today's mourners.

For whom is this book written?

If you are facing a profound transition in your personal life, I hope you will find comfort here. The book melds the commandments regarding the dying person, burial procedures, and mourning with psychotherapeutic exercises to help you forge a path toward consolation and personal growth. As you will see, this understanding of the commonality of emotions in those experiencing different kinds of losses has an ancient precedent.

Although the book is written from the perspective of those who are grieving after the death of a loved one, its principles apply to anyone facing a loss of any kind which has caused major disruption in his or her life. These may include divorce, deterioration of health, or moving to another city.

When should I use this book?

While this book is divided according to the time-line for mourning delineated by Jewish tradition, you needn't assume that the book or any section of it must be used at any specific time. You are welcome to explore the exercises in the book as you go through the period they describe, but it is more likely that you will use the book to reflect on your experiences afterward. Some people have found the material useful in healing themselves and their relationships before the death occurred. Others found it helpful decades later.

Go at your own pace, in the order that works for you.

The many questions and exercises that form the journal selections of this book address the various phases, moods, and needs common to mourning. But each person's experience, pace, and needs are different. The exercises and questions are yours to use—or not use—in the way that will be most helpful to you. I encourage you to go at your own pace and to pick and choose among the exercises, skipping around to find the order and the issues that are personally relevant. The book is laid out to make it accessible even to those whose attention span may be short as a consequence of their grief.

Write as much or as little as you wish.

You can write responses to the text's questions and exercises in the wide, white spaces of the book's margins. I encourage you not to be limited or intimidated by the amount of space allotted for any one of them. You may want to add many extra pages for one or write one word (or none at all) for another. Again, it is your healing process and the choice is yours.

The exercises and questions are designed to help you find your true feelings.

Don't worry about getting "right" answers. The questions asked in this book are designed to trigger emotional responses and stimulate a process of change which takes place unconsciously as well as consciously. Because of this there are no fixed "right" answers. In fact your answer to any one question is likely to always be in flux. I suggest that you read each question carefully and then take a deep breath and begin writing whatever comes into your mind—whether or not it is a direct answer to the question posed.

Prior familiarity with Judaism or the Hebrew language is not necessary.

While the book uses Jewish concepts and practices to organize the healing process, it does not assume a ritually "observant" or knowledgeable reader. This material has been useful to those unfamiliar with Jewish practice, including non-Jews, as well as to rabbis and other Jewish scholars. In the process of reading the book, you will be introduced to many elements of Jewish thought, which will be explored as tools of healing. Among the tools are the notes in the margins of the book. Some are quotations drawn from classical Jewish sources, including the Bible and its commentaries: the Talmud, the Midrash, the Zohar, and commentaries on them by ancient and modern teachers. I have also used quotes from my own journal, written as part of my healing process; these are indicated by the notation "Journal Entry," followed by the place and date of my writing. In addition you will find a sprinkling of inserts which begin with groupings of three Hebrew letters. These are the roots or *shorashim* of significant Hebrew words which are used in the text. Most Hebrew words are built upon these three-letter roots. Exploring a word's root and the other words which share the same three-letter source opens a window on the word's meaning and is a link to the evolution of Jewish thought and history.

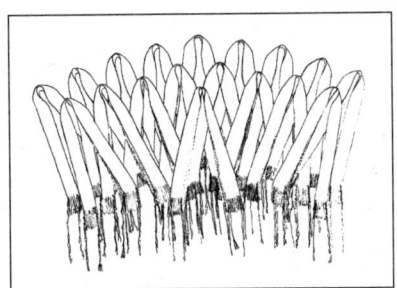

MOURNING & Mitzvah

25th Anniversary Edition

**A Guided Journal
for Walking the Mourner's Path
Through Grief to Healing**

• *with over 75 guided exercises* •

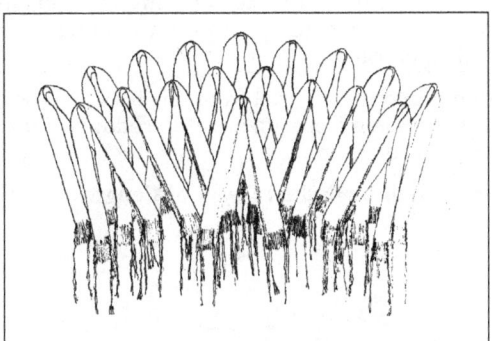

Rabbi Anne Brener, LCSW

For People of All Faiths, All Backgrounds

JEWISH LIGHTS Publishing

Nashville, Tennessee

Jewish Lights Publishing
an imprint of Turner Publishing Company
Nashville, Tennessee
New York, New York

www.jewishlights.com
www.turnerpublishing.com

Mourning & Mitzvah, 25th Anniversary Edition:
A Guided Journal for Walking the Mourner's Path through Grief to Healing

© 2017, 2001 and 1993 by Anne Brener

All rights reserved. No part of this book may be reproduced or transmitted in any form or by any means, electronic or mechanical, including photocopying, recording, or by any information storage and retrieval system, without permission in writing from the publisher.

For information regarding permission to reprint material from this book, please mail or fax your request in writing to Jewish Lights Publishing, Permission Department, at the address / fax number listed below, or email your request to submissions@turnerpublishing.com.

Cataloging-in-Publication Data available through the Library of Congress

Twenty-fifth anniversary edition

10 9 8 7 6 5 4 3 2 1

Cover design: Tim Holtz

Cover photo: *Ner Adonai nishmat Adam.* The human soul is the lamp of God.

Author photo: Andy Romanoff

Translation for the *Viddui*: Yaffa Weisman. Translation for the Kaddish: © 1991 Excelsior Computer Services. Other translations: © 1993 Excelsior Computer Services. Used with permission. The transliterations of the Hebrew do not attempt to preserve the Hebrew orthography. Instead Excelsior has used the English that is easiest to read.

Manufactured in the United States of America

לזכור
to remember

My mother, Eleanor "Honey" Brener (1923–71),
who gave me the gifts I needed

My sister, Jan Leslie Brener (1953–71),
that her name will live on

לכבד
to honor

My father, Mike Brener (1909–1995), who taught me
that generosity and humor are the source of healing

לחגוג
to celebrate

My daughter, Jen Tharler 1986-

My inspiration. My reason.

Contents

    iii **Guidelines**
    xv **List of Exercises**
    xix **Preface to the Twenty-fifth Anniversary Edition**
    xxiii **Kaddish de'Rabbanan:** *In Appreciation*
    xxvii **Foreword** by Rabbi Jack Riemer
    xxxi **Introduction to the Second Edition**
    xxxv **Introduction** by Rabbi William Cutter
    1 **Preface:** *My Time to Mourn; My Time to Dance*
    7 **Timeline:** *The Major Phases of the Jewish Year of Mourning*

Part I: Tzimtzum *Contraction*

The Jewish mystics described the creation of the world as having three parts. The first part is an act of Tzimtzum or Contraction. Recognizing that human creation is overwhelmed and blinded by the brightness of the Divine Light, the Divine Energy withdraws. This creates a darkness in which an as yet unknown creative process can emerge.

Mourning also begins with a contraction. It leaves one in a darkness whose value may seem unfathomable. In Part I of this book, we withdraw to examine the needs of mourning, your memories connected with death, and your resources for healing. This reflective process is created to help calm the overwhelming feelings that accompany mourning and is the foundation for the grief-work that follows.

  10 1 Avelut *(Mourning): The Mourner's Path*

  20 2 Hesped *(Eulogy) and Truthtelling: Mourning as a Process*

  32 3 Mekom Hanekhama: *Finding a Place of Comfort*

- 42 4 B'tzelim Elohim *(In God's Image):*
  Before Covering the Mirror

- 58 5 *The* Shekhinah *(God's Presence) at the Bedside:*
  Remembering the Illness and the Death

- 72 6 Aninut *(from Death to Burial):*
  Suspended between Two Worlds

- 86 7 Shiva *(First Seven Days of Mourning):*
  A Community Embrace

- 113 8 Sheloshim *(The Thirty Days Following the Burial):*
  Finding Your Footing in a Changed World

Part II Shevirat Kelim *The Breaking of Vessels*

The second phase of the creation process is Shevirat Kelim. *Here the vessels from which the Divine Energy has withdrawn break apart, shattering the world and hiding its holiness. In this section we confront the broken and uncontained feelings of mourning and face the most intense grief-work.* Avodah, *the Hebrew word for "work," was also the name for the sacraficial service performed by the High Priest in the ancient Temple in Jerusalem. It is also the name for the* Yom Kippur *service commemorating those Temple practices. I hope this connection will encourage you to embrace your grief-work as a holy journey.*

- 120 9 Keriah *(Tearing of Cloth After Hearing News of the Death) and Deep Feelings: Rending the Garment to Expose the Heart*

- 146 10 Keriah *and* Kaddish *(The Mourners' Prayer):*
  Keeping the Conversation Going to Heal the Hurt

- 164 11 Keriah *and* Prayer:
  Speaking Out from the Distress of Your Soul

Contents xiii

Part III Tikkun *Healing*

The final phase of the creation process, as seen by the Jewish mystics, is Tikkun or Healing. Here the holy sparks which were inaccessible during earlier phases are redeemed, reorganization takes place, and what was damaged is restored. In this section we will attend to your own healing by creating vessels to transform your loss into a living memorial and address your ongoing healing process.

186 12 *Immortality in* Olam Hazeh:
    Living On in the World of the Living

202 13 *Olam Haneshamot: Immortality in the Next World:
    A Walk through the World of Souls*

216 14 *Matzevah (Monument or Tombstone): The Unveiling:
    Raising the Curtain on the Rest of Your Life*

226 15 *Yizkor (Memorial Prayer),* Yahrzeit *(Anniversary of the Death), and the Cycle of Seasons*

254 16 *Shalom: Hello, Goodbye, and Peace*

260 17 *Those Who Say "Amen":
    How to Comfort the Bereaved*

273 *Epilogue: The New Mourner's Path—Navigating the Wilderness of Grief*

301 **Source Acknowledgments**

304 **Glossary**

309 **Books to Consult for Further Help**

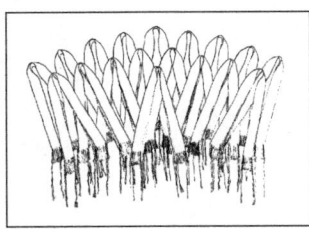

List of Exercises

Part I: Tzimzum *Contraction*

2 Hesped (*Eulogy*) *and Truthtelling: Mourning as a Process*
    Exercise 2·1   Beginning the Process: Creating Your Place of Comfort

3 Mekom Hanekhama: *Finding a Place of Comfort*
    Exercise 3·1   Hazkarat Haneshamot: Naming the Soul of the Person You Mourn
    Exercise 3·2   How Do You Feel about Changing Your Life?

4 B'tzelim Elohim (*In God's Image*): *Before Covering the Mirror*
    Exercise 4·1   Looking in the Mirror: A Commitment to Your Own Healing
    Exercise 4·2   How Do Mourners Behave?
    Exercise 4·3   How Did Those Close to You Deal with Intense Feelings?
    Exercise 4·4   *Shabbat* in the Midst of Mourning
    Exercise 4·5   The Major Deaths
    Exercise 4·6   Your Current Support System
    Exercise 4·7   Who Disappointed You?
    Exercise 4·8   A Last Look in The Mirror

5 *The* Shekhinah (*God's Presence*) *at the Bedside: Remembering the Illness and the Death*
    Exercise 5·1   Telling the Story
    Exercise 5·2   The *Viddui* (The Last Confession)
            Part 1 Life Review: The Sacred Trust
            Part 2 Concern with Relationships
            Part 3 Turning Toward God
    Exercise 5·3   Contemplating the Flickering Soul

6 Aninut (*from Death to Burial*): *Suspended between Two Worlds*
    Exercise 6·1   *Tahara* (Purification) and Forgiveness
            Part 1 Readiness for Forgiveness
            Part 2 Asking for Forgiveness—Past and Future
    Exercise 6·2   Create Your Own *Shemira* (Guardian) Liturgy
    Exercise 6·3   The Departing Soul as *Shaliakh* (Messenger)
    Exercise 6·4   The *Hesped* or Eulogy
            Part 1 Remembering What Was Said
            Part 2 A Private *Hesped*—What Should Have Been/Could Not Be Said
    Exercise 6·5   A Wish for the Soul

7 Shiva (*First Seven Days of Mourning*): *A Community Embrace*
    Exercise 7·1 What Disguises Do You Wear?
    Exercise 7·2 Meeting Your *Mekom Hanekama* (Place of Comfort)
        Part 1 Candle Meditation
        Part 2 What Obstructs Your Silence
    Exercise 7·3 What Kind of Contact Did You Get and What Would You Have Liked?
    Exercise 7·4 New, Renewed, or Severed Relationships That Are a Legacy of Death
    Exercise 7·5 Laughter in the House of Mourning
    Exercise 7·6 Setting the Table
    Exercise 7·7 How Do You Use Involvement?
    Exercise 7·8 When Did Reality Set In?

8 Sheloshim (*The Thirty Days Following the Burial)*: Finding Your Footing in a Changed World
    Exercise 8·1 Reentry Experiences
    Exercise 8·2 Your Continued Care
    Exercise 8·3 Writing Your End-of-Sheloshim Ritual

Part II Shevirat Kelim *The Breaking of Vessels*

9 Keriah (*Tearing of Cloth After Hearing News of the Death*) *and Deep Feelings: Rending the Garment to Expose the Heart*
    Exercise 9·1 Rending the Garment to Expose the Heart
    Exercise 9·2 Evaluating Your Depression
    Exercise 8·3 Nourishing Yourself in the Midst of Anxiety
    Exercise 9·4 Getting Things Done
    Exercise 9·5 The Soul-Breath: Focusing Your Feelings
    Exercise 9·6 Letters to the Living
        Part 1 Speaking Your Mind
        Part 2 Response
        Part 3 Last Word
    Exercise 9·7 "If Only" Statements
        Part 1 Regrets
        Part 2 Forgiveness or Sadness
    Exercise 9·8 Uncovering Your Own Shame
    Exercise 9·9 Cleansing Yourself of *Tumah* (Impurity)

10 Keriah and Kaddish (*The Mourners' Prayer*): *Keeping the Conversation Going to Heal the Hurt*
    Exercise 10·1 Moving Into the Gray Area
    Exercise 10·2 Letter to the Deceased
    Exercise 10·3 A Visitation
    Exercise 10·4 Invoking a Dream

11 Keriah and Prayer: *Speaking Out from the Distress of Your Soul*
    Exercise 11·1 Believer, Agnostic, Atheist, or…?
    Exercise 11·2 Sacrifice: Connecting with What Does Not Die
    Exercise 11·3 Crying Out in the Distress of Your Soul
    Exercise 11·4 Sound and Motion
    Exercise 11·5 Learning How to Pray
    Exercise 11·6 The Yearning to Be Healed
            Part 1 Reaching Out for Healing
            Part 2 Healing Reaches Out
            Part 3 Wholeness and Healing

Part III Tikkun *Healing*

12 Immortality in *Olam Hazeh*: *Living On in the World of the Living*
    Exercise 12·1 Biological and Physical Immortality
    Exercise 12·2 The Immortality of Influence
    Exercise 12·3 Counting Mitzvot
    Exercise 12·4 Writing an Ethical Journal
    Exercise 12·5 A Joint Ethical Will
    Exercise 12·6 Finding Your Deed: The Obligations without Measure

13 Olam Haneshamot *Immortality in the Next World: A Walk through the World of Souls*
    Exercise 13·1 The Soul Is "Gathered Into [Its] Ancestors"
    Exercise 13·2 The Pangs of the Grave
    Exercise 13·3 The *Kaf Hakela* (Catapult): Shaking Free of Dust
    Exercise 12·4 A Swim in the River of Light
    Exercise 12·5 The Purification of *Gehinnom* (Hell)
    Exercise 13·6 "The Righteous in Prayer"
    Exercise 13·7 Acknowledging the *Ibbur* (Impregnating Spirit)
    Exercise 12·8 Encountering the *Dybbuk* (Demon)
    Exercise 13·9 *Gilgul* (Reincarnation)

14 Matzevah (*Monument or Tombstone*): *The Unveiling: Raising the Curtain on the Rest of Your Life*
  Exercise 14·1 Making an Oath
  Exercise 14·2 Connecting with the Eternal
  Exercise 14·3 Contrasting the Funeral and the Unveiling
  Exercise 14·4 The Epitaph
  Exercise 14·5 Where are You Now?
  Exercise 14·6 Compassion for the Power that Runs the Universe
  Exercise 14·7 Making a Stand
  Exercise 14·8 Leaving a Pebble at the Grave

15 Yizkor (*Memorial Prayer*), Yahrzeit (*Anniversary of the Death*), *and the Cycle of Seasons*
  Exercise 15·1 Annulling Your Vow
  Exercise 15·2 Dealing with Regrets: "Averting the Severe Decree"
  Exercise 15·3 *Viddui* from the World of Souls
  Exercise 15·4 Resistance to Moving On
  Exercise 15·5 The Tears of Winter
  Exercise 15·6 Of Mourners' Bondage
  Exercise 15·7 Passing Through Egypt: A Guided Relaxation
  Exercise 15·8 The Four Children
  Exercise 15·9 Inflation and *Hummutz*
  Exercise 15·10 Questions in the Key of Passover
  Exercise 15·11 Retelling the Story
  Exercise 15·12 The Teachings of Your Relationship
  Exercise 15·13 Acts of Thanksgiving
  Exercise 15·14 First Fruits: The Thanksgiving Offering
  Exercise 15·15 Seven Praises
  Exercise 15·16 Affirming the Harvest—The Torah of What Is Gone
  Exercise 15·17 Acts of Thanksgiving

  Exercise 15·1 Dealing with Regrets: "Averting the Severe Decree"
  Exercise 15·2 The Tears of Winter
  Exercise 15·3 A Mourner's Bondage
  Exercise 15·4 Affirming the Harvest
      Part 1 The Teachings of Your Relationship
      Part 2 Acts of Thanksgiving

Preface to the Twenty-fifth Anniversary Edition

What an honor to be writing the preface to a twenty-fifth anniversary edition of *Mourning & Mitzvah* and to share my reflections on grief and healing as they have evolved since the last iteration of the book! *Mourning & Mitzvah* began almost thirty years ago with journal entries, written following the losses of my mother and sister. That my words resonated beyond my own needs for healing has been gratifying beyond belief.

That these gleanings of my own difficult journey have brought comfort to others speaks of the nature of healing, as understood by the Jewish mystics who described the transformative journey from what they called *Mochin de Katnut*, the contracted mind of narrow vision, to *Mochin de Gadlut*, the expanded mind, which is capable of seeing a much bigger picture. When we suffer, it is natural and necessary to focus on ourselves. In this state of *katnut*, we view our challenge from the narrow perspective of our own experience. This makes sense. When life kicks us in the stomach, we put our hands on our belly and wonder, "Why me?"

When I initially made the choice to address my personal grief, I remember wondering if my intense focus on myself was selfish in a world so filled with need. I came to see my individual focus become a gateway to something that reached beyond myself.

After we do the very necessary and individual work of bereavement, as I hope you will find outlined in this book, we discover that despite the uniqueness of each individual existential confrontation, our challenge is also a face of the human condition. In the state of *Mochin de Gadlut*, our necessary self-absorption in personal grief-work is loosened. We begin to feel a connection with others who have been similarly challenged. We learn to view our experience through a broader lens that takes into account all of humanity. This connection is also healing. I share this as a way of encouraging you to dive into your personal challenges, knowing that this journey will lead you to a more panoramic and generous embrace of life. I have come to believe that it is through our grief-work that we learn compassion, and that perhaps if we were to grieve fully our world would see a lot more kindness and a lot less war.

Re-reading *Mourning & Mitzvah* all these years later, I am grateful to reflect on changes in the culture since its initial publication. When I first wrote, there was a sense of stigma surrounding the subject of death. People rarely spoke about it. In truth, I was somewhat embarrassed to be writing about the journey through loss in a culture that denied death. Today, while we still face some of the consequences of denial, conversations about death are much more common. People are encouraged to address their finitude. They fill out advance directives, write ethical wills, participate in cyber-Shiva *minyanim*, and even attend "Death Cafes," where they share their experiences with loss and their fears about their own inevitable vulnerability and end of life, as well as their view on life after death. Grief is less often labeled as pathology and more often seen as an appropriate response to loss. I am heartened by this transformation. Most importantly, as we take grief seriously, we begin to look at trauma more appropriately. We address the needs of those who suffer in a more compassionate way. I am thinking in particular of our veterans who have so much to teach us about the horrors they have faced, if only we can create places in which their stories can be processed.

Another change that has taken place since *Mourning & Mitzvah*'s initial publication is in our attitude toward spirituality. As I admit, in the original chapter on prayer, the word "God" was not one always spoken comfortably at that time and the phrase "spiritual journey" was often dismissed as "new agey." Today, I believe that a new paradigm is emerging in which people are less wedded to purely material or psychological understandings of the self. As people practice meditation, explore their dreams, and speculate about the afterlife, there is greater comfort in embracing a broader definition of the self than one that is bounded by the contours of our bodies and individual psyches. This leads to a greater reverence for mystery and an increased willingness to explore the unknown places to which grief-work directs us, as well as the mysterious place from which healing emerges.

With the above sea change comes a broader definition that sees grief-work not just as a psychological journey, but also as a spiritual one. This recognition comes as we realize that when there is loss, not only do we mourn the loss of an individual, we also must mourn our shattered assumptions about the forces at the core of the universe whether or not we would name them "God." This knowledge opens a possibility of a much greater healing as we emerge from our personal struggle, having again found comfort in the world, ready to embrace others who walk this path that all humans walk. This is true whether or not we define that path in spiritual or secular terms. The epilogue, included in this new edition of *Mourning & Mitzvah*, charts grief's spiritual journey.

I want to thank Stuart Matlins and those who have midwifed much of this cultural transformation through their work at Jewish Lights Publishing and SkyLight Paths Publishing. I am grateful that they have stood with *Mourning & Mitzvah* all of these years, and continued to give me a place to let the book evolve as my understandings evolve. I am grateful as well to those at Jewish Lights' new home, Turner Publishing, for continuing to nurture this book. With this, I extend my hand in blessing to all of you as you walk this path yourself or attend to others who take this journey. In ancient words, which you will encounter in these pages, I say, *HaMakom Y'nechem*. May you find a Place of Comfort. And may you experience that place as Holy.

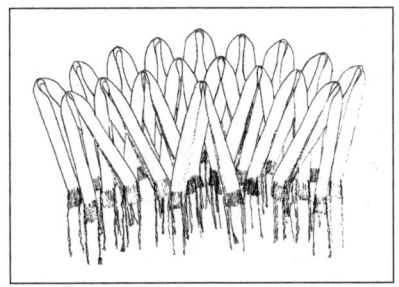

קדיש דרבנן

Kaddish de'Rabbanan

In Appreciation

The value of community is central to Judaism and certainly the belief that a mourner is sustained by a community is at the core of this work. Because of this I discovered that the deeper I went into my soul, the more company I was in. I have been blessed with a community rich with teachers who welcomed me as a friend. I will mention only a few of them. I am grateful for their scholarship and their generosity, which have helped to shape my understanding of the Jewish path of healing. I hope they will feel well represented in this work. However, in interpreting what they have taught me, I take full responsibility for any of my misunderstandings or misrepresentations.

Two women are on every page of this book. Deena Metzger taught me to listen to my voice and to write it down. Constance Corey (ז״ל) helped me to find my breath after my losses. She taught me to follow my feelings. And then I mourned her, too.

Reb Zalman Schachter-Shalomi, founder of the P'nai Or community, showed me the possibility of a Jewish path to healing. Reb Zalman is particularly felt in the chapter on the world of souls, which began in a workshop I took with him at Esalen Institute in the Winter of 1990. Rabbi Jonathan Omer-Man continually validates my experience of the spiritual journey of a Jewish soul.

Arthur Waskow's *The Seasons of Our Joy,* with its rich interpretations of the Jewish holidays, contributes to my enjoyment of Judaism and has shaped my work on *Yizkor.*

His work with the Shalom Center carries on the most sacred of Jewish tasks: healing the world. I am grateful for his example.

Much of this book was written while I was enrolled in classes at the Los Angeles campus of Hebrew Union College–Jewish Institute of Religion, where I began to find the Hebrew words that helped me make sense of my journey. My gratitude to that institution and its faculty and staff is enormous. I particularly want to thank: Rabbis David Ellenson, Michael Signer, Bill Cutter, and Lee Bycel, and Jerry Bubis, Rivka Dori, Amit Schtai, Edie Truisk, and Harvey Horowitz. I want to thank Yaffa Weisman for her help in locating resources and in translating the Viddui, and Marianne Luijken Gevirtz, who has initiated me into the joys and the responsibilities of serious scholarship.

Writing on the subject of Jewish mourning is possible because of the work of Rabbi Maurice Lamm, author of the modern classic *The Jewish Way in Death and Mourning*. Rabbi Jack Riemer's *Jewish Reflections on Death* and *So That Your Values Live On: Ethical Wills and How to Prepare Them* have also done much to bring the wisdom of the Jewish mourning practices into the world. I thank Simcha Paull Rafael, author of the forthcoming *Jewish Views of the Afterlife*, who has generously shared his work on the world of souls.

The work of many Jewish feminist theologians, including Marcia Falk, Rachel Adler, Rabbi Sue Elwell, and Judith Plaskow, has enabled me to find a place for myself within Jewish tradition that feels authentic and has affirmed my experience of the Holy.

Rabbis Kerry Olitzky, Leila Gal Berner, and Miriam Shapero were invaluable in the editing process. Thank you also to Rosalie Cohen, Rabbi Levi Meir, Marcia Cohn Spiegel, Andy Rose, Susan Schwartz, Jack Roth, Joan Schain, Shirley Kahn, the staff of *Elat Chayim*, Smidar Orlans, Jeffrey DeKrow, Rama Weizmann, Rabbi Mitchell Chefitz, Ellen Frankl, the women of Bat Kol and Shabbat Shenit and my *davening chevra:* the Moveable Minyon of Los Angeles. Ruth Egger and Mark Epstein were always generous with their computer resources, and Anna Montenegro and Paulina Amperez Lopez did much to make my life easier during this period.

Much gratitude is due the many people in the many settings where I have led workshops on mourning, especially the Freda Mohr Center, the Los Angeles Jewish Feminist Center, Beth Chaym Chadashim, the National Havurah Institute and P'nai Or. In these settings and in my private practice I have been privileged to work with so many people

Kaddish de'Rabbanan: In Appreciation

willing to feel their losses and allow them to be their teacher. It is because of their courage that I can assert that healing is possible.

Thank you to Arthur Magida, my editor, who took the expansive book of my heart and shaped it into something that I hope will be meaningful to many, and to the Jewish Lights staff, particularly Rachel Kahn, Jay Rossier and Carol Gerstein, whose diligence and friendship have made finishing this book a delightful process. Special thanks go to my publisher, Stuart Matlins, for sharing my vision and managing always to point to the parts of the book that seemed to have the most heart. His sensitivity, kindness, and judgment have been extraordinary.

I'd like to thank Jon O'Neal and Rachel Shields of Turner Publishing for their generous support of this third edition, as well as Victoria Curea and Rodger Kamenetz, who have nurtured the archeology of my soul that has led to its new insights. Thank you also to Susan Wyler, Darcy Vebber and Debra Linesch who have persisted with me as this edition has evolved. And Jen, always Jen.

And now, the most important—I would like to say thank you to my family, who have made possible not only the writing of this book, but much of my healing. My father, Mike Brener, has been supportive in every way. He is a man of conviction and generosity and has sought healing through acts of *tzedakah*. His loving example has taught me a great deal and I never forget how fortunate I am to have him in my life.

My husband, Gary Tharler, is the real hero of this book. His humor and genuine kindness are central to my life. He provides balance and respite when the work is too consuming. His belief in my work and his joyous and responsible embrace of fatherhood have made this book possible. Our daughter, Jen-Gavriel Brener Tharler has often had to share me with my work. She has been helpful and respectful and has come up with suggestions that are wise beyond her years. Gary and Jen are my best teachers and my best friends.

My life is incredibly rich and my gratitude goes to The Source—The Place from which all healing comes—המקום

A.B. 1993

Foreword

This is not a book for thanatologists or any other kind of professional "ists." It is only for those who are mortal, and know it.

It is the work of a human being who has been through all of the anguish and heartache and confusions that are an inherent part of the mourning process and who wants to reach out a hand to those who are now experiencing what she has gone through. Anne Brener has paid her dues to life. She knows what it means to love and lose. But she has also learned how to begin over again, and in this book she shares some of her hard earned wisdom with you.

For me, one of the great proofs of the existence of God is the fact that somehow, from somewhere, some way, human beings have the ability to endure losses and to start over again. One of my favorite words of Torah is the one that I learned from Elie Wiesel. He once pointed out that in the Jewish tradition, Adam is known as "Adam Harishon—Adam the First." That is really not an achievement; he just happened to be the first person created. The real wonder of Adam and of Eve, said Elie Wiesel, is that they lost both of their children in one cruel blow—one became a victim and the other became a fugitive—and so these two parents had every right and every reason to be bitter, to withdraw into themselves, to be warped by their loss, but instead they began over again. Anyone can begin: our libidoes make us do that. But to love and lose and begin over again, that takes courage and resiliency and the help of God. And it is for this that we need to be grateful to those first two earthlings. They are the models for all those losers in the world, and who isn't at some time in his or her life a loser? They never got over the loss of their first two children. No parent who suffers such a loss ever does. But they got up off their knees and tried again, and for this we must all be grateful to them.

What Adam and Eve did after their loss, Noah did after his. Every friend, every street sign, everything he knew went down in the Great Flood. When he came out on dry land he planted a vineyard and got himself drunk and wallowed in his tent, hoping in this way to forget. And who can blame him? Who, after losing as much as he did, would have done differently? But eventually, his hangover wore off and Noah began again. And therefore the human race is here.

What Adam and Eve did, what Noah did, Jacob did too after the loss of his love: Rachel. Years later, he still spoke of the day that she died with so much pain, as if it had just taken place, and yet he somehow learned how to live at least a partial life without her. And what these people did, Aaron did too. The day that should have been the day of his greatest joy, the day when he was officially installed as the High Priest of Israel with pomp and pageantry and parade, turned into horror when his two sons suddenly dropped dead. There are all kinds of reasons for their sudden death to be found in the tradition, but to a parent, the reasons do not matter. All that counts is that his children are dead and his moment of greatest glory has turned to ashes. Moses tries to comfort his brother with some religious cliché about how God is strictest with those that are closest to God—and Aaron just looks at him, with bloodshot eyes, and says nothing. And the Bible, which does not waste a word, records that silence.

What were his choices? He could have blasphemed and that must have been a tempting option. But if he had, whom would he have hurt? And what would he have done for an encore? He could have gone on mouthing the words of the rituals as if nothing happened, but he knew that God is not so hard up as to need praises that we do not really feel. So what he did instead was keep silent. At a time when there were no words, Aaron kept still. He withdrew into himself and then, when he was able to come back, he did. I am sure that the service he offered to God after he returned was different in tone, in kind, in spirit, from the service that he had offered before he lived through the agony of loss. It was probably a deeper, more mature, wiser kind of service that he offered then, but the Bible records, for our sakes, that when there were no words, Aaron kept silent.

The Bible gives us more tales to absorb in the time of our loss such as the story of Job who gritted his teeth and demanded to know "why" and whom God ultimately preferred to all those glib defenders and protectors of the Divine reputation who tried to make Job believe that what he was going through must somehow be his fault, so that it would not be God's. Or the story of David who lived more, did more, sang more, succeeded more, than almost any other human being in history and yet went on wanting more; who understood, long before Dylan Thomas, that we should not go gently into the night. The Bible contains the story of how David fasted and prayed and entreated God for seven days and seven nights for the sake of his sick child and then, when the child died, arose and bathed and dressed and ate "because I will go to him and he will not come back to me."

And the Bible contains the story of Moses, whose end is the theme of the last chapter of *Divarim.* In the Biblical text it is such a brief and simple tale: only eight lines. But what the Sages of the Midrash do with these few lines! They make it into a saga in which Moses tries to pierce the gates of heaven, in which he uses every argument that he can think of to persuade God to change the decree, in which he bargains and cajoles and protests and then finally, when he has no other choice, accepts the decree, makes the rounds in order to ask for and to give forgiveness to his people, and then gives back his soul to the God who loaned it to him.

What marvelous tales these are, each one! And to go with them, superimposed upon them, the Tradition has provided a whole network of rules and regulations, laws and judgments, through which we can sanctify the end of life and with which we can come to terms with our own mortality and with the losses that are the inevitable price that comes with love.

And now Anne Brener has created this journal in which she helps the mourner of our time to walk the lonely road that no one can detour for long. She understands that ours is a culture that denies death in every way it can. Instead of cemeteries we now have "memorial gardens." Instead of ripping a garment, as our people used to do when they felt anger and repulsion and all the other mixed emotions that each person feels in the time of loss, we now have these tiny snippets of ribbons that no one really takes seriously. Instead of getting our hands dirty and shoveling earth and hearing rocks and pebbles fall upon the grave, so that the reality of what has happened sinks in, now we have uniformed workers who do the shoveling, only after the mourners have been safely led away so that they need not see the truth or feel the pain.

It is hard to work through one's grief when there are so many cover-ups and so many different kinds of denial at work within the culture. And that is why this book is of such importance. Anne Brener has crafted a walkway through the valley of the shadow of death. The walkway has thorns and bramble bushes on it but it leads to the other side, beyond grief, for those who are willing to stay the course.

Keep this book for time of need and do the grief-work in which it instructs us and you will see that this long and wise heritage of ours still has the power to speak, to heal and to comfort—even in our time.

Rabbi Jack Riemer
Beth Tikvah Congregation
Boca Raton, Florida

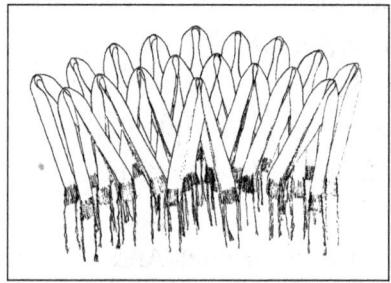

Introduction to the Second Edition

If you are holding this book you are either at a time in your life when you are most vulnerable or you are preparing to help people who are going through one of the most profoundly challenging periods of their lives. Either way, I extend my hand to offer comfort and support as you face these challenges.

If you are a mourner, about to read this book, I hold my hand out as someone who has walked the mourner's path in the past and knows both its difficulty and the fact that the journey does not need to last forever. In my mid-twenties, after my mother's suicide and my sister's death three months later in a car accident, I could not have imagined that I would be able to reach out to you to offer comfort. But as I hope the book will teach you, if you make a space to grieve, your relationship to your loss will change and you will not always have to mourn.

If you are not a mourner, I also reach out to you. I heartily encourage you to do the work of this book. It is a way of cultivating a relationship with the deep and rich nature of what it means to be human. It will make your life more meaningful. It will open your heart so that you will be able to live more fully. Doing this work will also make you a more credible and comforting comforter.

I am writing now almost a decade after I submitted *Mourning & Mitzvah* for publication. It is an uncanny experience to return to a snapshot of one's soul taken at a time of its most profound vulnerability. To prepare *Mourning & Mitzvah* for a second edition I chose to reread the well-worn copy that I have carried with me since the book's publication. The book is dog-eared, filled with jottings in the margins, and punctuated with sticky notes of all colors. These mark pages to be read out loud as I travel throughout North America,

Israel, and England, meeting with people suffering the challenges of loss and offering them the comfort of my words as a writer and a teacher. This copy is also filled with my own responses to the book's exercises as I worked my way through *Mourning & Mitzvah* two years after its publication when my father died, and I returned to the mourner's path.

In one of the book's early exercises, I ask readers to look back to previous losses in their lives to see what they might learn from them about their needs during times of great stress. This is because mourning can feel like a foreign country, and it helps to have a map.

I had a map when my father died in 1995. I did not have a map in 1971 when my mother and sister died. All three of the losses were excruciating. But healing was more accessible after my dad died, because I knew the territory. I had been there twenty years earlier, and I had taken notes. Those notes evolved into this book which describes my healing journey as I came of age while coming to terms with traumatic losses. *Mourning & Mitzvah*'s intention was to use what I had learned during that time to take mourners by the hand and help them navigate the world of mourning. When I wrote it, I did not expect that I would soon be forced to revisit that world. But when I did, it became my very own guide. Having a map made mourning a very different experience.

Having a map, I knew why I felt bad. I knew why it was hard to concentrate. I knew why my anger was sometimes out of control. These dark places had terrified me at age 24. Not having a map, I imagined each feeling as a black hole with gates that would slam shut once I was inside. Now I knew that each of these gates was an entrance to a place on the mourner's path where I would have to stop and pay attention. I had more confidence in the process. I knew I would pull through so thought I should take the time to learn what was inside of each of the holes. I hope this book will provide you with a map to make this journey less terrifying and allow you to surrender to the lessons that are part of the sea change of mourning.

In addition to creating a space for paying attention to your feelings and perceptions, I hope that *Mourning & Mitzvah* will also become a marker of your growth. As you look back to read or remember your responses, as I have done to write this introduction for the second edition, you will see that your feelings and you have changed. Evidence that change is possible, even in the most difficult situations, can give you the courage to grieve fully.

If you dare to grieve, if you use your grief to expand rather than to contract your world, your grief will make you a different person. Over and over in my workshops and in my sessions with individual clients, I see that the grief process is not about erasing pain.

It is about moving to another place so that your perspective on the loss, your life, and the nature of being human shifts in such a way that enables you to once again embrace life.

The person I am today would not write *Mourning & Mitzvah*. That in itself validates the message and process of the book. The insight and wisdom that I find in its pages are the insight and wisdom of one whose heart was broken and who wrote out of that pain and vulnerability. And in the writing what happened for me is what I hope will happen for you as you work your way through the book: the world shifted. I became a different woman than the woman who wrote the book. In paying close enough attention to my experiences and feelings to create the exercises that *Mourning & Mitzvah* offers you, my relationships with my deceased mother and sister, myself, God, other people, and the universe all changed. I wrote a new contract with life. I knew I would have to if I were to survive the trauma of those losses. This contract allowed me to acknowledge the losses while coming to see the world differently than I had before I became a mourner. I can think of no better affirmation for the process that the book describes than that.

Over the years since *Mourning & Mitzvah* was published, I have received countless words of gratitude. People tell me that what the book says is true. If you make a place for your grief, your grief will change. History won't change. What is lost will not return. You will still have times of yearning. But your world will get larger and there will be more possibility for healing, for growing, and for appreciating the awesome, broad and vast texture that is life.

One thing that I did not anticipate when I wrote *Mourning & Mitzvah* was how valid these rituals and exercises described in the book would be, not just in mourning a death, but also in making other transitions. So many people have told me of how they have been helped by the book after a divorce, serious illness, or other traumatic change. This reiterates the understanding that there are commonalities to the experience of loss. It enables us to draw on our previous experiences for help. As the book will tell you, this is ancient Jewish wisdom, known in the time of the Temple when a variety of people walked the mourner's path along with those who were mourning a death.

But the work of dueling with death and change, or confronting the constancy of change and loss in our lives, should not be limited to those catapulted into the work when catastrophe strikes their lives. All of us benefit from a world in which conversations about death, dying, and grieving are not hidden. The benefit of living in a world that is comfortable discussing death is that it becomes a world capable of embracing life.

As useful as this book has proven to be after a loss has occurred, I would love to see it used prophylactically before a loss occurs, as a tool for coming to terms with life's profound issues and deeper meanings. The exercises in this book can help to heal the relationship with the self, with the people in our lives, with God, with what it means to be human, and with the earth itself. These dialogues of purification can help to cleanse these relationships of the negativity of unfinished business. They can give us muscles for facing the inevitable challenges of loss and save us from the heartbreak of regret when loss does occur. When death is not a stranger, we open up to life. We cherish life and become more responsible to each other and to the planet. By breaking through the denial of death we are much more able to choose life. By making space for conversations about death we can overcome the fear of death. We also make it easier for those who grieve to be honest about their experience and thereby not be trapped in that experience with no hope of healing.

As a religion, Judaism encourages us to practice death. We do a version of the deathbed Shema every night. We go to sleep reciting a confession *(viddui)* and surrendering to sleep (which we are told is one-sixtieth of death) with the same words we are encouraged to say on our deathbed. We practice death on Yom Kippur when we don our burial shrouds, fast and recite another *viddui* in preparation for the atonement and symbolic rebirth of our souls. We practice death each time we cross a threshold and take the time to kiss a mezuzah or recite a Kaddish at a turning point in a prayer service.

There is a seeming paradox in a religion that impels us to choose life while encouraging us to cultivate a relationship with death. There is another paradox in the fact that this recognition of what is finite helps us to focus on the infinite. Perhaps the biggest paradox is that we can come again to love life even when we are mindful of death. Holding these apparent contradictions at once is a sign of wholeness—or healing—or shalom—words that have the same meaning linguistically. It helps us to love more courageously, to search in every moment for what is holy and eternal, to cherish each day and to cultivate life by caring for ourselves, each other, and the planet. Just as it brings personal healing, this relationship with death is a vehicle for bringing healing to the community and to the world. I hope your book becomes well worn and that in the process you learn the wisdom of walking the mourner's path.

Anne Brener

Introduction

I received a letter recently from a young man whose father had died some time before. I was reading Anne Brener's book at the time. The writer was surprised that he was still mourning after a year, and worried because he was having difficulty accepting his loss. "Was there a good book that could help him?" he asked. The book this young man needed was before me. But *Mourning & Mitzvah* is not just for him; people will use it in many different ways.

That is why I am pleased to have this opportunity to introduce *Mourning & Mitzvah*, and I want to say a few words about what it means to me, even though I know that every reader will assign a different value to it. Ms. Brener is an accomplished therapist, and a person of rich Jewish spirit. She has placed her technical accomplishments and her personal spirit in these pages. She knows as a professional that once we lose a loved one, there is no turning back. And she knows as a religious Jew that this harsh fact may be opportunity for fresh insight. One can take responsibility for new directions. And Anne Brener knows that Jewish rituals play a part in healing and return to richer life.

Mourning & Mitzvah draws on a wonderful range of sources. It draws on classical literature in the field of mourning study, like the work of Elisabeth Kübler-Ross, while reflecting the influence of classics of Jewish wisdom. In its pages the reader will find Bible, Talmud and the creations of medieval and modern sages. Its author mixes personal and professional anecdote in which the message may be delivered indirectly—with innocent innuendo, or with direct and sometimes hard-hitting advice that may surprise its readers. It is a book not embarrassed to express a point of view.

One of those "points of view" has to do with some of the clichés within our culture. Too often, our author frets, we hear terms like: "Be brave"; or "You'll get over it." She sees implied attitudes like the notion that love is unequivocal. She is particularly vivid in pointing out that mourners must experience their mourning fully, and let feelings surface. Public responses to the death of famous people often need to be turned on their head. Recalling an episode engraved in the mind of every adult over 40, she reminds us of Jacqueline Kennedy's legendary bravery at the time of President Kennedy's assassination. Ms. Brener is not afraid to say that this "brave behavior" may not be a helpful model for many people.

Readers will appreciate, also, the author's rich language—a language appropriate to the severity of its subject. The therapist in her urges mourners not to blame themselves for the deaths of loved ones; the writer in her refers to her freedom from an instance of that blame with the acknowledgement that her "mother was swallowed up by her *own darkness*."

Readers will be warmed by the light that encompasses them through this book of memory, personal exercise, and intelligent counsel. *Mourning & Mitzvah* may be read as a whole or its chapters may be seen as separate links in a larger chain of strenuous logic. One's reading may be heavy or light; but either way it will be a worthy workout.

One of the great joys of my life has been the opportunity to pay attention to the struggles of people in illness and mourning. My courses at the Hebrew Union College in chaplaincy have taught me far more than I have contributed. I have had the opportunity to edit a book, *The Jewish Mourner's Handbook* (Behrman House) on the strategies and requirements of mourning, and have enjoyed composing essays on aspects of visiting the sick. I work with the National Institute for Jewish Hospice in its encouraging people to accept the inevitable. This is a book I could not write, and wish I could. It is surely needed, and will be a welcome addition to the resources on which I depend in my continuing work.

Rabbi William Cutter
Hebrew Union College–Jewish Institute of Religion
Los Angeles, California

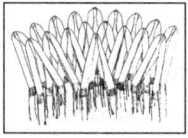

MOURNING
& Mitzvah

At the time when one should be joyous—
be joyous.
And when it is time to mourn—mourn.

— Midrash: Genesis Raba 27:7

עת לספוד ועת לרקוד

Preface

My Time to Mourn;
My Time to Dance

This book started with my own journey. It reflects my experience as a mourner, my work as a psychotherapist, and my struggles trying to live a spiritual life on a troubled planet.

While the book began with workshops in mourning that I led at Jewish Family Service of Los Angeles, the impulse to develop them this far has come from the many losses I had suffered while still in my early twenties. Among these were the suicide of my mother, followed three months later by a car accident which killed my nineteen-year-old sister—my only sibling.

These tragedies occurred in the early 1970s. Like many of my generation, I had been struggling to establish an identity during a time of great social upheaval. But few of my contemporaries were going through what I was. While many were coping with the Viet Nam war, mourning political leaders, and exploring new lifestyles, I was also suffering from the trauma of losing my mother and sister. I felt very much alone, and very lost.

I didn't have the Jewish mourning rituals to help me. I looked in horror at my father's cousin, who lovingly held out her arms to me and urged me to mourn, and I ran away. I left my hometown of New Orleans, deciding angrily that I was not going to spend my early adulthood mourning. I didn't even attend the unveiling of the tombstones seven months later.

I was in terror. And I didn't understand my feelings. Much of the time, I was alone and curled up in a ball. I wrote in my journal. I spoke to almost no one. I thought that I was damaged or that there was a curse on me. My friends certainly had no experience comparable to mine and were puzzled and impatient with my constantly changing moods and never-ending psychological pain. I did not know that my explosive, confusing, and all-consuming reactions were the natural—and, as I learned much later, predictable—corollaries of mourning.

If I had been able to concentrate long enough to read the books of Elizabeth Kübler-Ross and other psychologists who have studied death and mourning, I might have understood what I was going through.

For over a year, I kept very busy and tried to gather new experiences to put distance between myself and my history. I traveled with a backpack, a journal, and the expression of a child who had witnessed something horrible and incomprehensible. I put myself in challenging and risky situations, looking for a sign that I was really alive. I moved to a town where I knew no one. I hitchhiked. I took a raft trip through the Grand Canyon. When the cold water hit the back of my neck, I felt nothing.

A turning point came while I was swimming in the Umpqua River in southern Oregon. I got caught in the current. Struggling to cross the river, my energy ran out. I realized I was going to drown. I thought sadly of my beloved father, whose losses had already been so great. I took a deep breath and let the current carry me downstream.

This surrender to the swift current brought relaxation. When the river suddenly narrowed, I found the strength to swim to shore. What began with a deep breath of surrender had saved my life. It affirmed my instinct for survival.

ע.ב.ר **AVR:** to pass, cross over to the opposite side; past tense; to cross a river; pregnant; *Ivri*: a Hebrew

Months later, my breath brought more healing as I relaxed in a yoga class after achieving a new, strenuous position. With a full exhalation, I felt that veils were being pulled aside from deep places in my body, revealing connections I had never before felt to my pain, to my healing, and to those I had lost. I had the sense that my relationships with my mother and my sister had not ended with their death: that we remain connected in ways that transcended the physical. I had not really lost them. Sobbing uncontrollably, I spontaneously began chanting the *Shema* (Judaism's central prayer), lingering on the final word, *ekhad,* Hebrew for "one."

שמע, ישראל, יי אלהינו, יי אחד!
Shema Yisrael Adonai Elohenu Adonai Ekhad.
Listen Israel: Our God is One!

I soon learned that the Hebrew words for "breath" and for "soul" are related words, and that, in fact, Judaism teaches that life begins with breath: We are told

ק.ב.ל **KBL:** to receive, intuit, to be accepted, handed down; *Kabbala*: the Jewish mystical tradition

that upon our birth, God breathes our souls into our bodies. Because all things—living and dead—reflect the divine unity in the words of the *Shema,* holiness did not deny the pain I had been through. I began to feel that the separation I had felt from my mother and sister was not as absolute as I had previously believed. My body and my breath had intuitively understood the core of Jewish spirituality.

But my return to Judaism did not come with just two breaths. It was a full ten years before I found myself in a Jewish community again. In the meantime, I moved to rural Northern California. I grasped the implication of having been raised by a woman who had struggled with life since her own mother had died when she was two years old: my cells had not learned to be open to the spark of life. I set upon learning how to nurture myself. I began to run, to swim, to garden, to spend time in the wilderness, to write in my journal and to listen to my dreams.

Since that time, I have worked in many settings and with many different kinds of people. In Mendocino County, I worked with battered women and acting-out adolescents. In Los Angeles, I have worked with elderly Jews, incest survivors, widows, people who mourn parents and children and whose partners had died of AIDS or committed suicide.

From all these people and from my own pain, I have learned that one principle applies: *The only feelings that do not change are those that are ignored.* Only by facing our feelings do we learn and grow. Pain has a size and a shape, a beginning and an end. It takes over only when not allowed its voice.

I came to Los Angeles in 1981 to study at Hebrew Union College. I had the sense at the time, that the Jewish injunctions to choose life and to heal the world would give me a more profound understanding of the nature of healing.

That my search for healing has led me to the path of my ancestors speaks of the wisdom of the ancient Jewish mourning traditions. They can be as effective today as they were 2,000 years ago. I don't think you have to be ritually observant (or even Jewish) for the framework created by these rituals to help you heal. These rituals are embedded with universal truths about the needs of people in transition; they can be approached either for their psychological wisdom or as a spiritual guide and can be helpful whether or not one is part of a ritually observant community.

> While running I had a surge of energy and then it came to me: this is *not* a book about death. It is a book about living . . . about living a life that does not deny the fact that death exists. It is not a book that is obsessed with the dark side. It is a book that teaches how to treasure life in its fullness. (Journal Entry, Los Angeles, October 1988)

Whoever you are, I hope this book helps you, leading you to healing, growth, and a deeper understanding of Judaism as a rich and profound spiritual path. I hope it helps guide you through the sometimes frightening, but always interesting currents of your life, just as my own path led me safely through the currents of the Umpqua River.

The Major Phases of the Jewish Year of Mourning

THIS OUTLINE BEGINS our conversation on the Jewish Path of Healing and its understanding of the changing experience of grief. It is not intended as a rigid expectation for the timing of any individual's healing process nor as a comprehensive statement of all Jewish mourning practices. In fact, in today's society, where the concept of family extends to many different relationships, it is appropriate to say Kaddish for whomever one chooses for as long as mourning lasts.

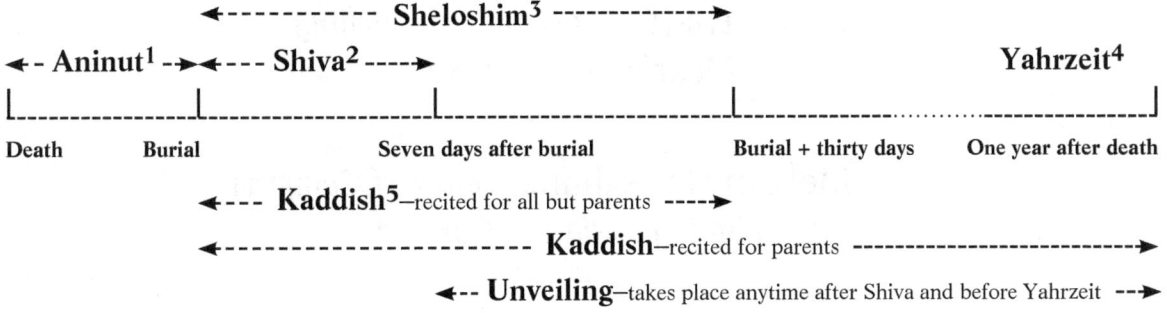

1. **Aninut**—The burial takes place as close as possible to the death, but not on Shabbat or on the High Holidays or on the festivals of Pesach, Shavuot, or Sukkot. This is the most restrictive period of mourning, during which mourners are exempt from performing many religious and social obligations. During this time the body is never left unattended. Members of the *Chevra Kadisha* prepare the body for burial and sit with it from the time of death until the funeral.

2. **Shiva**—The seven-day period following the burial is called shiva (seven). During this time, mourners remain at home and receive condolence calls from members of the community, who come to visit, pray, and provide food for at least the first meal after the funeral. The activities of mourners continue to be restricted. During prayer services, in the company of these visitors, the mourner recites Kaddish, the prayer said for the dead.

3. **Sheloshim**—The first thirty (*sheloshim*) days following the burial constitute the full mourning period for everyone but one's parents. Following the period of shiva, the mourner's actions are less restricted, although he or she generally avoids social events and does not cut hair or shave. The daily recitation of Kaddish takes place in the synagogue. The mourner continues to wear the back ribbon, given at the funeral, as a visible sign of mourning.

4. **Yahrzeit**—The anniversary of the death, according to the Jewish calendar. On this date, each year after the death, a candle is lit in memory of the deceased, Kaddish is recited and acts of *tzedaka* are performed in his or her memory.

5. **Kaddish**—This prayer is recited during prayer services for up to a year on behalf of parents, although it is generally recited for eleven months. For others it is recited for thirty days.

PART I

1   Avelut (Mourning):
The Mourner's Path

2   Hesped (Eulogy) and Truthtelling:
Mourning as a Process

3   Mekom Hanekhama (Place of Comfort):
Finding a Place of Comfort

4   B'tzelim Elohim (In God's Image):
Before Covering the Mirror

5   The Shekhinah (God's presence) at the Bedside:
Remembering the Illness and the Death

6   Aninut (from Death to Burial):
Suspended Between Two Worlds

7   Shiva (First Seven Days of Mourning):
A Community Embrace

8   Sheloshim (The Thirty Days Following the Burial):
Finding Your Footing in a Changed World

צמצום
Tzimtzum
Contraction

THE JEWISH MYSTICS described the creation of the world as having three parts. The first part is an act of *Tzimtzum* or Contraction. Recognizing that human creation is overwhelmed and blinded by the brightness of the Divine Light, the Divine Energy withdraws. This creates a darkness in which an as yet unknown creative human process can emerge.

Mourning also begins with a contraction. It leaves one in a darkness whose value may seem unfathomable. In Part One of this book, we withdraw to examine the needs of mourning, your memories connected with the death, and your resources for healing. This reflective process is created to help calm the overwhelming feelings that accompany mourning and is the foundation for the grief-work that follows.

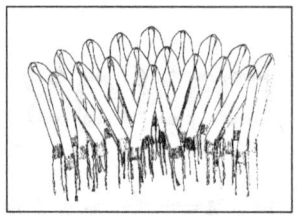

המקום ינחם אתכם
בתוך שאר אבלי ציון וירושלים

**May God comfort you
among the mourners of Zion
and Jerusalem.**

1

אבלות

Avelut

The Mourner's Path

THE TEMPLE IN the ancient city of Jerusalem had a separate path for mourners. Walking along it, mourners came face-to-face with all the other members of the community, who greeted them with the ancestor of the blessing we use today: "May God comfort you among the mourners of Zion and Jerusalem."

With a clear path to follow, and prescribed ways for the community and the mourner to relate to each other, it may have been easier for ancient mourners and their comforters than for those of today. Modern mourners often don't know how to behave. People who have suffered the loss of someone close may think their feelings are inappropriate or abnormal or that mourning should

> A mourner who enters the Temple Mount . . . may enter and walk around to the left . . . . They would then say to him, "May [the One] who dwells in this House comfort you."
>
> —*Semahot*

> Whosoever sees a mourner within thirty days should comfort him, but not ask him how he is feeling. After thirty days, but within twelve months, he should ask how he is and then comfort him. After twelve months, he should comfort him and then ask how he is feeling.
> —*Semahot*

צ.ו.ה TzVH: to lay charge, command, or order; *mitzvah*: a commandment

> The important thing is not how many separate injunctions are obeyed, but how and in what spirit we obey them.
> —*Baal Shem Tov*

be easier than it is. They may feel torn apart, yet try to hide this rupture rather than heal it. They find themselves in emotional chaos and may even develop physical complaints and health problems.

It isn't easy for those who want to help mourners, either. Would-be comforters often feel uneasy attempting to acknowledge the loss. They may not know what to say or how to say it. Because of their shared awkwardness, mourners and comforters often collude in denying the appropriate—and normal—discomfort and pain. Wistful affirmations, "You're doing great," and equally unrealistic replies, "Sure I am," imply recovery, often before the pain of the loss has fully registered. This collusion keeps the mourner from fulfilling obligations to the deceased and to the self. It robs the mourner of the mitzvah of mourning.

Mitzvah (plural: mitzvot) literally translates as "a commandment" or "an order." Orthodox Jews say that God revealed Judaism's 613 commandments—or mitzvot—at Mount Sinai. This comprehensive code delineates the behavior of individual Jews in all aspects of their life. A mitzvah, then, is a specific obligation of Jewish living.

But the word *mitzvah* also is commonly used quite differently. This word, familiar even to the most secular Jew, is understood by its Yiddish meaning: good deed. This meaning carries with it the sense of something one *ought* to do, not necessarily because one wants to, but because it is the right thing to do. A mitzvah may even entail something somewhat unpleasant, such as visiting a relative you really don't like. You do it because you "should." It's the kind of thing a mensch—a good person—would do, but perhaps not your idea of a great way to spend an afternoon. Still, you do it, and you feel better because you have "done the right thing."

In this book, I draw upon both the traditional meaning of the word *mitzvah*, as well as the colloquial understanding, which describes how people *feel* performing mitzvot. By creatively exploring the commandments connected with behavior before and after a death, I aim for the experience of transformation that is often lost in a world that does not honor ritual.

Finding Your Path to Healing

If you are facing a profound transition in your personal life, I hope you will find comfort here. The book melds the commandments regarding the dying person, burial procedures, and mourning with psychotherapeutic exercises to help you forge a path toward consolation and personal growth.

While I have written this book from the perspective of those who are grieving after the death of a loved one, its principles apply to anyone facing a loss of any kind which has caused major disruption in his or her life. These may include divorce, deterioration of health, or moving to another city.

Recognizing the similarity between different kinds of losses is part of Jewish tradition, for joining mourners on their path in the ancient Temple were others whose losses had been profound.

This book frames the seasons of bereavement according to the wisdom of traditional Jewish mourning rituals and the wisdom of a much more modern discipline, psychology. It will guide you along a path of healing so you can again live with zest and purpose.

> Who are they who circle to the left? A mourner, an excommunicant, one who has someone sick at home, and one concerned about a lost object.
> —Semahot

Chapter One

If you are a mourner, that last line might seem like the equivalent of saying that I'll teach you how to fly. You probably believe that your life and, especially, your frame of mind will never get any better. After all, nothing *will* bring back the person who has died. You may even be outraged at the thought that your life *could* get better. Such a notion may seem like an insult to the deceased.

Facing the Fact of Death

People tell you that time heals. You hear their words and you want to believe them. But you wonder: How can the world ever be set right when it has been so altered that it is no longer home to the person you have lost?

Judaism demands honesty. Our rituals are designed to help us directly confront death. We do not use embalmers or make-up artists to restore our dead to their former good looks. We hear the sound of each shovelful of earth hitting the wooden casket as we bury the dead. These rituals are part of our attempt not to distract the mourner from grim reality.

So, I will tell you the truth. To a large extent you are right. The person you have lost is not going to return. Contrary to what you may hear from others, you will never fully get over this loss. You are likely to miss this person for the rest of your life.

But there is something else—something that coexists with this sobering reality: Despite the fact that the death will remain the same, you—and life as you know it—can change. And in that change an entire world, filled with possibilities, can open up. This change comes through the *process of mourning*.

The process of mourning is the way in which the rupture created by the death of a person significant to you can begin to heal. Proper grief-work requires focusing on feelings associated with grief. It is the essential and indispensable labor of healing.

A Context for Your Healing

This book is about healing. It is about discovering the mourner's path and carefully walking it, with the help and the blessing of the community. As we walk the path, the feelings that once felt like obstacles to our growth become the vehicles for our transformation. We come to know and trust what once may have been frightening—our deep emotions become our friends.

The literal meaning of the condolence to mourners we recite today which is descended from the phrase used by Jews in Temple times is: "May The Place [a name of God] bring comfort to you among the mourners of Zion and Jerusalem." It addresses the need of mourners for a safe place for healing.

ק.ו.מ **KVM:** to rise, stand, endure, exist; *makom*: a place, locality, dwelling place; *Hamakom*: The Place, a name for God; *Mekom Hanekhama*: a place of comfort

Finding a context for this grief-work is one of the hardest things about being a modern mourner. The emotional chaos of bereavement makes it hard to settle down and face our lives. Between our limited involvement in ritual and a society that conspires to deny the darker side of life, there are few safe places for us to confront mourning. As a mourner, you need a non-threatening framework for your mourning—a *Mekom Hanekhama*. I hope you will find it here.

In creating your context, we will rely on traditional Jewish mourning rituals. The rituals create a safe context to encourage the full expression of grief and give it

נ.ח.מ **NKhM:** to comfort, console, have compassion; and condolence, a returned exile; *nekhama*: a comfort

Chapter One

a protective structure that progressively relaxes as time passes and the mourner heals. These mourning rituals are the inspiration for the exercises of this workbook.

Effective rituals translate concepts into actions. They connect participants to abstract beliefs and values that the rituals represent. They convey transcendent meaning and significance.

During their 2,000-year exile, the Jewish people recast rituals and symbols so that their tradition and its values could be carried across the earth. By weaving my own experiences into the tradition, I continue this practice. In doing so, I have been influenced by Jewish law and custom and by Kabbalistic (Jewish mystical) teachings about life, death, and the afterlife. Any liberties I take in interpreting Jewish practices, I do to recapture what I believe to be their intention and capacity to heal.

Journal Writing: A Creative Path for Your Mourning Journey

In addition to the Jewish rituals, we will use the guided journal to construct your safe place. This workbook will provide questions to facilitate the reflection and emotional release necessary for healing.

I have chosen this format because I believe that it addresses the isolation that is the reality of so many of today's mourners. Few of us live in rooted communities in which each death is felt by everyone, so that the community mourns together and thereby helps the mourner to grieve and to heal. I have adapted the rituals of those communities to the journal-writing genre. I hope this

> . . . the language of creativity—a language through which the self is carefully reconstructed out of pieces of itself.
>
> —Deena Metzger

will give you support and help you to find the resources you need for healing.

Writing in a journal helped me experience the feelings and the issues that the deaths of my mother and sister aroused in me. It gave me an anchor and a companion when I felt adrift and alone. It helped me recover a sense of myself. To this day it continues to transform my relationship with myself, with others, and with the Divine.

Journal writing is especially appropriate for the solitary journey of the mourner since it lets individual styles of coping emerge against the backdrop of the universal path of grief. A journal is also "someone" with whom to share a journey. Writing in my journal got me through some difficult times. Living alone in a cabin in rural northern California, my journal helped turn my agitated loneliness into tranquil solitude. During difficult times, I still awake in the middle of the night and pour my anxiety into my journal's pages until I am able to relax back into sleep.

Writing in my journal helps me to re-experience feelings that are locked inside myself: the knots which bind my emotional life. Whenever one knot is untied, the release of emotion brings relief, understanding, and a sense of homecoming.

Journal Writing Does Not Require You To Be a Great Writer

The journal is for your own eyes and soul. It's not a graded exercise; you don't have to be a skilled or experienced writer and your spelling or grammar don't need to be flawless. All you need is the desire to be honest and open with yourself.

Chapter One

ש.ר.ד **DRSh:** to seek, search, communicate, examine; *midrash*: a sermon, lecture, or investigation

In Judaism, writing is not a new tool for discovering personal meaning. The rabbis of antiquity wrote midrash (plural: midrashim), that is, stories, sermons, and other commentary on the Bible and the Talmud. "Midrash" means "to search," "to seek," "to examine," "to investigate."

One midrash says that the white spaces between the letters of the Torah are as filled with wisdom as the letters themselves. Our responsibility is to penetrate the wisdom of those spaces to live a life rich with meaning. Each of us must create our own midrashim, and in the process create our lives.

I believe in the wisdom of those white spaces. I believe in our ability to connect, through those white places, with the source of our healing wisdom. I often begin my workshops or classes by announcing that I am about to introduce the book in which I found the most support for my healing. As the workshop participants poise their pens to write down the title, I hold up a blank book. It is within those blank books that our personal truths are revealed. It was in one of those journals that this book began to evolve. I certainly would not have anticipated that so much would come out of it, when one winter night in 1975 in Mendocino County I decided that I had to face what my life had brought me. I wrote:

> It's very clear tonight . . . the path of pen and ink. . . . To take on all the legacies of death which have landed in my lap, armed with my pen, I will have to joust the personal truth that comes with all of these messages of death. I may lose, but I really have no choice but to try to write a new contract with life with terms originating in the generation of me. Everything else that I could do would be a lie. (Journal Entry, Redwood Valley, California, 1975)

I hope that you will fill in the white spaces of this book with a record of your own search for yourself, and that in those spaces you will discover meaning and growth.

Jewish law prohibits extending the usual polite greetings to the mourner. We do not say "Shalom Alekhim" ("Peace be with you") or "Good day" or "Good bye" because "Shalom" and "good" do not appropriately describe the days or feelings of a mourner. Rather than extend conventional greetings, it is suggested that someone attempting to provide comfort sit beside the mourner and share his or her grief. And so, through this volume, I will sit beside you, hoping to offer comfort and to ease your journey along the mourner's path.

> It is forbidden to comfort a mourner when the dead remains unburied.
> —*Talmud*

Chapter One

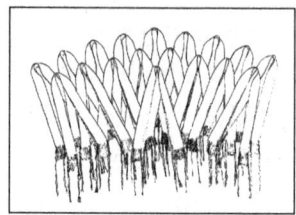

Lament the dead [in] words which break the heart . . . to cause much weeping

–Shulkhan Arukh: Yoreh Deah 344:1

2

הספד

Hesped *and Truthtelling:* *Mourning as a Process*

AS YOU BEGIN your walk on the mourner's path, I want to make sure that you understand one phrase: "mourning process." This will give you an idea of what lies ahead.

"Process" implies that things change over time and that there are ways to encourage that change to happen. It tells us that what we feel at one moment is not necessarily what we will feel at another.

Our society does not value process. We like things ready-made. We eat precooked food that is packaged for the microwave. We eat it without acknowledging the farmer, the trucker, the grocer, or the living spark of creation which is part of every fruit, vegetable, or lamb chop on our table.

So it is with our emotional life. We expect to be healed without acknowledging the rupture. We expect to arrive at our destination with no journey. But the process of healing requires a journey for which there is no shortcut. It requires us to acknowledge the variety of emotions which accompany a loss. Recognizing and expressing these difficult and varied feelings is the only way back from the world of mourning.

You May Not Recognize Your Behavior

You say that you don't recognize yourself? That you behave in ways that seem totally alien to you? You keep losing things or having outbursts of anger? You think that you are going crazy? Hearing this does not worry me. In fact, when one of my psychotherapy clients tells me that this is what is going on, I am often relieved. If this is true of you, it is likely to mean that your current difficulties are not the sign of a serious disorder that has been lurking for a lifetime. The fact that the behavior is so alien to you indicates that you are probably suffering a grief reaction or what my profession also calls a "situational" or "adjustment disorder." This is a direct reaction to a clear stress. It can be dealt with—*if* you are willing to risk opening yourself up.

This is not an easy thing to do. Suppressed emotion, stored near the surface, can be terrifying. Many fear that if the lid is taken off, the outpouring of tears or anger will never stop. But as I've said before, it is only the unfelt feelings that do not change. The pain or anger or whatever feeling is associated with the grief continues for a while, and then the bottom is reached, or things change, or a different emotion surfaces.

> A pilgrimage is not a journey toward transformation . . .
> but a transforming journey.
> —Jonathan Omer-Man

Avoiding your feelings means avoiding your own depth. It means avoiding the transforming experiences that life offers and failing to come to terms with your own personal history. Avoiding a feeling only prolongs it. Becoming familiar with the dimensions of the pain allows you to be less frightened and to cope more readily when the feeling comes up again. By overcoming the fear that suppresses the feelings, we become privy to the richness of our inner life.

Making the Choice to Heal

To say it simply: Our lives can teach us lessons. In this learning process, we have two choices: We can deny the learning and hold fast to our original vision of our self, the world and the way "it ought to be." Or we can let our history be our teacher. It is this latter path that yields wisdom and understanding.

I have certainly had to struggle with this choice. This isn't what I had planned for my life. I would not have set out to become an expert on mourning. But this is the life that I was given.

There is a story about Reb Zusia, an eighteenth century Chassidic Master. Zusia said, "When God calls me, I will not be taken to account about why I was not a better Moses or a better Abraham. I will have to account for why I was not a better Zusia."

Like Zusia I had a choice about whose life I would live. I could spend my life yearning for what might have been, railing against what was, or I could tell the truth about my life and use it as my teacher, taking every turn as a challenge for growth.

Life is what happens when you are busy making other plans.
—*George Santayana*

Chapter Two

The difficulty in surrendering to process is that there is no road map. I can't tell you what you will experience along the way, or who you will be when you get there. I can tell you that it isn't going to be easy, that it may get worse before it gets better, and that the alternatives to taking this journey are worse than the journey itself. These alternatives may include depression, prolonged numbness, decreased satisfaction with your remaining relationships, addiction, emotional difficulties which manifest as physical symptoms, or significantly less zest for living.

Do these sound like satisfactory alternatives to facing the feelings of loss? If you are open enough to have read this far, they probably do not.

I'll say it once more. The one thing that I do know with certainty from my own struggles and from being midwife to countless others as they face their dark sides: Feelings that find expression change. And *that* change is the process that brings transformation.

Hesped *Versus Eulogy: Telling the Truth about Death*

The understanding that mourning is a process is embedded in a Biblical word for "mourning": *Sapad.* The letters of this word form the root of the Hebrew word for *eulogy*: *Hesped.* Other words with this root mean "to smite the breast as a gesture of mourning," "to wail," and "to lament." This understanding of what mourners experience is vastly different from what *eulogy* conveys. The idea conveyed by the word *eulogy*, which is Greek for "good words" or "praise," seems to gloss over the difficult feelings associated with death. *Eulogy*, with its

ס.פ.ד **SPD:** to mourn, lament, or wail, to smite the breast as a gesture of mourning; *hesped*: a funeral oration injunction to speak only good of the dead, encourages glossing over the inevitable difficulties in relationships and the uncomfortable feelings associated with loss. It can result in a freezing of time and memory through which we struggle to hold on to an idealized sense of the person we have lost. This denial of death promotes a rigidity that makes healing difficult. *Hesped*, however, impels us to tell the truth about the person who has died and about the loss and its emotional consequences. It calls for the expression of the full range of feelings and enables us to use our lives as teachers. *Eulogy* calcifies memory, while *hesped* recognizes the fluidity of experience and teaches us that mourning is a process.

The attitude reflected in the word *eulogy* is also reflected in the Western approach to mourning, which is basically a denial of death. This denial is what makes it so difficult for mourners to honestly express their loss. Such phrases as "He's passed away to his final resting place," or "she's gone to a better place," keeps us from calling "death" by its name. Similarly, our excessive preoccupation with embalming fluids, cosmeticians, and garments and caskets that resist decay, mean one thing: "Let's deny that death exists." This attempt to conquer death stems from a misperception of the human condition that is totally inconsistent with Jewish thought.

The reminder that life is constantly waxing and waning is as central to Judaism as its calendar, which is based on lunar cycles. On Yom Kippur, traditional Jews wear a *kittel*, the white garment in which they will one day be buried. They recite the *Viddui*, a prayer of confession similar to the one recited by a dying person during the last moments before death. During the period preceding Yom Kippur, Jews are expected to put things

> Funeral orators and those who respond [Amen] after them are to be called to account for delivering eulogies that do not apply.
> —Talmud: Berakhot 62a

right between themselves and others, as if there would be no other opportunity for such repentance.

The impact of these practices can be enormous. When I questioned a woman in her mid-sixties about the calm way she appeared to respond to her diagnosis of breast cancer, she told me that she had learned that life and death are interwoven; at an early age she had observed the urgency of the men in shul, dressed in their white burial garments on Yom Kippur, as they sought forgiveness from each other. She said that her early experiences in synagogue had helped her to come to terms with death's inevitability when she was still a youth.

Grief Is Not an Illness; It Is Normal and Healthy

Today many people who are bereaved find themselves in the offices of doctors or psychotherapists, rather than the embrace of the community. They begin to believe that there is something really wrong with them. But this is rarely true. Grief is normal and predictable. Your story, your style of mourning, and the way you experience your grief is yours alone, yet the emotions accompanying your loss follow a pattern universally common to people facing profound transitions.

Understanding these phases of grief is a recent development in America. It is by no means the norm. Most commonly, psychological needs are ignored following a loss, as if nothing startlingly difficult has happened in the life of the mourner. Unfortunately, few values of our society have been more fully adopted into Jewish life than those regarding death and bereavement. This

> It was regarded as unnatural not to weep for the dead.
> —Ben Sira

is why I had such a difficult time in the period following the deaths of my mother and my sister. I did not know that my emotional extremes were not unusual. In addition to the agony of mourning, I had to deal with my fear that there was something really wrong with me.

In fact, while incredibly difficult to experience, these extremes represent a *healthy* psychological journey, that allows the psyche to do the emotional work essential to grief. Psychiatrist Elizabeth Kübler-Ross has determined that mourners progress though five stages as they grieve: denial, depression, anger, bargaining, and acceptance. These descriptions of mourning are modern formulations of the ancient understanding of grief embedded in the Jewish burial and mourning rituals. These stages will be reformulated within the context of the Jewish mourning rituals to form our framework for exploring the mourning process.

As Bad as It May Feel, Someone Else Has Been There and Made It Through

In the following descriptions of the mourning phases, you may recognize yourself and find comfort in knowing that you are not alone in what you are experiencing.

The *denial phase*, the first phase of grieving, is characterized by numbness, isolation, and separation. This can be a brittle and cold period before the flood of emotions, which follows. But it may also be marked by frenetic activity which keeps the bereaved from focusing on the loss.

Depression, anger, and bargaining occur in the middle phase. This is a time of chaos, guilt, and maybe even fear of losing one's sanity. Often during this phase,

> Your grief for what you've lost lifts a mirror up to where you're bravely working.
> —Rumi

Chapter Two

many unresolved issues of the mourner's earlier life come pouring through the window that the death has opened, even if they are not related to the death or to the person who died. This adds to the difficulty of the period, but also to its potential for psychological growth.

The final stage is *acceptance*. Acceptance is not synonymous with happiness. But it does represent a point at which a mourner begins to integrate the loss and to move toward a life less defined by attachment to the person who has died.

Although you may not experience all these feelings or go through them in the order that they are delineated here, some may sound familiar to you. That is good. It is important to know that your feelings are normal. While this won't make your pain go away, there is some comfort in knowing that other people share the same feelings. That is why I stress the predictable nature of the process of bereavement. As individual as mourning styles and personal histories may be, there is also this commonalty to human experience. As horrible as your experience may feel, someone else has been there—and made it through. Knowing this may not diminish your pain, but it may take the edge off your fear.

When Does Healing Begin?

Each person's needs are different. Some people begin grief-work even before the death has occurred. Ideally, it would not be necessary to wait for death to resolve issues between people. Ahead, you will find guidelines for addressing these issues at any point before or after the death.

It can often be difficult to fully engage in mourning in the months following the death. People who are just beginning to mourn are extraordinarily raw and vulnerable. Their sense of reality may be so blurred that it can be almost impossible to focus thoughts and feelings. Often, some time must pass before they can focus on the issues raised by grief. This was certainly true of me. My losses were so traumatic; it took at least two years before I could give them any focused attention. Mourn at your own pace. As I've already said, the time-line for healing is different with each individual. It is hoped that we have designed this book in consideration of the often attenuated attention span of those who grieve. Short blocks of print, empty space, with quotes and other information in the margins, should be easier to digest than the more traditional format. I hope this will lead you safely and with comfort into the deeper work of the book.

Many of us carry unresolved issues regarding separation and mourning for years after the loss. At any point in our lives, it can be appropriate to do grief-work. If it *has* been many years and your grief is now similar to what you felt in the first months after the death, then please consult someone experienced in working with bereavement, a rabbi, priest or minister, a clinical social worker, psychologist, psychiatrist, or physician. Grief, like other feelings, should change over time. If yours feels no different from the way it always has, a trained professional may help you find some relief. In addition, there are times when circumstances surrounding a death are so traumatic or the relationship prior to the death was so troubled, that it is essential to seek professional help.

Chapter Two

When Does Mourning End?

How long will mourning take? As long as it takes. Jewish tradition prescribes a formal period of up to a year. While the dead are also remembered on anniversaries and holidays, it is considered inappropriate to grieve beyond the first *yahrzeit* (anniversary of the death) for parents and thirty days for others. But unless mourning can be pursued with an intensity that is very difficult in our times, my experience in helping many mourners tells me that these time frames are unrealistic and insufficient for today's mourners to recuperate from their loss. They might be long enough in the more traditional Jewish communities that let a mourner fully engage in rituals which acknowledge the death and the mourner's change of status. But contemporary society minimizes the appropriateness of grief. Even when the importance of mourning is recognized, the outside world imposes many distractions and demands. In addition, contemporary mourners are often far from family and long-time friends who share the loss and whose companionship might ease the loneliness and sorrow. They may find that the people who are near have different needs while coping with this loss. With so many variables involved, it seems clear that the chronology of grief is unique to each person; this must be respected and never judged.

How to Begin Your Healing Process

The first thing to do is to stop holding your breath and counting the minutes until your pain is over. Mourning will end only by taking long breaths that help to deepen your focus on whatever you feel at any one time. This is the great paradox of the mourning process.

Whatever the timetable, feelings do change. The mourning process works, if you will engage in it. *Fully engaging in mourning means that you will be a different person from the one you were before you began.*

> Everything subject to time is liable to change.
> —Joseph Albo

Now, take a slow, deep breath.

This is where our work begins. With this breath, we will go on to create your mekom hanekhama—*your place of comfort—your place for telling the truth.*

What did you feel when you read the above sentence, "Fully engaging in mourning means that you will be a different person from the one you were before you began"? Respond honestly. Did you feel hopeful? Or did you feel a clutching in the pit of your stomach? While some people may feel almost giddy at the promise of relief, others are horrified at the thought that they could ever accept a world devoid of the person they have lost.

In the space to the right, tell yourself your reaction to the promise of change.

Exercise 2·1
Beginning the Process: Creating Your Place of Comfort

There are no right or wrong answers to the above question or to any of the questions you will find in this book. In fact, today's answer may be very different from the one you might give to the same question tomorrow or in a week. That's the nature of any process—change. Therefore our goal in raising the issues in this exercise is not to seek some immutable truth, but to create a path for *hesped*—a place where you can seek an honest and full expression of your feelings. And now we will move on—to continue to create your *mekom hanekhama*.

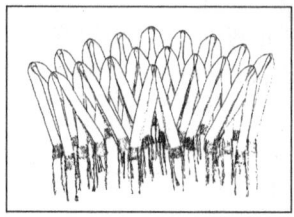

Here the heart is broken, here the spirit enters. The prayers of a broken heart call the spirit in, inevitably heal, are therefore whole.

–Deena Metzger

3

מקום הנחמה

Mekom Hanekhama

Finding a Place of Comfort

MANY JEWISH RITUALS are performed in community. Even a formal worship service requires a minyan of ten people in order for certain prayers to be chanted. But Judaism also acknowledges that a person who is opening his or her heart in prayer may need privacy. Even when one is a part of a group, a person may wrap him or herself into the cocoon of a tallit (prayer shawl) to acquire a sense of privacy.

Your journal can be a sort of tallit for you: a place of privacy and refuge where you can feel sheltered and protected, without losing your sense of the support of

ט.ל.ל **TLL:** to cover over, to hang, to depend, to roof; rained fine rain; night-mist, dew; *tallit*: a prayer shawl the community. It is also a place where you can gather yourself and become whole again, in the same way that a person, after saying the *Shema's* three paragraphs, gathers the tzitzit (the tallit's 613 fringes) in one hand to connect them to the 613 commandments and to affirm the Oneness of God.

How to Use Your Journal

Now you will continue writing in the journal. Remember to think of what you write as letters from your deepest self. They are to be treasured. Each time you write, take a few minutes to distance yourself from any voices that judge or censor your words. Don't worry about your handwriting or spelling or the style of your writing. If this is to be an effective tool for your healing, it must be in your most authentic voice and written for no one but yourself.

Remember our key word: "Process." Writing in a journal is not creating a product. We are not shaping literature. We are engaging in a process. I think of it as going fishing: I throw out my line, casting ink into a primal pool. I reel in my prize: awareness from my depths.

The best way to begin is simply to sit down, read a set of questions and write your thoughts as they come. You will discover your own way of doing the writing exercises, but here is the writing ritual that works best for me: I choose a time when I do not have to rush off somewhere, and when I do not expect to be interrupted. I do a little physical exercise to help me relax, perhaps walk around the block, ride on my stationary bicycle, or do some yoga. Then I sit down, take a few breaths, set a timer for twenty minutes and begin to write. For the full twenty minutes, I write anything that comes into my

> It is necessary to build a sanctuary within, brick by brick.
> —*Rabbi Jakob Petuchowski*

head, whether or not it makes sense. This stream-of-consciousness writing often leads me where I need to go.

I'm not always especially eager to write. Many of my journal entries begin with something like, "I really don't want to write today. I am tired, and I have so many things that I need to get done." I'm surprised how a statement like this will often lead me somewhere else. When I let my resistance vent itself, I am, often, right into the heart of some deep, unexpected material.

I try to keep writing no matter what occurs along the way, and I *never* stop to read what I have written. Even when I have had a difficult time getting started, I frequently find that when the twenty-minute alarm goes off, I still have a lot left to say. So, of course, I continue. But sometimes twenty minutes is just enough, and I am glad to come to an end.

It is sometimes helpful to begin writing with an awareness of your body. When you read an exercise's instructions, you may feel a strong emotion that may register as a physical sensation. Your stomach might jump or you might feel a fluttering in your chest. Perhaps your throat feels tight or you rub your eyes and tightly shut them. If you can connect with a feeling that is held in your body, you can often get a head start in writing from your deepest part (literally, in some cases, from your gut). Stay in touch with that feeling and let it speak to the exercise through your writing.

For example, I found that the awareness that I clenched my jaw when I was angry, helped me to resolve long-held resentments. Now, whenever I feel my jaw tighten, I ask myself what is making me angry. A little writing in my journal can usually give me an answer. But don't worry if you are not aware of the way in which

Chapter Three

your body responds emotionally. Just think about the questions the exercise asks and write your answers.

Find Someone with Whom You Can Share Your Journal

Ultimately to be Jewish is to be a part of a community. Certainly for a mourner, who may feel profoundly isolated, making contact with others is an essential part of healing. For this reason, I strongly urge you to find someone with whom you can share your writing. Ideally, you might find a partner or a group of people who are also bereaved. Together, you can work through the steps of this book, giving each other support. Even reading your journal out loud to yourself gives the words a new dimension. They feel more real and seem to have more conviction behind them.

Finding the right person to whom you want to read your journal may not be easy. Very often, for reasons that we will discuss later, the most obvious people—those to whom you are closest—are not the most helpful during bereavement. Instead, you might find people who are in a similar situation, but not related to you. Or you may want to find a therapist or counsellor who can listen to you more easily because he or she will not have to put aside pain or memories to give you support.

Note your feelings when the person to whom you read your journal entry responds to you. How you intuitively react to that response will let you know whether this is the right person with whom to share your journal. If you feel that you must alter your words as you read or if you feel you are being judged, you clearly have not found the right person.

> Do not separate yourself from the community.
> —Hillel

Naming the Soul

Your journal will help you to establish a satisfying ongoing relationship with someone who has died—a connection which transcends death. It will commemorate the deceased as well as mark the stages of your own healing process. This is in the tradition of *hazkarat haneshamot*, "the naming of souls," which is the reading of the names of the departed in the synagogue following the death, on the anniversary of the death (*Yahrzeit*) and at memorial (*Yizkor*) services.

Exercise 3·1
Hazkarat Haneshamot: Naming the Soul of the Person You Mourn

Use the space below to establish this book as the place where you will explore your connection with the person you mourn. If you like, attach a picture of the person; otherwise simply fill in the blank spaces.

This journal documents the mourning process for

_____
name of the deceased
who was born on _____ *in* _____
and who died on _____ *in* _____

photo

Honoring Your Ambivalence

The Talmud contains both law and commentaries on the law. The commentaries include advice, philosophy, and stories about rabbis. It often reads like a transcript of a conversation held two thousand years ago. These conversations often include opposing voices, each speaking to the same point.

Perhaps the most famous controversies were those of Hillel and Shammai, who were teachers in Babylonia during the early decades of the Common Era. For example, when a question was raised about the proper way to light Chanukah candles, the school of Shammai supported beginning the first night of Chanukah with all candles burning and lighting one less candle each night. The school of Hillel argued for lighting one candle on the first night and adding one more candle each of the next seven nights. While tradition has sided with the school of Hillel on the grounds that holiness increases and, therefore, so should the light, the Talmud quotes, as it often does, the different opinions rather than just giving a definitive answer.

As a mourner, you probably know that there may be more than one voice on the same subject. Mourners are often besieged by conflicting inner voices that make it difficult to sort out feelings and *impossible* to make decisions.

Exercise 3·2
What are your feelings about changing your life?

Let's go back to the question raised in the book's first exercise (Exercise 2-1, page 31) and acknowledge your conflicting voices. We will also treat them with the same respect that the Talmud treats opposing schools of thought. Remember your initial reaction to my statement at the end of Chapter 2, where I said that you would need to accept the possibility that your life will never be the same. Write more about that reaction in the space provided. Have there been any changes in your feelings since you first considered this question?

The suggestion that your feelings could change and that you could become a very different person from the one you are today probably elicited at least two different reactions: Hope and Fear. I want you to give voices to both feelings.

First, what are your hopes for this promise of change and growth? What would you like to gain from your mourning process? Write about who you would hope to be as a result of this process.

Now give voice to your resistance. Resistance is a powerful and a valuable part of you. You may be frightened of change, particularly when it triggers deep, volatile feelings. This voice may tell you that moving on is a betrayal of the person who has died. Or it may say that the process in this book will not work and may even be dangerous. Find that voice and allow it to speak.

Here is a record of my own ambivalent thoughts as I debated facing my own losses many years ago:

> I'm riding the trolley down Market Street. BART construction has torn up the area and the sight of the rubble around me is churning up the devastation on the inside. The whole world is changing, yet I'm here holding back the pain. Is it better to get in touch with these feelings or to ignore them? Looks from the other passengers, responding to the changes in my face, tell me I have no choice. The only one who doesn't see my pain is me. Where is the place I could scream and no one would hear me? What will become of me once I've retreated? Will there be anything left? (Journal Entry, San Francisco, 1972)

Balancing Your Opposing Forces of Growth and Resistance To Find Healing

In psychotherapy, two forces help the client move at the appropriate pace: The "growth principle" and "resistance." The first is like the heliotrope, a plant that turns toward the sun. It propels us forward toward growth. Resistance is like a bear which hibernates to get through a long winter.

I once had a client who wondered, after the death of her brother, if she had a right to have a baby. How could she, she asked, help in re-creating a world that did not have him in it? But despite the tormenting questions, her body had made a decision. She was pregnant. Clearly she wanted life to go forward; her body was getting bigger and bigger with the baby. But still she asked the mourners' questions: Do we have a right to distract ourselves from our pain with our joy? Do we have a right to happiness, those of us who are walking scars? Do we have the right to joy? To the future? I remember these questions. I asked them too.

Her pregnant body represented the impulse to move forward, which is the growth principle. Her questions represented the second principle, resistance. When the growth principle and resistance are in balance, they provide adaptation *and* protection. Too much sun can be as dangerous as too much sleep. For growth to take root, we must also have times of rest. Something we will explore in future chapters.

Having acknowledged these two parts of yourself in the above exercise, strive for balance. Ask yourself which voice to heed and which voice is distraction. Sometimes you will need to shut down the voice of growth and sometimes you will need to give your resistance a good swift kick so you can get on with the business of healing. You know better than anyone else what pace is right for you.

> If you want to find the truth, you cannot allow your resistance to continually motivate you. We are constantly hiding and posturing . . . instead of meeting with the pain and resistance which so cloud understanding. We continually elude our liberation because of an unwillingness to open.
> —Stephen Levine

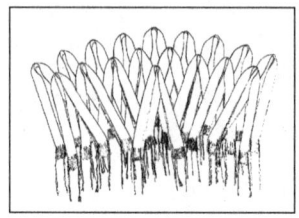

Comforting the mourner is an act of loving kindness toward both the living and the dead.

–Kitzer Shulkhan Arukh 193:11

4

בצלם אלהים

B'tzelem Elohim

In God's Image: Before Covering the Mirror

THERE IS A JEWISH mourning custom of covering the mirrors in the house from the moment of death until the end of *shiva,* the seven-day period following the burial. While the source of this practice is not clear, this much is known: Vanity, which is served by looking in the mirror, has no place in a house of mourning. After a death, we need to dwell upon issues of the soul, not on the external concerns that are reinforced by viewing one's own reflection. We are told that we are created in God's image. By covering a mirror, we may intuit that the Divine image that we reflect is not one that can be seen with the eyes.

-הת **HT:** prefix which can indicate a reflexive verb, meaning solitary acts undertaken for one's own benefit. התאבל ("to mourn") and התפלל ("to pray") are two significant words for mourners. Both are reflexive, indicating the private reflections that are essential in this transformative process.

Coming downstairs, the morning after my mother's death, I caught my image in the front hall mirror. I saw a face that did not look like me. I was frightened and puzzled.

Perhaps it was my look of horrified sadness that caught me by surprise. I was numb—not yet in touch with the feelings of grief my face was showing. It was a shock to encounter evidence of the pain I was feeling.

Withdrawn from the physical world, I was lost in emotional-spiritual wanderings. The physical connection to the closest person in my life had just been irrevocably and unexpectedly severed. I was taken aback at confronting any evidence of the physical me. My mother and I had been close. Part of me did not recognize myself in a world without her. In the past, when I looked in the mirror, I had probably seen her as well as me. But with her death, our bond was reconstituting. My heart told me: A significant part of who I was had gone. My eyes told me: I continued to exist. It would be the task of the next years to reestablish a relationship with my mother that was not based upon what I could see.

Using the Mirror and the White Spaces to Strengthen Your Inner Resources

Before we "cover the mirrors" to begin the mourning journey, there are a few things about yourself that we need to look at. This chapter has many exercises designed to build a foundation for the work of the rest of the book and to root that work in your own experience. As with all the exercises in the book, you may do them all or pick and choose which ones will most help you to see yourself.

B'tzelem Elohim: *Before Covering the Mirror*

Remember that mourning is not only a memorial to the person whom you have lost. It is also a testimonial to the process by which you summon—and strengthen—your own inner resources. In Exercise 1 of Chapter 3, you dedicated this book to the person you are mourning. Now I want you to do a second dedication. Write your own name and birthdate followed by an arrow extending toward the right margin—to remind you that your future is ahead of you, filled with possibility. Perhaps you will want to attach a picture of yourself as well; after all, this chapter is about looking in the mirror.

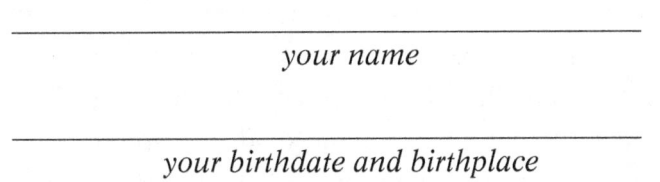

your name

your birthdate and birthplace

As prelude to covering the mirror and opening to the next part of your life, we will examine some factors which have shaped your life thus far. These will tell us a little about who you are and what we might expect of your mourning process.

It is easy to understand why we would want to honor the dead, but some of us may reject focusing on ourselves at such a moment as vain or self-indulgent. Please remember that mourning includes obligations to *yourself* as well as to the person you have lost.

Exercise 4·1
Looking in the Mirror:
A Commitment to Your Own Healing

photo

Chapter Four

Finding Healthy Models for Your Mourning Process

Properly confronting your grief is not self-indulgence. It is sound preventive medicine. The saying, by Dr. Henry Maudsley, an nineteenth-century British psychiatrist, "A sorrow that has no vent in tears makes other organs weep," underscores the importance of mourning.

Often, after the death of someone close, people have irrational fears concerning their health. In fact, physical symptoms often accompany grief. These many include heart palpitations, dry mouth or tightness in the throat or chest, which may resemble chronic illness. Unfortunately, although people often fear going to the doctor during mourning, seeing your physician can be quite reassuring. As you learn to deal more satisfactorily with stress in your life, the symptoms that are worrying you are likely to disappear. Some of the symptoms of grief are much like the symptoms of depression. However, grief is a normal, healthy response to loss, while depression is an illness. Far too often, mourners are given the medical diagnosis of "depression," and, with it, medication to treat it. This can short-circuit the grief process, denying mourners the healing that can come with these difficult feelings that are part of grief-work. It can also stigmatize grief by naming it as pathology.

If your own health is not a convincing enough argument for giving yourself permission to mourn, let us look to Jewish tradition for a role model. When one of the sons of King David died, David's servants were afraid to tell him about the death. They remembered that, when the child was near death, David's pain was so intense that he did not respond to their voices. "How

> The heart is king . . . wherever it leads, the organs follow.
> —M. H. Luzzatto, 1740

can we tell him the child is dead? He might do something terrible"(2 Samuel 12:18).

Seeing the servants whispering, David asked if the child was dead and was told that this was so.

At that point, David rose, washed, anointed and groomed himself, and prayed. He came into his house and ate the bread which his servants set before him. This surprised them. They pointed out the incongruity of the King fasting and weeping while the child was alive and eating and caring for himself when the child died.

"While the child was still alive," David responded, "I fasted and wept because I thought . . . [God] . . . may have pity on me, and the child may live. But now that he is dead, why should I fast? Can I bring him back again? I shall go to him, but he will never come back to me"(2 Samuel 12:22-23).

King David affirmed that, for mourners, life continues, despite the devastating loss. We have the *obligation* of taking care of ourselves. The message is clear in Judaism that we must continue with our lives. As the Book of Deuteronomy says, "I have put before you life and death, blessing and curse. Choose life—if you . . . would live" (Deuteronomy 30:19).

Public images of the mourner enormously influence our understanding of the expectations placed on mourners. King David demonstrated the need to care for oneself after a major tragedy. What other role models do you have? Think about how people you have known or observed have coped with the loss of someone with

Exercise 4.2
How Do Mourners Behave?

Chapter Four

whom they were close. They may have coped well—or quite poorly. Regardless of how they coped, write in the space to the left about a few people who have contributed to your understanding of how to handle grief. Try especially to remember people you observed in the early years of your life, as you first learned about death. What did you learn from each of these people? Discuss how you, as a mourner, are expected to behave and whether those expectations come from society at large, from your own family and friends, or from some other source.

Examining What You Have Learned about Mourning

Remember, we learn from both positive and negative examples. One of my clients spoke resentfully about her recently deceased mother, who frequently burst into tears when remembering her own sister, who had died as a young adult. "The shadow of that aunt hung over everything I did," she angrily told me. "I grew up thinking my life was a tragedy because of an aunt I never knew. I'll *never* do that to *my* children."

In a mourning workshop I led, one man described a grandfather who had never ceased grieving for his mother, who had died when he was a child. In another workshop, one participant remembered an aunt, who never mentioned the name of the husband who had died in World War II. The way these relatives expressed their losses made a lasting impression.

Your image of mourning may also come through public life or the media. When we hear the word "widow," many of us still see the face of a young Jackie Kennedy, frozen in silent grief. She was credited with great "dignity" in leading our nation through that trauma of her husband's assassination. But I often wonder about the personal cost of her "dignified" and public grief, as well as the danger of a role model who did not shed a public tear. In later years, it was revealed that the President's young widow, would go out on a boat, where no one could hear her. There, unable to be heard, she could scream at the horror that had come into her life and the lives of her children

While still mourning, one of my clients described a very different kind of "widow" when she spoke of being pressured to conform to what she considered to be an oppressive role. "Sometimes," she said, "I feel like Scarlett O'Hara, with her feet secretly tapping to the music of the Virginia reel, hidden below the heavy layers of her black taffeta dress of mourning. I can be walking down the street, feeling just fine, enjoying the chirping of the birds or a beautiful sky, and then I see someone who reminds me that I am supposed to be unhappy."

We are uniquely ourselves. Yet we are also a composite of all of the people who have influenced us. So when we look in the mirror, we also see the images of those who have so profoundly touched our lives that we often mistake their image (and their essence) for our own.

During mourning, we have the opportunity to strip away parts of our self-image that are not authentically our own, to bring clarity to our relationships and determine how strongly the deceased has influenced us. As we do this, we begin to reclaim our lives.

Chapter Four

Exercise 4·3
How Did Those Close to You Deal with Intense Feelings?

Think about how significant people in your early life expressed emotion. Do you remember what was said about someone expressing deep feelings? How did you know when someone was angry? How did family members show they were happy or sad? Try to recall specific examples of your family's attitude toward anger, sadness or joy. How did this affect your ability to express feelings effectively and with satisfaction?

Try to remember how the deceased coped with loss during his or her lifetime. How would he or she expect you to cope with this loss? Describe the deceased's way of expressing grief and other deep feelings, recording, if possible, specific memories which characterized the way you knew what he or she was feeling. You might want to remember an ideal time, when communication and tenderness were at their best. Or you might remember a day when the conflicts that were characteristic of the relationship were clear.

Choosing the Feelings That Are Yours

These attitudes of those to whom you have been close have influenced how you express your own deep emotions. Your father, for example, may have expressed anger explosively, without concern for how this affected others. You may be very much like him, or, after years of being intimidated by him, you may fear your own anger and repress it. It is difficult to predict how we will incorporate the influence of another person. This is often done unconsciously and over many years.

Becoming aware of such influence takes time but may help you find the style of grieving that will be most honest and fruitful for you. Understanding these influences will help you anticipate what mourning might be like for you. You can choose from the positive examples of those who shaped your early emotional life or you can be aware of some of the qualities that you might want to avoid, qualities that you might be prone to during a time of emotional pain, a time when we are all likely to regress emotionally. In the beginning of mourning, memories, even the good ones, are often painful. In your effort to get on with the process of healing, do not forget about the white spaces, even within your own words. Take the time to feel the feelings that these memories generate. If tears come, let them flow. If other feelings come to the surface, do not hold them back. I know that the longing and the despair can be difficult to face. But the feelings are there whether or not you want them to be. Perhaps by facing them something will change.

Time Off for Shabbat and Holidays

Tradition insures that the stringency of mourning is relieved by legislating that mourning is suspended for Shabbat and certain holidays. Rabban Gamliel, the leader of the Jewish community in Israel during the first century, whose imprint is on many of the rituals connected with death and mourning, said that "On Shabbat, it is as if a mourner is not a mourner." This tells us that despite the intensity of the shiva period, it is not expected to be relentless. There are times when you need to take a break from mourning and bring Shabbat's sense of renewal and restoration to your daily experience of mourning.

Chapter Four

Exercise 4·4
Shabbat in the Midst of Mourning

Make a list of things that you can do to nourish yourself. On the left is a list of ten things that have worked for me. Make your own list on the right, drawing from my suggestions or from things that have helped you in the past.

1. Exercise   1. _____
2. Write in my journal 2. _____
3. Meditate   3. _____
4. Call a friend   4. _____
5. Go to synagogue   5. _____
6. Take a hot bath   6. _____
7. Listen to music   7. _____
8. Go to a museum   8. _____
9. Get a massage   9. _____
10. Talk to a therapist 10. _____

You can refer to this list frequently during your griefwork, when you feel that you need a break from the demands of mourning. Perhaps you might want to make a copy of this list, hanging it in a conspicuous place where you will see it when you might need to be reminded to nourish yourself. As time goes on you may want to add new things to the list.

How Do You Cope with Change?

The final separation with which you are trying to cope has been preceded by what psychotherapist/philosopher Stanley Keleman called "daily little deaths." These day-by-day turning points can tell us much about how we will deal with major losses. As Keleman says:

> We are always dying a bit, always giving things up, always having things taken away. . . . Life can be described as a migration through many formative loops, many little dyings. Growth, change and maturing occur by deforming the old and forming the new. . . . There are no turning points that are not accompanied by feelings of dying. Each person handles them uniquely. Turning points evoke expressions of anger, pain, excitement, loss, sacrifice, grief and others. Becoming aware of how you handle turning points is . . . discovering how you live with little dying. Living your dying is learning about the transformation arising from your turning points. (*Living Your Dying*, p. 25)

Keleman's words remind us of the Temple's Mourners' Path which affirmed the commonality of the experiences of loss. To some people, the concept of "little deaths" may seem strange, even offensive. How can the change of a job and the loss of a loved one be compared? But there are usually some commonalties in the way each person experiences change. I know a woman who has spent years trying to decide to move from a totally unsatisfactory residence. She endlessly thinks and talks about moving, but never does. The same could be said about her pattern of obsessive behavior concerning the death of her brother. Decades after his death, she still grieves for him in the same way she did shortly after his death. While there is an obvious difference in the content and extremes of feeling regarding her attachments to her brother and her apartment, the way that she grieves for them is quite similar: She cannot move beyond them.

Exercise 4·5
The Major Deaths in Your Life

What have been the major "deaths" in your life? Include both the actual deaths of people to whom you have been close and the "little deaths" about which we have been speaking. These might be a change of residence or profession or of financial security. Recall events that altered your role or status. These events may have been either more or less traumatic than your current loss.

How were you able to cope with these changes and integrate the new situation that they created? How did you integrate the change they triggered? What did you learn that will help you cope with the major turning point at which you find yourself today?

Knowing the issues that are raised when we face turning points is helpful, because the emotional vulnerability of mourning invites all of our personal issues to come forward to be explored.

Exercise 4·6
Your Current Support System

You have written about people and events that have shaped your emotional life. But who is there for you now? When analyzing your current support system, think of family, friends, and community resources that you can count on to help you as you face your loss. List their names and how they have helped you.

I have rarely met someone who is mourning who does not feel that he or she has been profoundly let down by at least one close family member or friend. Often those with whom we are most intimate cannot offer the kind of support that we feel we need during mourning. There are many reasons for this. It may be hard for someone who has relied on you in the past to see you as vulnerable. Or, since a close relative or friend may also be suffering from the same loss that you are, he or she may also be needy now. Since each person's reaction to a loss is unique, he or she may have very different needs from yours.

When I left New Orleans after my mother and sister died, I also left my father. My journals from that time are filled with my sorrow at missing him, guilt at having abandoned him, as well as my recognition that he and I had very different needs during that time. We both found our way to healing, he through his work and his tremendous contributions to his community, and I through intensely pursuing my emotional and spiritual growth. Now we have also found our way to each other and are very close. We both regret that we were unable to reach each other during that difficult time, recognizing the differences in the path to healing we both needed to find.

Exercise 4·7
Who Disappointed You?

Describe how some people on whom you usually rely have disappointed or even pained you. Who are the people with whom you must exercise caution? It might be helpful to describe the limits you might need to place on yourself in each relationship. (For example: "I can speak to my daughter several times a week on the phone and ask her to help me with paperwork and other legal details regarding her father's death, but I can't get into lengthy discussions with her about how much I miss my husband and my fears of the future.")

By suggesting that you define the limits for these relationships, I am neither condoning nor judging the behavior of those close to you. I am only suggesting that you be realistic about the support people are offering, and what they actually can give. Acknowledging these limits should help you protect yourself when you are most vulnerable. Make sure that the limits you perceive are based on reality and not your imagination or desires.

Exercise 4·8
A Last Look in the Mirror

Now sit in front of a real mirror. Look at yourself. Describe whom you see, both physically and emotionally. Are you different today than before the death? How? Given your emotional history, the major turning points you have faced, and your support system, describe the major challenges you expect to face while mourning and the hopes you have for handling them.

Having taken this time to examine the emotional influences and supports that are factors in your mourning process, I hope you are ready to move forward. We will now cover up our metaphorical mirror and move together down the mourner's path.

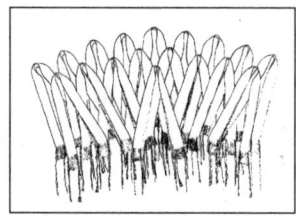

The Divine Presence ... is at the bedside of the sick.

–Kitzer Shulkhan Arukh 193:4

5

שכינה

The Shekhinah at the Bedside:

Remembering the Illness and the Death

ONE OF THE PRAYERS said at a Jewish funeral is the *El Malei Rakhamim*, which translates as "God, filled with Compassion." This asks the *Shekhinah*, God's compassionate and comforting presence, to shelter the deceased. Tradition tells us that when someone is close to death, the *Shekhinah* is near.

Meanwhile, as death is awaited, comfort is offered by family, friends, and health professionals. Jewish law is quite specific regarding care of the sick. Preservation

ש.כ.נ **ShKhN:** to dwell; a dwelling or neighborhood; indwelling; *Shekhinah*: God, the Divine Presence that dwells among us.

of life is the highest priority in Judaism and takes precedence over all other acts. Even Shabbat can be violated if a sick person needs care.

The Jewish rituals coming before and after death address the psychological needs of the dying person and articulate Jewish values and beliefs regarding deep philosophical issues. As we explore some of the traditional values and rites connected with the final part of an individual's life, we will elicit memories, raise unresolved issues, and stimulate philosophical reflections.

Jewish tradition and ritual give us the metaphors we will use to explore these issues. The goal of these explorations is the understanding that can lead to comfort. For some people this understanding will be entirely secular; for others it will be infused with spirituality. Religious rituals frame the process, yet the path can be useful to those of other orientations as well. These rituals are effective because they address universal human needs. Because of this the process has been useful both to secular and observant Jews as well as to non-Jews.

Judaism values practice over belief. It contends that certain feelings and beliefs will emerge in the course of performing prescribed actions. That is why ritual is so effective. For this reason, I encourage you to do the exercises even if you don't understand the principles on which they are based—and even if your orientation is determinedly secular.

> The effect upon the soul of . . . a work is not at all dependent upon its being understood.
> —Gershom Sholem

Remembering is Important

Let's shift back in time to explore events that led up to the death of the person for whom you are mourning. We will then review the period from death to the funeral and focus on the person you have lost and your memories connected with the loss. This period will be reviewed both from your perspective and from what you imagine to be the perspective of the person who died.

Memory is not always a friend. After a death, we are often told to cherish our memories. But the immediate memories of that death are often haunting or horrible. Of a death that came after a long illness, we may remember the excruciating pain of the patient or the anonymous, seemingly insensitive institutional settings, with tubes and monitors and scurrying by unfamiliar people all dressed in white or green. Of sudden deaths, we remember horror and shock. Mourners may relive over and over again the exact moment they received the unexpected news and the days of numb disbelief that followed. Of relationships that had many unresolved issues, the mourner may most remember his or her difficulties with the deceased. The death may trigger anger, guilt, or other uncomfortable emotions that are exacerbated because of the sense that the death has made their resolution impossible.

Mourners' assumptions about how they are *supposed* to behave sometimes make it difficult for them to share these memories. And since other people often do not want to hear these thoughts and emotions, mourning is made even less bearable.

There may be an image that you cannot get out of your head. A woman in one of my groups for widows couldn't stop thinking of her husband's fear of pain as he was being moved from their bed to the ambulance gurney while suffering from what would be a fatal stroke. His terrified expression was imprinted in her mind. One man kept remembering the icy hand of his eleven-year-old son, whose body was punctured by the tubes and wires that were keeping him alive after treatment for leukemia. He was embarrassed by the memory and didn't feel he should share it, even though it was bearing down on him. He kept feeling that cold hand, even in his dreams.

These people needed to talk about their memories, but each time they found the courage to share them, they were hushed by those who could not bear hearing them. "Don't do this to yourself," the man was told by his sister. She thought she was protecting him. In fact, she contributed to his inability to find a safe place to grieve.

Often, especially in the case of an unexpected death, the story of how the news arrived is what must be told. We frequently need to talk about the last moments spent with the deceased. This encounter frequently becomes magnified in significance. We feel as if we should have known what was ahead. We obsess over what were actually routine events, as if hidden in them is some magical truth that will make sense of the senseless.

I actually believed for a while that my mother's displeasure with the haircut I got a few days before her suicide was responsible for her death. The event took on extraordinary significance as I told the story over and over and thought about it obsessively. By telling and re-telling the story, I eventually realized that by believing that my haircut had somehow triggered my mother's death, I was attempting to persuade myself that I could have made a difference in my mother's life, despite reports that she had been swallowed up by her own darkness from a very early age. This grotesque reasoning is not uncommon as mourners examine all their final moments under a microscope. Sometimes it is easier to feel this kind of guilt, than to stand face-to-face with our helplessness in the face of the great mysteries of life and death.

Before mourners can find comfort in memory, it is often necessary for them to be purged of the haunting images that paralyze their grief process. So let's attempt this by telling the story of the events that led up to the death. Get the stories that you are longing—or afraid—to tell, off your chest.

Exercise 5·1
Telling the Story

Write about the events preceding the death. You may want to remember the moment when you were told of the type or the seriousness of the illness and the course of the treatment. You may recall a series of events involving doctors, nurses, hospitals, and long-term care. Or you may have one horrible moment when the unexpected news shattered your world. You may want to write about a special moment you shared with the deceased, perhaps your last time together. There may have been events that marked milestones in the medical treatments or in your relationship. Decisions had to be made, and certain people either helped or, possibly, even hindered you. Or were present, or should have been. There were things that you did or didn't do that satisfied you or that you wish you had done differently. There may be an event or image that you can't get out of your head. Tell your story in narrative form, and do not avoid any feelings that are aroused while you tell it. Cry if necessary. Rage if necessary. But focus on the telling and try not to judge what you did or what you feel now.

> Sabbath exists even in the midst of devastation.... This is the Sabbath: A little rain in the midst of drought, vision in the very moment of understanding nothing, a flash of beauty in a broken bowl, and the miraculous, insistent vitality of the body and the heart.
>
> —Deena Metzger

I rarely have met a mourner without a story, a memory, or something that he or she is longing to tell. As painful as these stories may be, they need to be told. After repeated telling, the stories lose some of their intensity.

Having told your story, this may be a good time to go back to the Shabbat list (exercise 4-4, pp. 51–52) that you made in the last chapter and find something that you can do to care for yourself.

The **Viddui**: *The Final Confession*

The mitzvot of *bikur cholim* (visiting the sick) and *kavod ha-met* (honoring the deceased) insist that up to the time of death, we focus primarily on the needs of the dying person; therefore, we now turn our attention to the deceased, remembering the events that may have preceded the death.

We will start by imagining how the deceased might have reviewed and assessed his or her life. Our context for such an assessment comes from a traditional Jewish perspective for reviewing a life.

According to Jewish law, the dying person should recite the *Viddui*, the final confession. In this prayer of repentance, God is asked to forgive the dying person's sins and to protect his or her surviving family. It ends with an affirmation of faith in God and a recitation of the *Shema*.

The Hebrew word for repentance, *teshuva*, means "return" or "turning." Reciting the *Viddui* on the deathbed is an act of *teshuva*, a turning from evil toward good. One *returns* to behavior appropriate to one created in God's image. Since this act of *teshuvah* is the last act in life, one senses that the notion of *return* is central to Judaism's understanding of the nature of death.

But what are these offenses for which one must repent as the last act of life? The concept of sin in Judaism is similar to an arrow that has fallen short of its target. Among the Hebrew words for sin are: *het*, "to miss" or "fail"; *averah*, "a breach"; and *avon*, "crooked." These ascribe sin to acts which fail to live up to one's obligations or fulfill one's potential.

There are essentially two kinds of sin: Those against God and those against other humans. A human life stretches from dust to dust. In between, it is animated with the breath of God's soul. A human being has that soul "on loan" and is obligated to use it to its full potential to fulfill God's precepts. To sin against God, then, is to miss the mark in living up to that trust. In secular terms, this kind of transgression represents a failure in meeting goals consistent with an individual's unique ability and destiny. This requires soul-searching, the expression of regret, and a recommitment to living a life aligned with purpose.

A sin against another human being is a different matter. If I've done something wrong to you, it is not enough to confess to God and ask forgiveness. I need to make amends to you directly.

Traditionally, in Judaism, it is God who forgives our trespasses against our own potential, for these are sins against God. But forgiveness for transgressions that one human commits against another must be worked out between those individuals. Violating the rules that govern human interaction requires amends to the person who has been sinned against. Therefore, a dying person

ש.ו.ב **ShUV:** to return or repent; an answer; *teshuva*: repentance, returning to a path of righteousness.

is encouraged to settle all debts to others, whether they are material or emotional, before death.

As forboding as the idea of intoning a final confession may be, Jews are familiar with the process. Many observant Jews recite a version of the *Viddui* every night before closing their eyes to go to sleep. During the High Holy Day period Jews confess their transgressions against their God-like potential and against other humans. These can be considered a rehearsal for reciting the *Viddui*.

The *Shema*, an affirmation of God's oneness, is a basic statement of Jewish faith. It is said many times daily, both privately and with the community, including before going to sleep each night. Ideally, the familiarity of the process of saying the *Shema* while preparing to go to sleep gives comfort to one affirming God's oneness and closing his or her eyes one more time.

To understand the *Viddui* as a ritual intended to heal transgressions, we can look at the practices in the time of the Temple which were associated with expiating sins: Worshippers at the ancient Temple who wanted forgiveness for their sins brought animals or other offerings to the Temple for sacrifice. These sacrificial offerings were symbolic. They represented the person who had sinned and who hoped that the sacrifice would assure his or her personal purification and forgiveness for the transgression resulting in their realignment with the path of Holiness. The sacrificial rites in the Temple can be compared to the fast and other practices of prayer and self-denial on Yom Kippur, where food and other comforts are sacrificed for the purposes of purification and forgiveness. But when a dying person recites the *Viddui,* there is no symbolic ritual. The person's own life is the offering.

We should repent every day. As R. Eliezer said: Repent one day before your death. Since no one knows the day of death, all our days should be spent in repentance.

—*Talmud: Shabbat* 153

The *Viddui* will help us focus on the deceased. By exploring the perspective of the deceased toward life and death, we acknowledge that his or her perspective may have been different from ours. This begins the process of separation.

The starting point of the following exercise is a prayer of supplication and affirmation. Some people may be uncomfortable or, at least, unfamiliar with appealing to God. Nevertheless, see if you can put these feelings aside while responding to the first two parts of the exercise, because even without belief in God, the exercise raises important psychological issues.

The first two parts of the *Viddui* will be used to review the life of the deceased and to express concern for you as the survivor and mourner. These are concerns which are appropriate to all of us confronting our mortality, regardless of our spiritual philosophy. For the third part of the *Viddui,* which includes the *Shema,* you can describe the beliefs of the deceased.

All dying persons must confess. Everyone who makes confession has a share in the world to come.
—Kitzer *Shulkhan Arukh* 193:13

Part 1: Life Review: The Sacred Trust

This exercise is done from the imagined perspective of the person who died. Try to imagine the deceased at the moment of death as he or she prepares to account to God for the life that is ending—its meaning, its achievements, its failures. Would the deceased say that his or her life fulfilled the sacred trust with God? From his or her perspective, what would be counted as promises kept or broken, or sins committed? Use the space next to the translation of the prayer for your journal entry.

Exercise 5·2
The *Viddui*

The Viddui

מודה אני לפניך, יי, אלהי ואלהי אבותי, שרפואתי
ומיתתי בידך. יהי רצון מלפניך, שתרפאני רפואה שלמה.
ואם המות כלה ונחרץ מעמך אקחנו מידך באהבה. ותהי
מיתתי כפרה על כל חטאים ועונות ופשעים שחטאתי
ושעויתי ושפשעתי לפניך. ותשפיע לי מרב טוב הצפון לצ-
דיקים. ותודיעני ארח חיים שבע שמחות את פניך נעימות
בימינך נצח.
אבי יתומים ודין אלמנות. הגן בעד קרובי היקרים
אשר נפשי קשורה בנפשם. בידך אפקיד רוחי פדיתה
אותי, יי, אל אמת. אמן ואמן.

My God and God of my ancestors,
let my prayer come before you.
Do not ignore my plea.
Forgive me for any wrong
I have done in my lifetime.
Please accept my death as an offering,
bringing atonement and forgiveness for my wrongdoings,
for against You alone have I trespassed.

May it be your will, God of my ancestors,
that I live in alignment with your Holy Name.
With your great compassion, cleanse me of my misdeeds,
but not through suffering and disease.
Send a perfect healing to me and to all who are stricken.
My God and God of my ancestors,
I acknowledge that my life and recovery
depend upon You.
May it be Your will to heal me.
Yet if You have decreed that I shall die of this affliction,
may my death atone for any wrongdoings,
which I have committed before You.
Shelter me in the shadow of Your wings;
grant me a share in the world to come.

Part 2: Concern with Relationships

The next part of the Viddui *is concerned with the protection of those left behind. Which survivors would the deceased be concerned about? Why? This explores transgressions the deceased may have committed*

Part One

against others which God cannot forgive until attempts have been made to make amends to the injured person. You might want to list major relationships that the deceased had and write how you imagine the deceased felt about each of these as death approached.

> God:
> Parent of orphans,
> Defender of widows,
> protect my beloved family,
> with whose soul my
> own soul is bound.

Part 3: Turning Toward God

At its conclusion, the Viddui expresses the traditional belief that confession will bring redemption and forgiveness. At this point, the final Shema is recited, giving the dying person one more opportunity to affirm God's oneness. The God of the Viddui's final paragraph is a God of truth, judgment and compassion. How would the deceased have described God? Was he or she a believer, an agnostic, or an atheist? What do you imagine this person felt as death was imminent? Describe what he or she may have felt about the fate of the soul and the nature of God.

> Into your hand I deposit my soul.
> You have redeemed me, God of truth.
> *Shema Yisrael*
> Adonai, *Elohenu*
> Adonai, *Ekhad.*
> Hear O Israel
> Our God Is One
> Adonai *Hu Ha Elohim.*
> Adonai is God.
> God the Judge, is God the compassionate.
> *God the Judge, is God the compassionate.*

Light—the Symbol of the Divine

Traditionally, when a person dies, a candle is placed near the head of the body. Light is an important symbol in Judaism. The flickering light of a candle and of the eternal light in the synagogue symbolizes that which does not die. It represents God and the spark of God that is in each of us. In the Bible, human life began as God breathed the breath of life, or the soul, into Adam. Since we are told that life does not begin until God has breathed a soul into each human being, it is as incumbent upon each of us to develop his or her unique potential as it is to remember the realm of breath. It is with breath that we embody God. This is the place within and without each of us, a place that we share with all other souls and with God. As a person dies, the soul and the breath leave the body and begin to find the way back to The Source.

> The human soul is the lamp of God.
> —Proverbs 20:27

Exercise 5•3
Contemplating the Flickering Soul

Contemplate the soul symbolized by the light of a candle. Sit in a darkened room, light a candle, watch it, and breathe deeply. As you breathe, recall the discussions about soul, repentance, and forgiveness earlier in this chapter. Consider how those concepts relate to your sense of what became of the deceased after death. Now consider your attitude toward these concepts. What do you think the soul is? What, if anything, do you believe to be eternal? You may have a strong sense that there is something that exists beyond flesh and blood, or you may believe that there is nothing but "dust to dust."

These questions may leave you with more questions— and no conclusions. No matter. Just contemplate these questions and see what comes into your mind's eye.

No matter what you feel about the soul and eternity, your willingness to explore such issues indicates an openness to the opportunities mourning brings for growth and transformation. Let's move on to confront the death itself.

One who cares to pierce into the mystery of the holy unity of God should consider the flame as it rises from a burning coal or candle.

—Gershom Sholem

Chapter Five

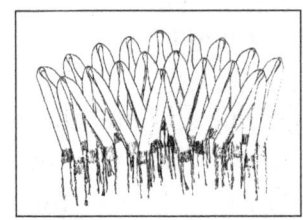

Rav Nachman showed himself to Rava [in a dream after his death]. Rava asked him, "Was death painful?" Rav Nachman replied, "It was as painless as lifting a hair from a cup of milk. But were the Holy One . . . to say to me, 'You may return to that world where you were before,' I would not wish to do it. The fear of death is too great."

—Babylonian Talmud: Mo'ed Katan 28a

6

אנינות

Aninut

From Death to Burial: Suspended between Two Worlds

We are now at the moment of death. According to Jewish tradition, our attention still rests with the deceased. Only after burial does attention shift to the needs of the mourner. During *aninut*, the period between the death and the burial, the behavior of mourners is tightly restricted. In addition to the prohibitions on prayer and study, almost every action of the mourner's life is curtailed.

Among the activities forbidden to mourners during this period are: eating or drinking to excess, sitting on a chair, greeting friends, engaging in sexual contact, or working. Attention is directed to rituals involving the body of the deceased.

א.נ.נ **ANN:** to complain, murmur, wail, be sorry for, lament, grumble; *aninut*: the period between death and burial; *onen*: one who mourns during this period

Before the interment, the mourner . . . should not utter any benediction, nor respond "Amen" to the benedictions of others. [S]He cannot be included in a [minyan].
—*Kitzer Shulkhan Arukh* 196:1, 2

Kavod Hamet: *Honoring the Dead*

A dead body is equated with a damaged Torah scroll, no longer fit for use, but still deserving reverence for the holy purpose it once served. The community is responsible for protecting the body and keeping it company while awaiting burial. These responsibilities specifically fall to the *shomrim* (the "guardians" or "watchers"), who can be either friends, relatives, or members of the esteemed *Chevra Kaddisha* (the "holy society"), although they should not be members of the immediate family.

The *Chevra Kaddisha*'s practices include *taharah*, the ritual washing of the body. This is considered a final act of love and respect by the community toward someone who had been part of it. It may also be a way for the community to forgive the deceased for any transgressions committed while a member of that community.

Just as there are two kinds of sins, there are also two very different purification rites. The first is the *Viddui*, in which the dying person directly asks God to forgive his or her shortcomings. The second, which parallels the *taharah*, requires the *community* to forgive transgressions that were interpersonal. These two practices allow the deceased to leave the world with the same spiritual purity, cleanliness, and innocence with which he or she entered it. It may also be a formal way for the community to say goodbye to one who no longer dwells within it.

In contrast to the work of the *Viddui*, which was from the perspective of the deceased, the *taharah* gives us a framework for your ongoing evaluation of the life of the deceased and your relationship to him or her. This evaluation is a prerequisite to your eventually letting go of the connection you once shared to enable its

---

א.ר.נ **ARN:** a chest, coffin, closet; *Aron Hakodesh*: the ark which contains the tablets of the law or the Torah; a casket containing a body

ט.ה.ר **THR:** clean, pure; *tahara*: the ritual cleansing of a body before burial

Naked came I out of my Mother's womb, and naked shall I return there.

—*Job* 1:21

transformation from a physical to a spiritual connection. The entire process of mourning, in fact, can be considered a form of *taharah* since its goal is to help you find the peace that lets you release the person who has died and accept what has transpired. This means coming to terms with all aspects of the relationship, including the changes in it brought about by the death. It also means having integrated the death into your newly transformed life and being ready to allow your own life to go on despite the dramatic new reality.

In case you are not ready for this separation yet, we will undertake the *taharah* in stages. We will do part of it now and part of it later in the book, when you explore some of the remaining unfinished aspects of your relationship.

Exercise 6·1
Taharah and Forgiveness

Part 1: Readiness for Forgiveness
Focus on yourself as the one who will perform this rite of release and forgiveness. Are you ready? Can you imagine saying goodbye? Are there areas that feel especially unfinished where forgiveness and release seem impossible? What are they? Projects that were left undone? Issues in the relationship? Feelings that came with the death? Don't expect these feelings to be rational, kind, or fair. Acknowledge in the space provided here the extent to which you are ready to forgive and to say goodbye.

Part 2: Asking for Forgiveness—Past and Future
It is customary, after a death has occurred, for family and friends to enter the room where the body lies and speak to it, reviewing their relationship and asking

> One is not held liable for what is said when suffering.
> —Talmud: Baba Batra 16B

forgiveness for any offense that might have been committed. Similarly, the taharah *begins with members of the* Chevra Kaddisha *asking the body to forgive them for any indignities that might occur while cleaning it.*

This is a good opportunity for you to ask forgiveness for any unresolved issues for which you may feel responsible. It is also a time to state your intention to go through the healing process with honesty. Since relationships are a complex mixture of many feelings it is likely that you will grapple with emotions or memories that contradict the concept of eulogy, or only speaking favorably about the dead.

Address the deceased as if you were writing a letter to him or her and ask forgiveness for your past transgressions. You might also want to ask forgiveness for the healing process itself. This is suggested because many mourners often feel that choosing to move on with life feels like a betrayal of the person who died. In addition, since honesty is essential to healing, your grief-work may require you to tell stories about the deceased that may have been secret or may feel like a violation of trust or be a negative portrayal of the deceased. Ask for forgiveness in the space to the left.

In choosing to write this book, I have had to ask several people, living and dead, for forgiveness. Because I believe that the values of the *hesped*—honesty and deep feelings—are the essential tools of healing, I have had to reveal personal stories about a difficult time in my life. In sharing these stories I hope that others will be encouraged to face their own experience directly and that the tragedies I had to face so early in my life will have some redeeming qualities, as others learn and grow from hearing of my experience. Ultimately, I feel that by telling the truth, I am honoring the lives of those I have mourned. And in using their stories to help others, I am giving the people I remember the opportunity to continue to perform acts of *tzedakah* (charity and justice) and *gemilut chasadim* (acts of loving kindness) despite their death. (Journal Entry, Los Angeles, 1992)

Shemira: *Guarding and Honoring the Deceased*

The duty of the *shomrim* is *shemira* (watching). Since it is believed that leaving the body alone violates the dignity of the person who has died, one of the important tasks is to guard the body. Some feel this is a way of comforting the newly departed soul; others feel it is a way of honoring the dead. The *shomrim* sit with the body around the clock and read aloud passages from the Book of Psalms.

> You will find refuge under God's wings. . . . You need not fear the terror by night. . . . God's angels will guard you wherever you go and carry you in their hands.
> —Psalm 91:4–11

List below readings or musical selections that you would have liked to share with the deceased as a way to say goodbye. They may be designed to comfort yourself or to ease the passage of the soul. You might choose favorite poems or songs—yours or the deceased's. You may include your own writings or passages from the Bible or other works of literature or music. They may or may not address death and might include music or poems that evoke moments you shared together or that describe what you feel now. Perhaps you will want to make a booklet or an audiotape of your selections.

Exercise 6•2
Create Your Own *Shemira* Liturgy

It is said that the departing soul is a shaliakh, or messenger, from the world of the living (Olam Hazeh) to the world of souls (Olam Haneshamot), or perhaps a direct

Exercise 6•3
The Departing Soul as *Shaliakh* (Messenger)

Chapter Six

line between God and the earth. This is seen as a time when prayers are especially likely to be heard. If this were so, is there a message you would want to send up with the soul of the deceased? Perhaps a prayer for your own healing or the safeguarding of the soul would be appropriate or, perhaps a prayer for the healing of the planet. Write the wish or the prayer you would like to have carried to the higher realms by the soul of the one you are mourning.

Remembering (or Imagining) the Funeral and Burial

The burial of the body changes the focus from *kavod hamet* (honoring the dead) to *yekare de'hayye* (the needs of the survivors). This transition is made through three hallmarks of the burial service: the *hesped,* or eulogy; the *El Malai Rakhamim*; and the Kaddish. These give a final public accounting of the life of the deceased, release the soul to the *Shekhinah,* and shift attention to the responsibilities and concerns of the living.

Exercise 6·4
The *Hesped* or Eulogy

As we have said, a hesped *should accurately represent the life of the deceased. It is as inappropriate to laud an evil person as to malign a good one. We have already explored the difference between "eulogy," the English word that most approximates a* hesped, *and "hesped" itself. In this difference lies the Jewish determination to directly and honestly confront death and the feelings it elicits.*

Part 1: Remembering What Was Said

Do you remember the hesped *that was delivered at the funeral or memorial service? If it was read by the person who officiated at the funeral, you might be able to insert here a copy of what was actually said. Otherwise, write what you remember was said. If no service was held or if you were not present at the funeral, write what you imagine was said.*

Eulogies invariably concentrate on the positive deeds of the deceased. This is consistent with honoring the deceased and comforting the mourner. But it is hard to capture the total person, and frequently the eulogizer is not well acquainted with the person who has died. Unfortunately, people close to the deceased often complain that the person described in the hesped was not the person they knew. This can often leave those who knew the whole person burdened with secrets.

Part 2: A Private *Hesped*: What Should Have Been/Or Could Not Be Said?

Were you satisfied with what was said about the person who died? If you were dissatisfied with what was said, or feel that something was omitted, take this opportunity to write another hesped *that fully describes the deceased—one that could possibly never be recited in public. You may know of good deeds sworn to secrecy or not-so-good deeds that could not be mentioned for the sake of propriety, loyalty to the deceased, or protection of the living. Since tradition requires that you be honest and realistic, you can include whatever you want. Such focusing on your true feelings begins the transition from honoring the deceased to caring for yourself as a mourner.*

El Malai Rakhamim: *A Prayer for the Soul*

In Judaism, God has many names, but there is only one God. Each name describes a different attribute of God.

The world is a field of compassion.
—Deena Metzger

Chapter Six

מ.ח.ר **RKhM:** the womb; *rakhamim*: mercy, compassion, love; *Harakhaman*: a name for God: the Compassionate One

Various prayers invoke these different names as a way to draw on the various qualities which God reflects.

The *El Malai Rakhamim* is intoned during the burial ceremony, following the interment of the body. It calls upon God to embrace the soul of the deceased with compassion as it is bound up with all the other souls, under the nurturing wings of the *Shekhinah*. The *Shekhinah* portrays God as being present, close, personal, and nurturing. Often described as the feminine side of God, inclusion in the tradition is evidence that the familiar image of "God the Father" is not the complete picture.

Rakhamim refers to God's compassion. Its root, *rekhem*, means "womb." It alludes both to God's maternal attributes and to the nurturing, loving quality of the ever-present *Shekhinah*. *Rakhamim* is central to our work. Without compassionately understanding the life of the deceased, we may not be able to say goodbye. Nor will we find release from the burdens connected with the death of the relationship. That we pray for the deceased to find rest in God's nurturing womb, gives us insight to Judaism's understanding that life is a journey from womb to womb. It alludes to the possibility that our earthly task is to remain in alignment with what Deena Metzger calls the "field of compassion."

But the full awareness that may enable us to feel compassion is not always available soon after the death, when our hearts are crowded with a mix of feelings. This womb-love which unconditionally accepts and forgives and does not stand in judgment, often eludes us when we are in the early stages of mourning. It comes only after extensive grief-work, which encourages the honest settling of accounts between the mourner and the deceased and requires acknowledging resentments and gratitudes.

Without appreciating both sides of the ledger, it is difficult to close the account so that we can accept what has happened and say goodbye with compassion.

Compassion is also central to our work on ourselves. Mourners subject themselves to destructive self-judgments: shame, guilt, anger, and embarrassment. *Rakhamim* helps us see ourselves as we are and to heal, with love, our vulnerabilities, imperfections, and disappointments. This compassionate encounter with ourselves is essential to change, since only by truly seeing ourselves and what has shaped us can we lift ourselves out of the shadows and into the light. We come to know that frightened, hidden self and to understand and finally love it. Such healing with love is *rakhamim*. It is what the community prays that the newly departed soul of the deceased will encounter as it rises to the place where souls go. This self-compassion and divine compassion elevate us and help make our lives whole and less troublesome.

El Malai Rakhamim

אל מלא רחמים, שוכן במרומים, המצא מנוחה נכונה תחת כנפי השכינה, במעלות קדושים וטהורים כזהר הרקיע מזהירים את נשמת... שהלך לעולמו (שהלכה לעולמה). בעבור שנדרו צדקה בעד הזכרת נשמתו (נשמתה), בגן עדן תהא מנוחתו (מנוחתה). לכן בעל הרחמים יסתירהו (יסתירה) בסתר כנפיו לעולמים, ויצרור בצרור החיים את-נשמתו (נשמתה). יי הוא נחלתו (נחלתה). וינוח (ותנוח) על משכבו (משכבה) בשלום, ונאמר: אמן.

El malei rachamim, shochein bamromim, hamtzei m'nucha n'chona tachat kanfei hash'china, b'ma'alot k'doshim ut'horim k'zohar haraki'a mazhirim et neshmat… she'halach l'olamo (she'halcha l'olama). Ba'avur she'nadru tz'daka b'ad hazkarat nishmato (nishmata), b'gan eden t'hei m'nuchato (m'nuchata). Lachein ba'al harachamim yastireihu (yastireiha) b'seter k'nafav l'olamim, v'yitzror bitz'ror hachayim et nishmato (nishmata). Adonai hu nachalato (nachalata). V'yanu'ach (v'tanu'ach) al mishkavo (mishkava) b'shalom. V'nomar: amen.

God full of mercy (womb God), who dwells on high, grant proper rest under the wings of the divine presence, in the heights of the holy and the pure, who shine as the Earth shines, for the soul of … who has gone to his/her world. For those who swore righteousness to remember his/her soul, may his/her rest be in the Garden of Eden; so may the Master of Mercy shelter him/her in the shelter of God's wings to the ends of time, and may God bind his/her soul in the bond of life. Adonai is his/her heritage. He/she will rest in peace on his/her resting place. Let us say: Amen.

Exercise 6·5
A Wish for the Soul

The El Malai Rakhamim *is recited after family and friends begin to shovel earth into the grave after the body has been lowered into the ground. It is a moment at which the body and the soul are believed to be forever separated: The body returns to "dust" and the soul rises to meet other souls. As we watch the body being sealed away from us forever, it is also a moment when our own sense of separation is most intense. Write the wishes, thoughts and feelings you might have had as the body of the person you are mourning was lowered into the ground or the feelings you have now when contemplating this separation.*

Many, especially those who have witnessed agony and pain in the final days of life, often say goodbye with a wish that the soul will finally be at peace. Not everyone feels compassion at such a time. When my mother committed suicide, her sister wished that she would find the peace she had never known. But I stood, looking into the grave, and was overwhelmed with horror. How could my mother have chosen to leave me? Later,

I could not forgive myself for thinking of myself when my mother had been in such pain. Yet my anger was as appropriate as my aunt's compassion and my healing required me to feel compassion both for my mother's choice and my anger about it.

"Like Grass of the Earth"

One practice often performed toward the end of a funeral very graphically addresses the separation of the body and the soul: This is the ancient custom of plucking a few blades of grass and throwing them over the shoulder, when leaving the cemetery. Through the centuries this has been interpreted as an ancient ritual performed to dispel evil spirits, as well as a representation of the return of dust to dust. The gestures associated with this act play out symbolically the entire cycle of mourning—its desperate yearning as well as its potential for healing and growth. It seems appropriate that this act takes place at the moment that tradition encourages us to change our focus from *kavod hamet*, honoring the deceased, to *yekare de'hayye*, attending to the needs of the mourner.

In grabbing onto the living plant, we see the intense desire of the mourner to literally hold on to the living physical being who has just been surrendered to the ground. In opening the hand and throwing the grass, we see the greatest challenge of mourning: to let go of the physicality of the relationship with those who have been lost and reach out to the wind—the spirit, opening up to a continued relationship that does not rely on physical presence. The major vehicle for this transformation to a spiritual connection with the deceased is the Kaddish.

> Out of the city may they flourish like grass of the earth.
> —Psalm 72:16

ר.ו.ח **RVKh:** wind, breath; *ruakh*: spirit

Chapter Six

The First Kaddish

The Kaddish is one of the most familiar Jewish prayers. It is commonly thought of as the prayer that the living say to remember the dead. But different versions of the Kaddish are recited in different contexts. The Burial Kaddish is recited at the funeral, and the Mourner's Kaddish is repeated at services during the year after the death, on the anniversary of a death (*yahrzeit*) and at memorial (*yizkor*) services throughout the year. The Kaddish is used in other situations, which we will explore to enrich our mourning process. For now, we are concerned with the Kaddish as it is recited for the first time—as the body is placed in the ground.

While the burial Kaddish acknowledges death, most versions of this prayer don't even mention death. It is concerned with life in the world. It asks that God's name be sanctified among the living and calls for a world of holiness and peace. It reminds us of one of the most central obligations of Jewish life: *tikkun olam*, healing the world, making it so holy that the gap between the world that we know and the world in which *tikkun* (healing) is fully realized is ended. The Kaddish also reminds us of our obligation to continue the task of living, carrying on the values of those who have died and the obligation of the Jew to choose life.

We say the Kaddish for the first time at a moment when we are stunned, searching for what is no longer among the living. It confronts us with the assertion that there is purpose to our remaining in the world, reminding us of our role in the world at a time when we may not be sure the world is where we belong. As such, it helps anchor the bereaved on the earth. We say the Kaddish and then turn to face the world without someone who has, until that moment, been central to bringing meaning to it.

The Kaddish is also used to punctuate transitions. The prayer is recited at various parts of a service to mark the end of one part and the beginning of another. Certainly the living make no more profound transition than when we turn our backs on a fresh grave and move into a world without those we have just buried. So with the awareness of the difficulty—and the holiness—of this transition, we move into the period of *shiva* and observe the first seven days of mourning.

Kaddish

יתגדל ויתקדש שמה רבא בעלמא די-ברא כרעותה, וימ-
ליך מלכותה בחייכון וביומיכון ובחיי דכל-בית ישראל, בעגלא
ובזמן קריב, ואמרו: אמן.
יהא שמה רבא מברך לעלם ולעלמי עלמיא!
יתברך וישתבח, ויתפאר ויתרומם ויתנשא, ויתהדר
ויתעלה ויתהלל שמה דקודשא, בריך הוא, לעלא מן-כל-
ברכתא ושירתא, תשבחתא ונחמתא דאמירן בעלמא, ואמרו:
אמן.
יהא שלמא רבא מן-שמיא וחיים עלינו ועל-כל-ישראל
ואמרו: אמן.
עשה שלום במרומיו, הוא יעשה שלום עלינו ועל-כל-
ישראל, ואמרו: אמן.

Yitgadal v'yitkadash sh'mei raba b'alma divra chir'utei, v'yamlich malchutei b'chayeichon uv'yomeichon v'chayai d'chol beit yisra'el, ba'agala u'viz'man kariv. V'imru: amen. Y'hei shmei raba m'vorach l'alam ul'almei almaya. Yitbarach v'yishtabach v'yitpa'ar v'yitromam v'yitnasei, v'yit'hadar, v'yit'ale v'vit'halal sh'mei d'kud'sha b'rich hu, l'eile min-kol-birchata v'shirata, tush'b'chata v'nechemata, da'amiran b'alma, v'imru: amen. Y'hei sh'lama raba min-sh'maya, v'chayim aleinu v'al-kol-yisrael, v'imru: amen. Oseh shalom bimromav, hu ya'aseh shalom aleinu v'al kol yisrael, v'imru: Amen.

May Your great name be magnified and hallowed, in the world created according to Your will, and may Your reign be quickly established, in our own lives and our own day, and in the life of all of Israel, and let us say: Amen. May Your great name be blessed for ever and ever! All praise and glory, splendor, exaltation and honor, radiance and veneration and worship to the Holy One of Blessing, even beyond any earthly prayer or song, any adoration or tribute we can offer, and let us say: Amen. May there be great peace from the heavens, and life for us and for all of Israel, as we say: Amen. May the one who makes peace in the high heavens send peace for us and for all of Israel, as we say: Amen.

Chapter Six

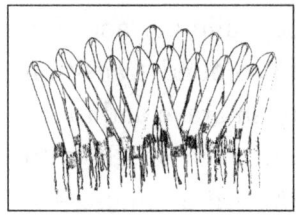

**It is better to go to
a house of mourning
than to a house of feasting;
for that is the lot of [all]. . . .**

–Ecclesiastes 7:1–15

7

שבעה

Shiva

A Community Embrace

A JEWISH FUNERAL ends amid potent rituals. One by one, family members and friends of the deceased file past the grave. Each takes the shovel and fills it with earth. The shovel turns and the soil hits the coffin with a distinct sound. This occurs again and again until the coffin is covered and the cycle of "dust to dust" enters its final stage. The mourners then walk through a double line formed by members of the community who reach out to support the mourner with the traditional words of comfort. This is a vestige of the ritual acknowledgment of mourners in the ancient Temple in Jerusalem.

The smell of the fresh earth piled by the grave site, the sound of the earth hitting the coffin, the double row

> Dust you are and dust you will be.
> —*Genesis* 3:19

of comforters—all these penetrate the dulled senses and spur the mourner into acknowledging the tasks of the early stage of mourning.

Today, it is not uncommon for people to eschew the Jewish mourning rituals, including choosing cremation over burial. I am hoping that this book will be a testament to the wisdom of opting for the Jewish path of healing. To some contemporary minds these ancient arguments advocating for in-ground burial, may seem archaic. However, we are at a time when both our species and the future of the earth are profoundly in peril. The affirmation of the intimate connection implied in "from dust you came and to dust you will return," reminds us of the sacred bond between the human and the earth, as well as our obligation, expressed in the early chapters of Genesis, to serve and protect the earth.

There is a Midrash explaining God's mysterious statement, in the first chapter of Genesis, preceding the creation of the human being: "Let us make a being in our image. " From the earliest times, Biblical commentators have questioned to whom God was speaking: Who was the other half of the "us" in that statement? One legend says that God was speaking to the earth, positing the human being as the fruit of the union between earth and God. When we return a body to Mother Earth, we affirm the holiness of our relationship with the earth, reminding us of our obligation to care for and protect it.

"Until you return to the ground—For from it you were taken. For dust you are, and to dust you shall return."

The Ambivalent Needs of Early Mourning

The psychological tasks of this stage are contradictory. You can retreat to a world where the natural anaesthetic of denial and numbness protect you from the brutal reality of loss. At the same time, sights and sounds of your immediate environment remind you of the reality of the loss. The challenge is to learn to travel safely between numbness and awareness in order to incorporate the new reality when possible and summon defenses when the pain is overwhelming.

Jewish law provides for graduated stages of mourning. Its initial activities are quite restrictive, and provide a tight frame to enclose the early intense feelings. The practices gradually become less restrictive and support the mourner's reentry into the communal stream of activity.

The Hebrew word *avelut* is used to describe the response to a calamity. When it refers to a human, it means "mourning." But when referring to a plant, it means "fading," "languishing," and "withering." The latter meaning, though not actually relating to humans, describes the emotional experience of early bereavement, in which many mourners withdraw into an almost vegetative state. Acknowledging this, tradition has legislated a highly protected period for the first seven days after the funeral—the *shiva* (seven). Sephardic Jews call this period *siete*, the Spanish and Ladino word for "seven."

Ideally, during this time, mourners are protected. At a time that they might feel an extreme sense of separation or isolation, they are surrounded by a supportive community, which gently encourages them to face the reality of the death.

א.ב.ל **AVL:** to mourn, languish, fade, or wither; *avelut*: mourning; *avel*: a mourner

ש.ב.ע **ShVA:** seven: an oath, a week; *shiva*: the first seven days of mourning following the funeral

Chapter Seven

> Visitors coming to a shivah house to bring comfort should wait for the mourner to begin the conversation. The mourner sits in a central place, surrounded by comforters and shakes his or her head to indicate that it is time for comforters to move on.
> —*Shulkhan Arukh, Yoreh De'ah*

During *shiva*, mourners stay at home and members of the community visit, reaching out to the grieving family. Effectively, the synagogue and the community change venue. Daily prayer services are usually held at the home of the deceased, and comforters are expected to come to pray and sit silently with the mourners.

Mourners withdraw into a tight cocoon circumscribed by the community and the withered emotions of early mourning. They are exempt from many obligations of economic, social, and religious life and encouraged to focus on the loss. Breaking one's daily routines underscores the profound rupture of the mourner's world. Hair cannot be cut. Because the wearing of leather is prohibited, shoes are not worn. Clothes cannot be washed. Greetings or inquires into the mourner's well-being are not permitted and mourners cannot sit on regular chairs or couches, but sit on low benches on the floor. Reading from the Torah is forbidden except from such books as Job or Lamentations, which focus on loss. Immediately following the death, during the period of *aninut*, mourners are even exempt from the recitation of certain blessings. These exemptions not only free mourners from obligations but recognize the isolation that mourners may feel, *even from God.*

Disguising Feelings to Hide Your Grief

Feelings of denial characterize the early stage of mourning. During this phase, a mourner may need to deny—consciously or not—the emotional impact of the loss that has occurred. He or she must begin to muster psychological defenses to protect him or herself from the too-bright light of reality.

While intellectually acknowledging the death is impossible to avoid, emotions can resist what the mind may clearly know. They may even cause the mind to play tricks. For a full month after her husband's funeral, a woman woke up each morning with a sense of relief—until she realized that the car accident which had crushed her ribs but had killed her husband was *not* just a bad dream. Many people report, with absolute conviction, that they have heard footsteps or seen the shadow of the person who has died. A nine-year-old girl showed no signs of grief, and insisted that her daddy tucked her in each night. These phenomena provide insulation from the reality of the end of physical contact.

People may experience physical as well as emotional numbness. One man said he was so dissociated from his body that he believed either he was dreaming—or that *he* was the one who had died. Others report feeling *nothing* during the funeral and the months following it. They experience this profound change in their lives with the emotional detachment similar to watching an intellectually interesting movie. Later, they may not even remember this phase of their lives.

These powerful emotions might make mourners withdraw from all social contact, or spur them on to become obsessively involved in activities or thoughts that prevent them from focusing on or feeling the loss. A man whose twin brother died after surgery so busied himself with the details of the funeral and caring for his brother's family that not until seven months later did he feel the impact of the death.

Chapter Seven

Some Disguises Can Be Particularly Harmful

Finding activities or relationships—or indulging certain personality traits—that can help you accept the loss *at your own pace* is important. But some of these defenses may be destructive. What begins as a way to cope can become emotionally disabling.

It may be hard to tell a destructive mode of coping from a healthy one. Sometimes a mourner who seems to be "dealing well" with the loss may actually be withdrawing from difficult feelings that need to be confronted. Known to psychology as a "flight into health," this is a common phenomenon. An extreme example was the seventy-three-year-old widower who remarried within three months of the death of his wife of forty-seven years, having gone through no period of adjustment.

During this period, you may also be vulnerable to alcohol or drug abuse, compulsive eating, and other obsessive behaviors designed to numb your pain. Or there may be a rush to a false serenity that is unwittingly encouraged by friends and relatives saying such bromides as "It was God's will" or "She's at peace now." These may unintentionally persuade you to deny the questions, angers, or other deep feelings so necessary for a healthy adjustment to loss. These difficult emotions can be the vehicle for the unbidden growth that death spurs as we confront the reality of death and come to terms with our own mortality.

After her forty-four-year-old husband died of a heart attack on a family vacation, a formerly zestful woman said, in a voice so tranquil that it sounded drugged, "He's in the hands of the Lord." For the next few years, she continued to affirm God's higher wisdom, without acknowledging the range of other emotions which attend loss. She participated only in solemn activities that she saw as fitting memorials to her husband, and required her daughter, who was eleven when her father died, to participate in them also. Although she was still a young, attractive woman, she never deeply connected with another partner. Her joyful, close relationships with family and friends withered away.

Shortly after she turned fifteen, the daughter began experimenting with drugs and sex. Unable to cope with the girl's behavior, the mother finally saw a psychotherapist, and began to see that she had been hiding behind a facade of false spirituality. She had used her faith in God to block her deeper feelings about her husband.

As she began to open up to the feelings from which she had retreated a decade before, she reviewed her life with her husband. She had idolized him from the day that they met when, as an eighteen-year-old, she had attended a workshop he was leading. He was charismatic, successful, and ten years older than she. Quickly becoming her mentor, he brought her into his stimulating, creative world. Her awe and gratitude blocked her ability to see all of him and his effect on her. For as he was contributing to her growth, he was also remaking her in his image and controlling her interests and activities. By the time they married, on her twenty-first birthday, she was almost completely dependent on him.

In addition, her husband was fifty pounds overweight. His family had a history of early death from heart disease. He had ignored his doctor's repeated entreaties that he lose weight, improve his diet and lead a more relaxed lifestyle. Her recovery came when she cried about his death, felt terror and outrage at being abandoned by the man she expected to always care for her, and raged at him for ignoring his doctor's advice—and at God for letting her life be so devastated. She realized that her rush to serenely accept his death had been disastrous to herself and her daughter.

Soon, she could give more of herself to her daughter and her daughter, in turn, could expect from her mother the very attention that her outrageous behavior had covertly been attempting to elicit.

Eulogizing Can Be Harmful

Eulogizing may also contribute to the denial process. The tendency to speak only good of the dead often delays our mourning. A sixty-five-year-old woman's husband was celebrated for his philanthropy and untiring participation in communal activities. Throughout their marriage, she was by his side, relishing the stimulation, stature, and adventure that his projects gave her. But she always knew that her own work had to be dropped in a minute to cater to her husband. Her four children supported her when she complained of being unappreciated and psychologically abused.

Yet when her husband died, the woman moved from the role of "Helpmate of the Great Man" to "Widow of the Great Man." She could not remember any difficulties in their marriage or tolerate her children's discussion of resentments or difficulties connected with their father. Now, fifteen years after his death, she has become the self-appointed keeper of the flame and bitterly resents that her husband's name is no longer reverentially invoked with what she considers

> Who thinks of death improves himself.
>
> —Bahya Ibn Pakuda

sufficient frequency by current business and community leaders. Even worse is that her denial of her husband's dark side has estranged her from her children and prevented her from realizing a creative, useful, and independent life.

The expectation of eulogy can also be frustrating if a mourner has long-standing anger or resentment that was not resolved during the life of the deceased. The belief that "we only say good of the dead" can make you feel that expressing these negative or ambivalent feelings is not permissible once a person is dead and healing is possible, even when these were difficulties in the relationship. The truth is that relationships continue to grow and change, even after one of the parties to them is dead. A great example, both poignant and humorous, was the statement a husband made to his wife about her mother, with whom she had had a troubled relationship. Over ten years and much therapeutic grief-work later, when the wife recounted a story about her mother, her husband said, "You know, she hasn't been so bad lately!"

Another form of isolation can occur when someone close to the deceased tries to protect others who are mourning that same death by not sharing his or her thoughts or feelings. After the loss of his father, a young man took a new job, which required that he move to another city. His mother, thinking she was protecting him from deeper pain, did not inform him when the tombstones were to be unveiled, nor ask him to help when she moved from the family home. Consequently, not only did the chances for intimacy between the mother and son decrease, but the son never had a sense of saying goodbye to the family home and the family life that had flourished within it.

Chapter Seven

Exercise 7·1
What Disguises Do You Wear?

Did you recognize yourself behind any of the disguises described? Did you withdraw or isolate yourself? Did you keep very busy? What were some of the things you did to protect yourself from the pain you felt following the death? What can you do to assure that these benignly protect you and do not become destructive?

What Lies Behind Your Defenses?

Let us see if we can explore what lies behind your defenses. Traditionally, upon returning home from the cemetery, a candle is lit that burns for the entire seven-day period, while the mourner is surrounded by family and friends. Even in the midst of so much support the mourner often feels alone with his or her loss. While the candle burns, the mourner may sit silently or cry out hysterically—out of reach of the community surrounding him or her. Either response characterizes the mourner's sense of isolation. But detachment from others can have other meanings. It can also represent awe.

At the point when the slender line between life and death is so clear that one feels the profound connection between them as well as their overwhelming separation, the sense of detachment is a sensible response. This can represent a withdrawal to a place of comfort and refuge—perhaps a *mekom hanekhama*—a place deep within yourself that is your own source of protection and security. That place can be an enormous resource for healing. Of course, while so much is feeling bruised and wounded, it may also be a place to which the gates seem to be shut.

Part 1: Candle Meditation

On the floor or a low stool, sit in front of a candle. Rather than contemplate an idea or concept, find your own silence. You may do this by watching the candle and taking deep breaths to relax your body or by closing your eyes and turning your thoughts inward. Set a timer and sit for either five or ten minutes, and observe where your thoughts go.

Part 2: What Obstructs Your Silence?

What happened during the candle meditation? Were you in touch with deep feelings? Did you cry or moan? Perhaps you were anxious or heard an inner voice that would not stop. Did images of the deceased or of other people arise? Were you preoccupied with tasks that need to be done or with such desires as hunger or wanting a cigarette?

Whatever was elicited during the meditation may need to be heeded. It is likely you need to focus on those images or voices and explore the memories, issues, or relationships they represent to help you find comfort in silence. Evaluate whether the thoughts that kept you from finding silence are genuine needs which must be addressed or obsessive ideas which keep you from your deep feelings and ultimately your sense of peace. Write about what you learned from the experience.

Exercise 7·2
Meeting Your *Mekom Hanekham*

Understanding the obstacles between you and your own inner nourishment is a key task of mourning. Once this is understood, you will have a rough blueprint for the path your grief-work will have to take. As I have said before, it is unlikely that this understanding can be reached in isolation. This understanding is central to the practice of *shiva*, which provides the mourner with a communal embrace.

Kaddish Guarantees the Contact You Need

Finding nourishing contact should be a given. The traditional image of the barefoot mourner, sitting on a low stool for seven days while the community files by in silence, symbolizes the need of mourners to be supported, yet not intruded upon. Rarely is this need fulfilled. Following a funeral, people are more likely to return with the mourner to the *shiva* house and participate in something akin to a cocktail party. While tradition mandates that the community is responsible for having a meal waiting for mourners upon their return from the cemetery, often mourners become distracted from their emotional tasks and get consumed with the details of hosting the people paying condolence calls. These visitors may chat loudly and incessantly, distracting the mourner's attention from his or her feelings. Then the guests leave and are not heard from again. These responses on the part of would-be comforters are all signs of the prevalent need to deny death. Meanwhile, the mourner's needs for protection and consolation are rarely met.

In fact, one of the primary purposes of Jewish grieving rituals is to communally embrace the mourner. An example of this is the community created through the mourner's recitation of the Kaddish. Practices regarding the Kaddish vary with respect to the people for whom the prayer is said and the length of time it is recited. However, in religiously observant communities, mourners say Kaddish in a prayer service three times daily

> They sat with Job on the ground seven days and seven nights. None spoke a word to him for they saw how very great was his suffering.
> —Job 3:13

> The consolers are not to speak until the mourner speaks. The mourner sits at the front of the room, and once he nods to indicate that the consolers should leave, they are not permitted to remain any longer
> —Shulkhan Arukh

for a period of as much as a year following the death of parents or for thirty days for other close relatives. Traditionally *the Kaddish cannot be said alone.* It is said as part of a prayer service that requires the participation of a minyan or a group of ten people. This guarantees that the prayer is said in the consoling embrace of others, at a time when one is most likely to feel alone.

The Kaddish as a Tool for Helping Mourners to Find Their Mouth

So often, I find myself exasperated with what takes place in the House of Shiva. Mourners are often besieged by an over-stimulating and intrusive social event instead of the protective cocoon they require in order to literally "come to terms" with their loss.

The Kaddish provides a formula to recite to help mourners find their voice. Both mourners and comforters have a role, as the mourner learns the Kaddish and becomes accustomed to reciting its words. When this is done properly, the Kaddish can be the vehicle for transforming the silence of grief into healing words, as the mourner, literally, "find[s] his mouth" in the silence of grief. Kaddish takes the mourner through all four worlds in which Kabbalists tell us that the soul dwells: *Assiyah*/the Physical World, *Yetzirah*/the Emotional World, *Beriah*/the Intellectual World, and *Atzilut*/the Spiritual World. In each world, the Kaddish empowers the mourner to conjure healing in ways beyond our understanding.

As mentioned above, the Kaddish is said in a language that's unfamiliar. We don't say it in English. We don't even say it in Hebrew. The Kaddish is written

> Why do we bring round foods to the house of mourning? Because round things have no mouth. The work of shiva is to help the mourner to find his/her mouth.
>
> —*Pesiqta Zuta (Leqah Tov)*

in Aramaic, a language that few people today speak. I think that is purposeful. I think it tells us that the act of doing the Kaddish is in some ways more important than understanding what the Kaddish says, at least at the beginning. Aramaic is the same language as another word that is as mysterious and magical as the Kaddish: "*Abracadabra.*" "*Abracadabra*" is actually an Aramaic word that means "I create as I speak." This is true of the Kaddish, Judaism's therapeutic tool. Invoking this word in connection with the magic of the Kaddish is appropriate. "*Abracadabra,*" we speak the Kaddish, and we create a bridge toward healing.

Healing comes from a place of mystery, a place we don't know yet, can't possibly know, because nothing in life has prepared the mourner for facing the gaping hole that death brings. Death, shatters all assumptions about how the world works. However, if the mourner is curious about this mystery and open to the possibility that there is something that he/she does not yet know, if he or she says the Kaddish with this uncertainty and with questions and curiosity, the Kaddish can take the mourner to a place that is not yet imaginable. It is a place we cannot conceive of when our grief is new. If we are willing to explore the unknown and open ourselves to this mystery, we are likely to find ourselves transformed by our grief on the wings of The Kaddish.

In the early stages of grief, in the World of *Assiyah*, The Physical World, that bridge connects us to community at a time we feel most lost. It tells us to stand in the middle of a minyan, at a time we might otherwise not be sure what to do.

When the mourner first begins to say the Kaddish, at the gravesite and in the house of mourning, he/she often feels as if the words are being mouthed from deep inside a thick balloon. Numb, uncertain, there is no sense that things can change, or that healing is a possibility. As the mourner begins, the words of the Kaddish may be nothing more than black letters on a white page, and it may seem like a miracle to get from the beginning to the end. But those black letters can be a lifeguard's rope extended from the tradition to save the mourner's life. And that miracle can be a sign that other miracles will come.

As the mourner says the Kaddish, the balloon in which he/she feels trapped begins to rise, like a hot air balloon. The Kaddish slowly takes those who mourn to that place of mystery, where miracles happen and transformation is possible.

While the mourners ascend, those below, the comforters, first at the graveside and then at the house of shiva and in the synagogue, say *"Amen"* to the mourners' Kaddish. These members of the community hold the tethers that keep the mourner and their balloon connected to the ground. Those *"Amens"* say to the mourner, "Go. Let the Kaddish take you to that mysterious place where healing happens. Say the Kaddish with every emotion, with every question. Say it with sadness. Say it with anger. And as you do that, we are here, tethering you to your life, tethering you to your community. With our *"Amens"* we promise: We are here. We will help you through this." The mourner hears these words of comfort and support as the air balloon lifts off, taking them to the mysterious land where mourners confront the unimaginable. The mysterious land from which healing comes.

Then *"Abracadabra"* and the mourner is in the Emotional World, *Yetzirah*. The Kaddish becomes a wireless connection between the worlds. Mourners speak and the Kaddish creates the vehicle for the most important task of mourning: continuing the conversation with the one who is lost. Buoyed by the Kaddish, mourners discover that the part of them that lives in that conversation is still alive. They can still say the things that were left unsaid. In this world, the person mourned remains a presence, even while the mourner is engaged in the most excruciating challenge of being human: transforming the physical connection with one who has died to a spiritual connection. All the unsaid words, all the emotions are transmitted, as the Kaddish becomes a vehicle for communication.

Then *"Abracadabra,"* and the balloon rises higher. Mourners look at the words of the Kaddish. They read its translation. They can be taken aback, even repelled. The words of the Kaddish, "Magnify and sanctify the Great Name," may challenge them. They ask the most basic existential questions. "Why would I want to magnify the name of such a God? What kind of God would cause such pain? Why do good people suffer? What does it mean to be human and to live on a planet where living things must die?"

With these questions, asked in *Beriah*, the World of the Intellect, mourners confront their shattered faith and their understanding of the God that they may feel has betrayed them. They explore the boundaries of mortality and ask profound questions, not just about the person who has died, but also about their own lives. Kaddish becomes a kind of crowbar, in Bob Dylan's words, "knock-knock-knocking on heavens door."

Then, *"Abracadabra"* and seemingly out of nowhere, the words hit a sweet spot. The balloon rises higher, to a place where a much bigger universe can be seen than the universe in which the mourner lived before the loss. This births a new kind of spirituality and a new understanding of God. As mourners take comfort in this new vision, they recognize that they have not only not lost God; they have also not completely lost the person they mourn. They feel the combined presence of God and the one who is gone. The two feel linked, fulfilling the El Maleh Rachamim's hope that the deceased will "rest under the wings of the Shekhinah (God's Presence)." This is the world of *Atzilut*, The World of Spirit.

A process that began on the side of awe that is filled with fear and horror has been transformed into the awe of radical amazement and wonder. *"Abracadabra,"* the mourner has spoken the Kaddish and created a new universe for a home. This universe can hold the paradoxes of horror and wonder in one heart at the same time: life can be beautiful even in the midst of pain. The fact of the death remains, but the mourner and the universe the mourner inhabits, is different.

With this mysterious insight, the balloon returns the mourner to earth, into the loving arms of those who held its tether–those who said *"Amen."* The mourner returns, carrying the *reshimu*, the residue of mystery.

When the Community Disappoints

After the death of her husband, a woman in her mid-sixties expected support from the couples who had been friends of her husband and herself since the early years of their marriage. But it soon became clear that the others were uncomfortable in her presence. Her husband was the first of their group to die, and the thought of his death and her widowhood made the others aware of their own vulnerability. She felt she had to mourn her friends as well as her husband.

When his twin brother died, a man in his mid-twenties expected support from his peers. Yet since few of them had experienced any significant losses they had difficulty empathizing with him. They were uncomfortable in his presence and could not understand why he grieved so deeply and for so long. Another man who had always appeared to be the tower of strength among his family and friends, was hurt when few people offered help after his wife's death. Yet, he had created an image of himself that made it hard for people to see him as vulnerable. Comfortable only in the role of giver, he was not aware that he was unreceptive to support from others and actually closed off when people tried to help him. People wanted to help, but did not know how.

Exercise 7·3
What Kind of Contact Did You Get? What Would You Have Liked?

Compare the support you received with what you actually needed. What kind of support did you get from those around you? Who was helpful? Who was soothing? Who was irritating? Who disappointed you? What might have been more useful or comforting to you?

What prevented you from getting what you needed? Were friends or relatives uncomfortable in dealing with the death? Were you able to express your needs? Could you allow people to help you?

This is not about discovering who is to blame. It is about discovering—perhaps for the first time—what your needs were, and what they may still be.

Shiva Chevra: *Companionship in the House of Mourning*

Sometimes, after a funeral, family or friends may find themselves relating in ways they have not in years. The environment and state of mind after a death can help transcend the problems of distance, time, or issues that have created tensions in the past. Intimacy that may feel very nourishing is often possible. A seventy-eight-year-old woman who died was the last survivor of a family of nine children. She had no children of her own, but her brothers and sisters all had large families. Following the death, a contingent of fifteen nieces and nephews, representing three generations, came from many cities and two foreign countries to attend her funeral. Some were first, second, and third cousins who had never met. Most had not been in contact with each other for many years. Nevertheless, they realized they had followed each other's milestones over the years through the aunt, who had been a prolific letter writer. While mourning her, relationships were rekindled or established.

ח.ב.ר. **KhVR:** a friend, member, study partner; *chavurah*: a community, a group that meets together for study, prayer, and/or personal growth; *chevra*: a group of like-minded people

The bonding that often occurs in a house of mourning can create new relationships or reinvigorate old ones. This is frequently an unexpected legacy of a death. But the opposite can also occur. The raw feelings of mourners may make them easy to offend, causing rifts that may become long-standing. Or further estrangement may result if mourners try to protect each other by not sharing their intimate needs for fear of burdening the other mourners. Thus opportunities for intimate connection are missed.

Exercise 7·4
New, Renewed, or Severed Relationships That Are a Legacy of the Death

Did you make any new friends in the days immediately after the death? Did you renew any old friendships? Describe these. What will you do to make sure that you maintain any new closeness that you felt? If there are hurt feelings, describe what happened and any action you might take that might change the situation for the better.

Exercise 7·5
Laughter in the House of Mourning

Surprisingly, in the special bonding of the shiva house there are often funny stories that emerge either about events during the period itself or in the rekindling of memories. What are yours?

The Meal of Consolation

Traditionally upon returning from the funeral, the community's first act on the mourner's behalf is to provide the *seudat havra'ah* (the meal of consolation). The meal is intended to nourish the mourner physically while he or she is in spiritual and emotional turmoil. It is a way to cut through the numbness which might make one forget to eat and risk falling ill. It reminds us of King David, who shifted his concern from his son to his own nourishment after the son's death. The meal of consolation is also a way for the community to provide care at a time when self-care may not be possible.

> At the first meal following the funeral, mourners may not eat their own food. It is a mitzvah to prepare food for the mourner.
> —*Shulkhan Arukh, Yoreh De'ah* 378:1

Using the meal of consolation as a model, imagine the community as a banquet set out specifically for your nourishment. The menu for this meal traditionally includes round foods, such as eggs and lentils, which symbolize the cyclical nature of life. Think of yourself in the center of a circle, embraced not just by people but by all the resources of your community. Picture all that is available to you. Imagine a table specifically set out to nourish you and indicate the activities or services from which you might draw nourishment.

Mourning's Push and Pull Can Confuse You

The fact that a mourner's needs vary is quite clear in the conflicting pull between our needs for isolation and connection that are played out repeatedly during mourning. As we have seen, one can be isolated or connected while alone or with others. Since we have affirmed the value of both of these poles, you need to understand how to use them to help you.

After his thirty-two-year-old son died from AIDS, an architect felt compelled to return to his firm and continue his daily routines. He found solace by continuing the part of his life that had not been ruptured. His wife also returned to her work at a travel agency, but it provided neither distraction nor emotional satisfaction. In therapy, it became clear that she needed to continue focusing on her relationship with her son. She ended her outside activities and stayed home for several months, sometimes sifting sadly through her son's belongings under the pretense of cleaning out his room, sometimes doing nothing.

Exercise 7·6
Setting the Table

Why are peas the proper food for mourners? As the pea rolls, so does mourning roll from one person to the other. Today's mourner is tomorrow's comforter and today's comforter is tomorrow's mourner.
—Talmud: *Baba Batra* 16

This couple represented the two poles to which people can withdraw. Was the husband's rush to return to work a form of denial that represented an inability or unwillingness to grieve, or was it a healthy affirmation of what still functioned in his life? Was his work productive for him, or an escape? Did his wife's inability to connect with the world indicate depression? Or was it a wise retreat so she could recuperate?

In fact, both of their choices could have been either regressive or healing, depending on what they did with them. This was not a dysfunctional couple. Husband and wife were able to use their very different forms of withdrawal to heal their wounds. In addition, each used their relationship to slowly open the part of the self that had been shut down. She guided him into his inner world. Every night when he came home, his love and concern for her would open his heart—first to her pain, then to his own, and they would mourn together. He soon became her guide to the outer world. Clinging to his arm, she accompanied him to events and activities until she could socialize comfortably without his constant support. Despite the differences in their styles of coping, they were able to use each other as resources. They found safety in each other's company. They did not grow apart. By taking care of themselves individually, they helped each other to heal.

Exercise 7·7
How Do You Use Involvement?

Let us look at your own experience with the poles of involvement. Can you remember when you found comfort by being alone? Or comfort by being with others? Where and with whom do you feel safe enough to

Part One

be authentically yourself without having to hide your feelings? To what extent does this distract you from your concern with the death? What activities, if any, feel productive to you? Can you think about subjects other than your loss for any amount of time? Do you get projects finished? When involved with others, do you long for the moment when you can be alone? Describe satisfying places, people, and activities and how you might find others.

As with all the questions that mourners ask, there are no right or wrong answers. Mourning is a necessary form of regression. We do what we do because we need to do it. The behavior of mourning should not be judged. We examine our behavior to help bring it into consciousness, and that consciousness helps us progress along the path toward healing. The inner wisdom that guides us should be respected. We are cultivating compassion. It is the compassion we feel for ourselves that helps us in healing.

Nevertheless, some behavior *does* raise red flags. We need to be on the lookout for behavior that is destructive in a way that might have long-term effects. Examples of such behavior might include reliance on drugs, alcohol, or other dangerous substances, food, abusive behavior to others, or severe withdrawal. If you fear that you may be involved in these or other potentially dangerous behaviors, you should discuss your concern with your doctor, psychotherapist, spiritual counselor, or other support person at once.

But I cautiously alert you to the fact that many of the appropriate emotional responses to grief mimic the symptoms of depression. Medical professionals may be likely to prescribe medication. While sometimes this

Chapter Seven

approach is wise, it can sometimes inhibit the necessary expression of grief. Paradoxically, these painful experiences of numbness, tears, and anger, and the overwhelming exhaustion, as each cell works overtime to accommodate a world in which all previous assumptions have been shattered, can be important experiences on the road to healing.

זכור את השבת *"Remember Shabbat!"*; the fourth of the ten commandments

And remember Shabbat! Many of the obligations of *shiva* are suspended during Shabbat and certain holidays. Look back at the list that you made in Chapter 4 to help you cope with the conflicting emotions of this period.

The Seventh Day

The end of *shiva* is marked by performing an act that is forbidden during these seven days of mourning, such as cutting the hair or studying Torah. In some Jewish communities, for example, *shiva* is ended by hammering a nail into a wooden board. This rich image acknowledges that it is time to end the period of numbness and withdrawal and begin to face the reality of loss. The loud rap of the hammer is a sensory alarm clock. It wakes up the mourner and penetrates the layers of his or her withdrawal, just as the nail penetrates the board.

Exercise 7·8
When Did Reality Set In?

When did the reality of the death begin to penetrate your awareness? Was there a specific event or activity that woke you up to the fact of the loss or was it something that your psyche just gradually absorbed? Are there parts of you that still have not accepted the death?

Part One

More commonly, the end of *shiva* is marked by mourners putting on their shoes, leaving the house, and walking together around the block. This walk seems to symbolize the return to the activities and obligations of daily life. *Halakha* (the Jewish code of law for daily living) walks the Jew through all aspects of daily life including those from which the mourner is exempted during *shiva*. *Halakha* has the same root as the Hebrew word for "walk." In the next chapter we will begin our walk from the House of Mourning.

ה.ל.כ **HLKh:** to go, walk, step, continue or proceed; *halakha*: code of Jewish law delineating how to live a Jewish life

Chapter Seven

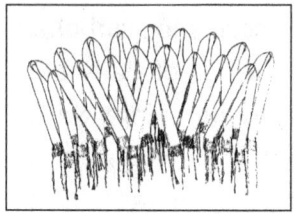

After thirty days, but within twelve months, he should ask how he is and then comfort him.

–Semahot

8

שלושים

Sheloshim

Finding Your Footing in a Changed World

שלושים Sheloshim: The number thirty, the thirty days following the burial

When my father died, two years after the first publication of this book, the walk from the house of *Shiva* was a strange mirror of my inner world. Following my father's burial, it began to rain. It hadn't rained that hard in 500 years. New Orleans filled up with what had been its greatest flood in history (surpassed, ten years later, when the levees broke after Hurricane Katrina). As I walked around the block, accompanied by members of his community, I had to climb over fallen trees and other debris left by the receding waters. The outer world looked as chaotic as I felt inside.

This is rarely the case. As I said above, the walk from the protection of the House of Mourning can be a rude awakening. The world does not reflect the mourner's experience. It moves at a different pace than one who still walks the mourner's path. *Sheloshim* provides continued protection to honor that difference.

For all losses, but the loss of parents (for whom one mourns for a year), *Sheloshim*'s thirty days (which include the week of *Shiva*), is the full term for halakhically-defined mourning. During *Sheloshim*, mourners continue to recite the Kaddish, but the venue changes. They return to the synagogue, where traditionally, they attend services three times a day while members of the minyan say "Amen" to their Kaddish.

Traditionally certain stringencies still apply. Mourners are not allowed to travel, they are not supposed to shave or cut their hair. But the real task of *Sheloshim* is to create a safe cocoon for the mourners as they tiptoe back into the world again.

During *Sheloshim*, one continues to wear the *kriah* ribbon, which is rent either upon hearing the news of the death or at the funeral. This ritual tearing of cloth will be discussed in depth later in the book and will provide the metaphor for much of the deep emotional work of mourning. This makes the transition smoother.

I remember returning to Los Angeles after my father's death. In New Orleans, I had been acknowledged as a mourner. The support I had received in the embrace of my Dad's community had been a tribute to him. He was a generous and gregarious New Orleans businessman, who had spent all of his nearly eighty-six years in that community. He was well known and well loved.

The community held me in tight embrace of a traditional house of *shivah*.

In New Orleans, many people carried my father's stories and our family memories. They shared my sorrow at his death, and mirrored my own grief. That brought me comfort.

In New Orleans, I was part of a community. In Los Angeles, no one shared my loss. No one besides my immediate family mourned my father. I felt invisible. Back in Los Angeles following my father's *shiva*, I found relief in continuing to wear the cut black ribbon that had been given to me at his funeral. It was the only visible sign of the profound change in my life. It signaled to the world that I was in the cocoon of mourning.

I appreciated the compassionate nods of recognition I had received from those who understood the significance of my little ribbon, even from strangers. Their silent deference, which came with their awareness of my status as a mourner, continued to provide reassurance. It helped me to stay connected to my feelings and to focus on my grief work. People were less intrusive and I felt protected. While wearing the ribbon, my father seemed less far away. I felt acknowledged as one walking an ancient and venerable path.

What were your experiences as you tried to reenter your familiar world, following your loss?

Exercise 8•1
Reenetry Experiences

_____

_____

_____

Chapter Eight

Exercise 8•2
Your Continued Care

Recognizing that mourners continue to be out of step with most people that they encounter in their daily life, how will you continue to care for yourself, as you walk the less restricted path of the year of mourning?

Ending Sheloshim

In contrast to the silence of the House of *Shiva*, where the voices of others may sometimes feel intrusive or strident, or the mourner may be too numb to take in what is being said, there comes a point when mourners long to hear the voices of others. They yearn to hear people, not only offering them comfort, but also speaking of the deceased. In the house of *shiva*, we observed the awkwardness of those who sometimes stay away during the earliest stages of grief for fear of saying the wrong thing, as well as those who carry on as if they were at a cocktail party. Around the time of *Sheloshim*, this ineptness can make another unfortunate showing.

Out of fear that speaking of the person who has died, will make the mourner "feel bad," people often stop talking about the deceased completely. Instead of protecting the mourner, this can give them the sad impression that the one they have lost has been forgotten. I often encourage mourners to create a ceremony to mark the end of *Sheloshim*. Inviting carefully chosen friends, they might share something about how their grief is going or perhaps they read words that were special to the deceased. Perhaps they take off the *kriah* ribbon that they have worn throughout the thirty days and say a Kaddish with their community.

As *Sheloshim* comes to an end, I believe that it is most important to give members of the community the opportunity to speak, in ways that might have been inappropriate in the house of *shiva*. They might be invited to talk about their own experiences of mourning and should be encouraged to talk about the deceased, at a time when the mourner may yearn to know that the one they have lost is still remembered.

Imagine that you are convening a ceremony to mark the end of Sheloshim. *Whom might you want to attend? How would you structure the ritual?*

Exercise 8·3
Writing Your End-of-*Sheloshim* Ritual

_____

_____

_____

_____

_____

PART II

9 Keriah (*Tearing of Cloth upon
Hearing News of the Death*) *and Deep Feelings:
Rending the Garment to Expose the Heart*

---

10 Keriah *and* Kaddish (*The Mourners' Prayer*):
Keeping the Conversation Going to Heal the Hurt

---

11 Keriah *and Prayer:
Speaking Out from the Distress of Your Soul*

שבירת כלים
Shevirat Kelim:
The Breaking of Vessels

The second phase of the creation process is *Shevirat Kelim*. Here the vessels from which the Divine Energy has withdrawn break apart, shattering the world and hiding its holiness. In this section we confront the broken and uncontained feelings of mourning and face the most intense grief-work. *Avodah*, the Hebrew word for "work," was also the name for the sacrificial service performed by the High Priest in the ancient Temple in Jerusalem. It is also the name for the Yom Kippur service commemorating those Temple practices. I hope this connection will allow you to see your grief-work as holy.

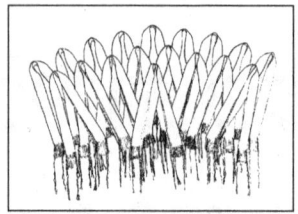

. . . all garments must be rent opposite the heart . . . for the mourner has to expose the heart.

–Kitzer Shulkhan Arukh 195:3–4

9

קריעה

Keriah *and Deep Feelings: Rending the Garment to Expose the Heart*

THE WALK FROM the house of mourning may be the most difficult of your life. For many, it may feel like learning to walk with new legs as you struggle to regain your equilibrium. The walk begins with the careful, measured steps of early mourning and must find footing amid the chaos and raw emotion of the middle stage of loss. The transition marked by *Sheloshim* can also be a difficult one, as well, as it also represents the loosening of some of the protections provided the mourner in the early stages of bereavement.

When Does Mourning End?

The formal mourning period lasts up to a year for a parent (although it is usually observed for only eleven months, for reasons we will discuss later) and thirty days for others. At the end of thirty days, when *sheloshim* is observed, which marks either the end of the mourning period or the beginning of a less restrictive mourning period for those mourning their parents. But as was said before, these time-lines represent the values of a much earlier time, where communities had different attitudes toward death. In my experience, it is often only after the formal mourning period ends that deep, healing mourning begins. This is the subject of this section of the book.

Naming Your Feelings

We now begin to sort out the relationship with the person who died and with the fact that we have survived him or her. In the process we must also sort through our relationships with those who remain in our life and with God and the universe. These are monumental struggles. But they are the struggles of any mourner determined to come to grips with grief and to move on with life. And they are fundamental tasks of living. The centrality of these issues is embedded in the name of the Jewish people, for Israel means "one who struggles with God."

Go at your own pace. Much of this work is done on an unconscious level. You will not be abandoning the effort, even if you put the struggle aside for a while. But if you decide to skip an exercise, be aware of the

ש.ר.ר **SRR:** to struggle, wrestle, or strive; a minister or govern-ment official; *Sarah*, the Matriarch; *Israel*: one who struggles with God possibility that the voice telling you to stop may be the voice of denial, which needs to be confronted.

Remember, one of the underlying themes of the mourning process is that feelings change, and, by following them, we change. As if walking on a spiral staircase, we experience our feelings again and again from different perspectives, until we make peace with ourselves and our own stories.

Feelings often ricochet from one to another. Experiencing one emotion may take you directly into another and that emotion can take you someplace else. Yet that emotional tripwire may turn into just the guideline you need to find a way out of the dilemmas that may now seem to be overwhelming.

The experience of one of my therapy clients illustrates the way our feelings can guide us. She first came to me because she was depressed after the death of her older brother, with whom she had always been close. After several sessions of solemnly extolling his virtues, she cautiously admitted that she was angry at him for having neglected his health. She then began to feel the terror of being without him. That terror, in turn, led to her feeling powerless, which led to resentment at having been abandoned by her brother. Facing this helped her confront her loneliness and became the basis for her becoming responsible for areas of her life which she had previously abdicated to him. Alternating between anger and fear helped her experience being alone in a new way, and helped her to feel less like a victim and more responsible for herself. All of these feelings—as well as her healing—had been locked inside her depression.

Chapter Nine

Job and Hannah: Biblical Role Models for Expressing Deep Feelings

One role model for this part of the journey is Job. Although often remembered for his patience, Job, who had lost everything he treasured, had the same powerful, complicated feelings that you probably do in this stage of mourning.

"I will not speak with restraint," he said. "I will give voice to the anguish of my spirit; I will complain in the bitterness of my soul" (Job 7:11).

In his profound sorrow, Job confronted his neighbors and God, angrily trying to bargain for the justice which mourners never find. Job's rage is an excellent example of this phase of our journey. By railing against what he knew to be God's unjust decree against him, Job asked the questions that many mourners ask. These questions may have no answers. But asking them is essential to transforming the numbness of the early phase of mourning and the depression that often follows into an energized reentry into the world of the living.

Another Biblical role model for this stage is Hannah. While praying silently for the birth of a child, she had such a strange expression on her face that the priest, Eli, thought she was drunk.

Defending herself, Hannah said, "I have been pouring out my heart [before God.] Do not take your maidservant for a worthless woman. I have only been speaking all this time of my great anguish and distress" (1 Samuel 1:15-16).

Hannah asserted her right to express her feelings without being judged for her appearance or her words. Job resisted his friends' efforts to silence his outrage,

> I am disgusted with life; I will give rein to my complaint, and speak in the bitterness of my soul.
>
> —Job 10:1

because they believed that questioning God's justice was blasphemy. These Biblical heroes sanction our need to find our deepest voice and express it freely. By "speaking out of the fullness of . . . misery and grief," we cleanse our souls and purge our sorrow.

Keriah *and the Release of Feelings*

Let us begin as Job began. When he received word of the calamities that had befallen him, he "tore his robe. He cut off his hair, and threw himself on the ground." He said, "Naked came I out of my mother's womb and naked shall I return there. [God] has given and [God] has taken away. Blessed be [God's] name" (Job 1:20–21).

Upon hearing of the death of a loved one, Jews traditionally tore their garments "to expose the heart." This practice began in the Bible with Jacob, who tore his cloak and began to mourn when the bloodied coat of his son, Joseph, was brought to him. Tearing a garment symbolizes the severing of a relationship. It permanently mutilates something valuable that cannot be mended. By "exposing the heart," we also expose our vulnerability before others. This emotional nakedness, which Job speaks about, is the raw material of our transformation. And it often feels horrible.

Today this practice, which is called *keriah,* usually takes place at the funeral home or at the cemetery just before the actual burial. Modern mourners are given black ribbons to tear or cut symbolically rather than ruin their clothing. Yet no matter what material is torn, it is the act of tearing that is significant. The sharp sound of the cloth being ripped punctures the numbness

Jacob rent his clothes, put sackcloth on his loins, and observed mourning for his son many days.

—*Genesis 37:34.*

ק.ר.ע **KRA:** to split asunder, tear, or rend; a rag, torn garment; *keriah*: the ritual of tearing a garment upon hearing of the death of a close relative

Chapter Nine

of the mourner and helps release his or her feelings. Harnessing that energy to bring release is the work of the middle phase of mourning.

When the cloth is torn, the mourner recites a blessing that praises "God, the True Judge." It is hard to imagine being willing or able to praise a God who has just taken away a loved one. Perhaps this prayer is designed to remind us that there may be a wisdom, greater than ourselves, which we cannot understand. Perhaps in ancient times, the fact that death was part of life was so well understood that the act of *keriah* took the mourner through all the stages of emotional recovery, stages that will take us three thick chapters—almost half the book's pages—to cover.

Praise God, the True Judge

ברוך אתה, יי, אלהיני מלך העולם, דין האמת.
Barukh Attah Adonai Eloheinu Melekh Haolam Dayan Haemet.
"Blessed are You, God, Ruler of the universe, the true Judge."

Exercise 9·1
Rending the Garment to Expose the Heart

Find a piece of cloth, about the size of a face towel, that is so thick that tearing it requires some effort. While thinking about your loss and its effect on your life, tear the cloth repeatedly. (A small cut at the edge of the cloth will make this easier to do.) Does the sound and the feel of tearing put you in touch with a feeling? If you want to make sounds to accompany the sound of the ripping cloth, make them. If there are words you want to say to accompany these sounds, let them come.

After a few minutes of this exercise, describe your experience. How did the act of tearing feel? Were any memories generated? Have there been times recently when you felt such a need to release or express some feeling that you might have liked to rip something?

I could have used a cloth to tear upon hearing of my sister's death. When I arrived at the hospital, I was ushered into a small examining room in the emergency clinic. My father was waiting to tell me that my sister was dead. After a few horrible moments that remain blank in my memory, I began screaming "It's a lie. It's a lie!" I walked over to the sink in the room's adjoining bathroom, put one hand on each side and started to tear the sink from the wall; suddenly I stopped myself and froze completely. I have always wondered what might have happened if I had gone ahead and ripped that sink away. It seems to me that the damage done to hospital property would have been minor compared to the cost that the pattern of repression of deep feelings, which began at that moment, had on me in the years that followed.

For some mourners, the sound and feel of the ripping cloth puts them in touch with their deepest feelings. One woman, who could not talk to anyone for months after the death of her six-week-old son, said that she heard the sound of the tearing cloth, not with her ears, but with her whole body. She then told me—for the first time—details of her son's funeral, which occurred when her body was still sore from childbirth and her breasts engorged with milk. The tearing of the cloth reminded her of the physical pain she had felt when her child, still so much a part of her body, was ripped from her.

Chapter Nine

Exercise 9.2
Evaluating Your Depression

Could you tear the cloth? For some mourners, still numb in the aftermath of the death, such an energetic act is impossible. The ability to feel anything beyond the numbness is thoroughly suppressed. If you have felt this way for several months, let's look for other signs that will indicate if your depression reflects your bereavement or has become something which may be more chronic and might require help from a mental health or medical professional. Was this depression a new feeling for you? Did it come only after the death? Chances are that if you don't recognize your usual self in these depressed feelings, it is a grief reaction and not a sign of an ongoing problem. How is your appetite? Is sleep disturbed? Too much or too little sleep or eating may indicate a problem beyond the mourning.

Do you feel things other than depression? Can you get caught up in a book, movie or TV show? Can you enjoy, at least briefly, a social situation? Can you laugh? Can you cry? Tears that bring at least momentary relief indicate that you are capable of a variety of feelings and that you are not in a chronic depression. Write your answers to these questions below. If there is any indication of a persistent depression, consult with a mental health professional to help you distinguish between chronic depression and depression that is a symptom of bereavement.

More often the blocked feeling that feels like depression is not a chronic problem, but a kind of barrier that needs to be pushed through by focusing and expressing our feelings. This breaking through to expose our deepest vulnerabilities and release our emotions is the goal of *keriah*.

Anxiety: Emotional Free-Fall

Anxiety frequently accompanies mourning. It feels like free-falling in space as we pass from one set of intense feelings to another with absolutely no idea where we are headed. It often masks deeper feelings and distracts us from those feelings that need to be released. Anxiety seems to have a life of its own. When it hits, it is difficult to avoid. And it can be very unpleasant.

Following are two exercises to help you manage anxiety and the other unrelenting and difficult feelings that are part of mourning. They are followed by a third exercise designed to help you transform the feelings and learn more about yourself.

> The Holy One hears the prayers that a person prays at night.
> — S. Y. Agnon

During times of anxiety we must take very good care of ourselves. This is a time when we are most at risk for accidents, illness, or misusing substances that we hope will help us control the feelings.

Concentrate on helping your body tolerate the anxiety. Make sure you exercise, eat correctly, and try to get enough sleep (during anxious times, sleep is often disturbed). Refer back to Exercise 4-4 (page 52): "Shabbat in the Midst of Mourning." Use that list to create a Shabbat for your soul when it is overwhelmed by feelings. Note some things you will do to help yourself.

Exercise 9·3
Nourishing Yourself in the Midst of Anxiety

You may feel you are suffocating under the avalanche of emotions racing through you. Besides anxiety, you may feel sorrow, anger, panic, fear, loneliness, regret. Any one of these would be overwhelming by itself. Together they can throw your life so far off balance that you find it difficult to concentrate on even the most ordinary of tasks.

Exercise 9.4
Getting Things Done

To help you function in a time of emotional chaos, make a list of tasks you need to accomplish, but feel that you can't. These may range from concrete goals, such as changing the name on your safety deposit box, to harder to define tasks, like making time for you to heal.

Making such a list can make these tasks seem less oppressive. Arrange them so the least anxiety-provoking tasks are on top and the more terrifying are on the bottom. Start at the top of the list and work your way down. Cross out a task with a thick, dark line after you have completed it. Each line will boost your confidence as you progress to the next, more challenging task.

Even if there is only one thing on the list that is crossed off, give yourself credit. Anxiety consumes energy. It is hard work. Anything else you get done is a major accomplishment. This is not a time for global resolutions. This is the time for getting through a day—or an hour—at a time. Any kind of follow-through is a triumph. Set small, specific, and concrete goals. This is not a time to decide to lose twenty-five pounds. How about getting through one day without eating sugar? This is not a time to decide to clear out and renovate your entire office. But you could sort out the pile behind the desk.

A woman who was overwhelmed by paperwork after the death of her husband—an accountant—used this technique each day. Each day she added to the list when she brought in the morning mail. By the time the page was nearly black because she had crossed out so many completed activities, she was confident she could handle her new responsibilities.

Keriah and Deep Feelings: Rending the Garment to Expose the Heart

Deep Feelings: The Gate to Healing

While it is important to find techniques for coping with anxiety and the other difficult feelings that are part of mourning, we must also spend time with these feelings. They are the gate to our healing. Some people find that this exploration works best in solitude. Others prefer the presence of a trusted friend, a therapist, or a group of others in similar situations who can help them focus and not get distracted. Below is an exercise that may be helpful with anxiety and the other difficult feelings experienced during this phase. These feelings—loneliness, despair, panic, anger, or great sorrow—often overlap, making it difficult for you to focus on one feeling or get anything done.

The following exercise may help you to focus. It may even help you to relax. It is often good to do when you awake in the middle of the night and are overwhelmed by feelings. It would be useful to dictate the instructions onto your phone or other device, so you can listen to them, rather than reading them when you do the exercise. Also prepare some relaxing music to listen to when you have finished the exercise. When you finish the exercise, refer again to your Shabbat list (Exercise 4-4, page 52)—and nurture yourself.

First, lie down. Close your eyes and take ten slow, deep breaths. As you breathe, remember the connection Jewish mystics make between God, the Soul, and the Breath. Invoke that Breath of God, which created your Soul, as a Breath of Healing.

For several minutes, simply be aware of your breath. Feel it as it fills your body and as it leaves it, creating an

Exercise 9·5
The Soul-Breath: Focusing Your Feelings

Chapter Nine

exchange between your deepest soul and the soul of the universe.

Survey your body, looking for places where there is tension.

Focus on a part of your body where you feel tense. You may sense butterflies in your stomach, tension in your throat, clenching in your jaw. Imagine that you are drawing deep, relaxing soul-breaths into the specific area that is tense.

If that part of your body does not relax, exaggerate the tension: Tense the muscles in it even more. For example, tighten your shoulders, clench your fist, or point your toes. Then, try to relax those muscles, drawing in full, deep breaths. If, after tensing and relaxing a few times, that part of your body still will not relax, let it express itself. Find a sound or phrase that expresses the feeling that the tension represents. Possibly it could be the sound of deep relaxation or of frustration, yearning, or sadness. Feel your tension. What is it trying to tell you?

With each exhalation, repeat this phrase or sound and be aware of whatever feelings emerge as you do so.

Once that tension is either soothed or has fully expressed itself, you might want to stop and write about what you felt or you might want to move to another part of your body and repeat the process above. Continue to breathe deeply, tensing and relaxing, until your tension dissipates or finds its voice. Each time, be aware of the feelings that are evoked. Very often feelings are trapped in the anxious contractions of our bodies. In the act of relaxation, you may find them. Let them express themselves. Seek support from others if it is too difficult.

Write about your experience during this exercise.

Part Two

While sometimes anxiety won't budge until it is ready to, the preceding exercise often breaks through the tension. It may relax you or it may lead to an expression of deep feelings. This expression frequently frees the energy that the anxiety has demanded and lets us confront deeper issues or the details of daily life. While doing the above exercise, a thirty-three-year-old man whose throat had been constricted since the death of his mother six months earlier, emitted a low, slow moan. A widow, left with three young children, began to gnash her teeth and snarl like an angry cat. Another young man, whose wife had divorced him, felt a queasiness from what felt like a hole in his belly. Focusing on that feeling eventually led to the phrase, "Come back." He repeated this phrase over and over. As the voice and the feeling amplified, he broke into deep sobs. This was painful, but it broke through the paralysis he had been feeling. When he finished crying, he felt better, and that night he slept more comfortably than he had since his wife had left.

Anger May Be Your Turning Point

Anger or outrage are often associated with the death of someone close. We may search for someone to blame and, often, we do find someone whom we can implicate (justly or unjustly) in the death: doctors who may not have caught the symptoms in time or who chose one treatment over another, family members who didn't help the deceased the way we feel they should have, or friends whom we think haven't helped us sufficiently in our grief. We may blame ourselves for a million tiny infractions that "if only" we had done differently. . . .

We might also blame the deceased, God, or the universe, although accusing them may seem irrational, unfair, or guilt-provoking or make us feel guilty. But our feelings exist, even when we tell ourselves that they shouldn't. And so, often in silence or with great guilt, we accuse the deceased, who should have taken better care or gone to the doctor earlier or not left affairs in such a mess, or simply should not have abandoned us. We may also accuse God and the universe for injustice and cruelty.

Sometimes this outrage is valid. Mistakes are made. People do not always act appropriately. We might have done more for the deceased. Justice is not always apparent.

Sometimes our thinking is irrational. The deceased probably would not have chosen to die. Doctors are not all-knowing. Even the best of us—including you—is imperfect. And perhaps there is a plan to the universe to which we are not privy. We wonder: Do we dare question the force that runs the universe?

> . . . do not placate a person at the time of rage.
> —Mishna: Avot 4.18

For now, none of this matters. What is important right now is not to look for the truth, but to find the feeling. Find your outrage. Find your anger. Find your clenched fist and grinding teeth. In my personal experience, and in my work as a therapist with so many others, I have found that acknowledging anger is the turning point. It won't bring back the dead or change history. It won't make thoughtless relatives kind or God more attentive. But it can help you to mobilize your energy and gain control of your life.

Our society has so many rules about anger that few people feel entirely comfortable feeling it, let alone expressing it. The guilt we may have about anger is magnified many times during the especially vulnerable period of mourning, when eulogies are the standard form of expression. The guilt might be magnified many times again if your anger is directed toward the deceased.

For the mourner, it is easier—and, sometimes, more comfortable—to rage at the living than to turn our wrath on the dead. We may feel furious for the sense of abandonment that we feel, and it is easier to rage out of control at an otherwise insignificant social slight than to vent our primal and irrational wrath at the deceased. If the person were living, there would still be a possibility of working something through, but, we feel, that possibility has been taken from us, leaving us to feel both bereft and angry about the loss, and often displacing those feelings by focusing on areas where change may still be possible. This is far easier than facing what we feel we cannot work through with those who are gone.

Exercise 9·6
Letters to the Living

Part 1: Speaking Your Mind
Are there people for whom you carry grudges regarding the death, or other matters that seem to be consuming your thoughts? Write a letter that will not be sent. Say exactly what you feel. Don't worry about the consequences. By not sending this letter you can ventilate, clarify, and honestly express your feelings without alienating the person. After you have explored the issue more fully, you can decide on what may or may not be appropriate for you to send.

Part 2: Response
Now imagine yourself as the person to whom you directed your wrath. Imagine what he or she might have

felt when they did whatever angered you. Really try to mentally change places with that person so as to see the issues from his or her perspective. How would they respond to your letter? Write a letter from that person to you.

Part 3: Last Word

You will now have the last word. How did imagining yourself as the other person affect you? Do you have the same feelings regarding the person that you had before you wrote the letter in Part 2? Respond to the imagined reply to your letter, using the format below. This exercise uses the language of assertive communication, encouraging you to express your deep feelings directly and responsibly. This differs from Part 1 of this exercise, in which the goal was to ventilate your feelings, with no concern about the effect your expression might have.

After reading your letter, I understand that you _____

_____

_____

At this point, I feel _____

_____

_____

I wish that initially you had _____

_____

_____

Part Two

At this point, I want _____

_____

_____

Perhaps this process gave you some insight that can help you resolve these angry feelings. Perhaps not. There are many instances when resolution of anger may be nearly impossible, such as the anger that a Los Angeles attorney felt at two teenaged boys who raped his daughter a week before her eighteenth birthday. But bear in mind that while there are times when anger that will not budge is legitimate, sometimes these apparently unresolvable angers can represent a subtle form of denial.

Such anger can be used by mourners as a way of freezing time. By focusing on what they felt was a bad medical decision that led to the death of their fifteen-year-old daughter, her parents' attention froze on the period before her death. It became an obsession that distanced them from their pain. Expressing anger through a lengthy lawsuit was easier than confronting their hurt. They sued the doctor for malpractice. When they finally won the case several years later, they began to express the deep, painful feelings associated with mourning. For the years of the court battle, they had been insulated from much of their grief by the fact that they were fighting for their little girl. When the fight was over, they were overcome with sadness. They were finally forced to confront the reality of their loss.

I'm not saying that these angers are not legitimate, important vehicles of mourning or that it isn't important to express them. But they need to be monitored. Moving back and forth among different feelings is characteristic of mourning. Being frozen in a particular feeling for a length of time may need to be questioned.

Guilt: Your Anger Turned Inward

Anger directed toward ourselves might manifest itself as depression, guilt, shame, or obsession. Depression occurs by repressing feelings that should be directed outwardly. Guilt, which is often anger turned inward, focuses on actions we did or did not take and which we assume might have made a difference in the relationship with the deceased or in his or her survival. By focusing on things in the past, we promote the illusion that time stands still. We get frozen in reworking a past that cannot be changed—a defense which keeps us from facing the present. Perhaps we derive a false sense of power from this behavior, which helps to insulate us from the vulnerability we feel. This is what I was doing when I blamed my haircut for my mother's death; I was trying to believe that I could have made a difference. But while the truth is that we cannot change history, we can change our relationship to it.

> If a person incurs guilt . . . when the guilt is recognized . . . it shall be confessed. . . . the priest shall make expiation on behalf of the sin and it shall be forgiven.
> —*Leviticus*: 1–11

Exercise 9·7
"If Only" Statements

Part 1: Regrets
Reflect on some of the things you wish you had done differently, and feel the pangs of regret that go with each statement.

Part Two

If only _____

_____

_____

If only _____

_____

_____

If only _____

_____

_____

If only _____

_____

_____

If only _____

_____

_____

_____

How do you imagine the deceased would feel about what you wish you had done differently? Would he or she feel that your remorse is appropriate? Would you be forgiven? Write yourself a letter from the deceased responding to your regrets.

Part 2: Forgiveness or Sadness

If forgiveness is possible, let yourself feel that sadness. While many times our feelings of guilt are unnecessary ways we punish ourselves, sometimes we have genuinely done something wrong. If this is so, this is a deep regret—the kind of sadness that we all have about mistakes we have made. Now is the time to let yourself feel it. Perhaps an energetic expression of the regret will help to move intractable guilt. It is your turn to write a letter to the deceased apologizing and asking for forgiveness.

These are some of the most tender feelings with which a mourner must deal. As I write, I can feel myself wanting to cheer you up, and spare you your pain by telling you that it will be better. In fact, we will talk about reparations and memorials to the deceased in another chapter. But this sadness is an important truth in your story, and you must not turn it away or you may act out some sort of behavior that can be destructive to yourself or others.

Please know that all of us who have faced this kind of tragedy have had to face our own version of this terrible pain. I hope that knowledge can comfort you as if we were the silent visitors at your House of *Shiva*, extending our hands and our hearts.

> When one repents out of love, the previous evil acts are considered changed into good deeds.
>
> —Rabbi Levi Yitzchak of Berditchev

Tears and Sadness: Finally, the Heart Exposed

Tears are a natural reaction to loss. Even some animals shed tears at separations. So much of the sadness, despair, and panic that accompany a death can only be expressed by crying. Tears are an important way to break through the barrier to action and fulfillment created by uncomfortable feelings. They are essential, not only to grief, but also to health. They release important enzymes into our systems. Yet some people have a hard time getting those tears to flow.

Often the anxiety, anger, guilt, and obsession that we feel cover our sadness. As difficult as those other feelings are, they may sometimes be easier than facing the sadness that is the bottom line of loss. But that sad truth is what must be faced, so it is important to find your tears.

In Talmudic times many mourning practices were intended to exaggerate tragedy in order to help mourners find their tears. If a young person died before getting married, the shrouded body would be carried to burial under a chuppa or wedding canopy. This underscored the tragedy and caused a cathartic outburst of feeling among mourners in the community.

If its hard for you to cry, find something that will help you shed your tears. See a sad movie, listen to a song, or read a poem that you know will be a tear-jerker. When your tears come, don't hold anything back. Continue to cry as you think about your own losses. Try not to be afraid of your tears. I know that I always feel better after crying. I think you will too.

> Shedding tears evokes Divine Providence.
> —*Rebbe Nachman of Bratzlav*

> From the day of the destruction of the Temple, all gates to heaven have been closed, but the gates of tears are always open.
> —*Talmud: Berakhot 32b*

Chapter Nine

Tumah: Shame Versus Awe

Shame also directs our anger against ourselves. It is closely related to guilt and obsession. When shame accompanies mourning, the mourner feels as if he or she has done something wrong. Unlike guilt, shame is not a feeling of responsibility that can be attached to specific acts. Nor does it necessarily have much to do with the loss itself. It is a global discomfort, experienced as if we are somehow marked or blemished as a result of what happened and our reaction to it.

Shame is a discomfort we feel with our vulnerability. We are embarrassed by our wounds. Our loneliness, pain, confusion, anger, and inability to cope are humiliating. It is as if our garments have literally been torn and some private and grotesquely ugly part of us is hanging out for the world to see.

Of course we are embarrassed by what we feel. If death is a taboo, as it is in our culture, then the mourner is an embarrassment. We become ashamed of our most appropriate feelings.

> Humiliation is worse than physical pain.
> —Talmud: Sota 8b

Exercise 9·8
Uncovering Your Own Shame

Have you been embarrassed by anything you have felt since mourning began? Are you convinced that any of your feelings are improper or inappropriate? Is there anything that you have experienced that has made you feel shame or that you have felt you should not share with anyone else?

I remember how ashamed I was of my pain. It breaks my heart to read the following words that I wrote in my journal:

> I speak to no one. I don't want to bother them. I am too heavy . . . too intense. I can't let it go. What is wrong with me? It has been six months since Jan died . . . nine months since my mother died. Why can't I get it together? (Journal Entry, Berkeley, 1972).

Of all the feelings connected with mourning, these are the only ones that anger me. They are so unnecessary. They are unrelated to the emotional needs of mourning and instead reflect both society's ignorance of the needs of mourners and its oppressive attitude toward death and mourning.

Jewish tradition gives us a different model for handling the profound experiences that in our modern society often leave us feeling blemished. In Judaism, those who have come into contact with the most awesome of life's experiences are given rituals which affirm the sense of strangeness they might feel. These rituals help transform them so that they can once again comfortably walk in the mainstream.

Those who have stood at the juncture where life and death almost touch are considered to be *tamai* (or in a state of *tumah*). Among those is the person who has come into contact with a dead body. A menstruating woman is also in this state and is forbidden physical contact with her husband until she immerses herself in the ritual waters of the mikvah (ritual pool), following her menstrual period.

Unfortunately, the term *tamai* has been translated, not by its description of the altered path we take when confronting profound experiences, but as "impure." Given our society's attitude toward profound truths, this pejorative term is not surprising. But it is nonetheless damaging. Many women feel that being labeled "impure" during their menses is demeaning and destructive. It negates the significance of a woman's menstrual cycle and the awesome power of her body to nourish life.

While technically mourners are not considered *tamai*, their proximity to death and the response of society to them leaves them feeling "impure" and ashamed of their appropriate response to life's most awesome truths. When we accompany someone to death's gate, we come face-to-face with the very limits of human existence. Death is part of being human, but its total mystery invokes awe in us and draws us closer to the unfathomable mystery of being human.

When the Temple stood, those in a state of tumah immersed themselves in a mikvah and were sprinkled with the "water of lustration," a mixture composed of the ashes of an unblemished red heifer that had been ritually slaughtered and burned on the altar of the Temple mixed with water and the ashes of herbs and branches. Today, upon leaving the cemetery after a burial or upon entering a house of *shiva*, mourners and their comforters ritually wash their hands to cleanse themselves of tumah.

Use the following water ritual to help transform whatever shame you feel into a sense of awe. You may do this exercise as a guided fantasy or actually find a source of water in which you immerse yourself.

> God leads me beside still waters and restores my soul.
> —P*salm* 23

Exercise 9•9
Cleansing Yourself of Tumah

Imagine yourself entering a pool whose waters are perfumed with the herbs, oils, and ashes used for cleansing since the time of the Temple. As you approach these waters, acknowledge any sense of shame or of being blemished that you have felt during your mourning. Recognize any sense you might have that your feelings were inappropriate. Pay attention to any judgments that were made—either by yourself or others—regarding your experiences during the mourning process: how long it has taken you, the intensity (or lack of intensity) of your feelings or any other part of your experience.

Now, accept any aspect of your mourning experience that you felt you needed to hide. With a deep breath, imagine that you are immersing yourself in the warm, healing, and sweet-smelling waters. As you remain beneath the surface, feel the waters swirl around you, saturating you with the Divine Essence and transforming your feelings of shame and impurity to entitlement and awe.

With this empowered vision of what had seemed like shameful vulnerability, you are now ready to confront your deepest feelings and focus further on God and the universe, the deceased, and yourself. With Job's sense of outrage, you will "speak out in the fullness of your soul."

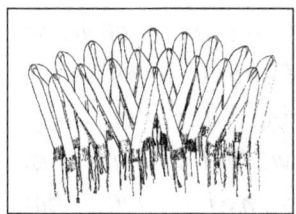

. . . because the son said the Kaddish for his departed father or mother, they were saved from judgment.

—Kitzer Shulkhan Arukh 26:1

10

קדיש

Keriah and Kaddish: Keeping the Conversation Going to Heal the Hurt

MAINTAINING AN ONGOING connection with our ancestors is a primary concern of Judaism. Continued connection with the dead is also an important goal of grief-work. But we encounter obstacles as we seek to transform our relationship with someone who has died from a wound to a blessing.

Coping with What Feels Unfinished

Perhaps the biggest obstacle is the unbearable sense that the relationship is over, that we will never again see—or talk to—the person who died. We feel that we are left in the middle of a conversation which can never be

> God of all Generations . . . You remember the faithfulness of our ancestors, and in love bring redemption to their children's children.
>
> —*Gates of Prayer*

finished. How can we express the full range of feelings toward a person who has died? How futile (how embarrassing) to cry out from such need, to someone who cannot hear us!

For some, these feelings are about yearning, longing, and loneliness. We can't believe that we will never see them again. We miss them. We want to see them. We want to tell them something. And it overwhelms us. We are left with feelings that we think will never end.

Others are left with "unfinished business." There are issues that haven't been worked out and difficulties that were never properly confronted. We need to get something off our chest, or even rage at the person who has died. We need answers to some serious questions. And the sense that it is too late weighs heavily on us. We wonder: How can these unresolved issues ever be worked out?

We hold back all these unfinished feelings. We're not even sure these feelings are "appropriate." While we feel that certain subjects can be confronted, others seem to be off-limits. So these strong and unyielding feelings are repressed, and they become embedded in our psyches. We don't cry out; we enter the next phase of life lonely, lost, depressed, embittered, cynical, or angry.

Yet we are told that there are precedents for crying out in this way. When the Jewish people were suffering greatly while in Egypt, they cried out in despair and anger. According to the Torah, God heard them. This was the beginning of their redemption.

One of the ways Jewish mourners cry out is by saying the Kaddish. In this chapter, we will expand our understanding of Kaddish to continue the *kriah* process. You have already rent your garment and psychologically exposed yourself. Now reach even further into the hole that rip created. Our goal will be nothing short of the goal of the slaves in Egypt: redemption. We seek to redeem ourselves and to transform our lives. We also seek to redeem the soul of the person whom you mourn as we address the continuing issues of the relationship. In the process, we hope to create a vehicle for continued communication with the person who has died.

Kaddish: Continuing Your Conversation with the Deceased

Death does not end the relationship. Of course death changes the relationship profoundly. But there is still the possibility of saying what needs to be said. Even after a death of one of the members, a relationship can still grow and change and issues can still be explored. The Kaddish can be the vehicle for continued communication, a line between the living and the dead.

Over the years, I have learned to use the Kaddish as a way to communicate with the people I have lost. When I say the Kaddish, I focus on the person I am remembering and think about what I would like to tell him or her.

Through saying the Kaddish, I have watched my relationships continue to evolve. I have watched as, over time, what I need to say changes. When I first began saying the Kaddish for my sister, all I could feel was sadness as I focused on her soul and struggled with how much I wanted to hold her again.

After awhile I began to communicate other things as I either said the prayer or stood there in silence hearing its words recited by others around me. Sometimes there is a burning issue that I need to resolve. Sometimes I

ק.ד.ש **KDSh:** to set apart, separate; holy, sacred, consecrated; *Kaddish*: the mourner's prayer; *kiddush*: prayer sanctifying wine want to share something that has happened to me. More and more, I have less of a need to share a message than to feel the connection. I have come to relish the time of Kaddish as a time I can spend in the presence of my dear little sister.

> Dream: My mother was calling from far, far away, perhaps from another world. The telephone was a model from the time of my birth: black, heavy and with a rotary dial. But its cord was shimmering: translucent, somewhat metallic and pulsating—filled with veins and blood—an umbilical cord, connecting us after her death. It is the silver cord that links the worlds, before and after we take our human breaths. The cycle, like the circular dial, rotates, yet the connection remains. The Kaddish is the silver cord. (Journal Entry, Los Angeles, 1992)

The Jewish mystics tell us that the living play a part in the redemption of the dead. This redemption means that the significance of a person's life can be enhanced, even after his or her death, by the actions of those who remember that person. Redemption cleans the slate, allowing the positive value of a life to be the full measure of the person. We are told that one of the ways redemption occurs is by reciting the Kaddish for up to a year after a death.

Few people recite the Kaddish for a full year because of the kabbalistic belief that following death, the soul resides in *gehinnon*. While *gehinnon* is often translated as "hell," many feel that it is closer in concept to "purgatory," for it is here that souls are said to reside for a maximum period of a year, during which time they can be purged of the impurities or wrongdoings they accumulated during their lifetimes. Since the length of time spent in purgatory is based on how much purgation is necessary (based on the number of sins that were

---

In a dream, a sage encountered a spirit loaded with wood he was sentenced to carry to Gehinnon because of evil committed during his lifetime. "How can I help you?" asked the Rabbi. "I had a son. If he should go to the synagogue and publicly praise God, my sin will be remitted." The Sage [found] the boy [and] taught him the Kaddish.

—Aseret Madebrot: Midrash on the Decalogue

committed while the person was alive), survivors rarely recite the Kaddish for the maximum possible term, because that would indicate that the soul being remembered required the full term for cleansing!

The fact that survivors, reciting the Kaddish, can take part in this redemptive purgation indicates that on some mysterious level, the dialogue continues between the living and the dead. This mystical concept tells us that the living can still have an effect on the dead and that even after death there is the possibility of change. Thus, we still have the opportunity to work out unfinished business and work through many of the feelings that continue to churn within us. Through the vehicle of Kaddish we can still confront the deceased, expressing the words and feelings we did not or could not share while he or she was alive. Kaddish keeps the conversation going until we have said all that we need to say.

Whether or not we share the spiritual assumptions of the Kabbalists, the concepts of Jewish mysticism translate into metaphors which can work to help us communicate what remains unsaid. By continuing our dialogue with the deceased, we advance the work of Kaddish, redeeming the relationship so that we and the person we mourn can be free from persistent and difficult entanglements. This removes the weights that bind the souls of the dead to the souls of the living and permits the departed souls to join the other departed under the wings of the *Shekhina*. It also frees the souls of the living so they can focus on the concerns of living.

We can also see Kaddish as a continuation of the *tahara,* in which those among whom the person once lived do the work of cleansing and purification. But this time, it is not the body that is purified. It is the soul.

Chapter Ten

Beyond Eulogy or Rage—Beyond Black and White

No relationship is perfect. There is almost always some conflict between people who are close. The opposite is also true. No relationship is without some redeeming qualities. After a death, survivors often tend to idealize the person who died, forgetting some of the tensions that marked the relationship, or remembering only the hardships without acknowledging what might have been positive.

Remember the widow who alienated her four children by enshrining the memory of what had been a very difficult man? Her idealization made successful bereavement impossible and she became a hostage of her selective memory. A young woman whose father had molested her could not move beyond her anger. Her anger was justified, but it was constricting her life. She could not get beyond it.

The truth is that often good people do bad things and bad people do good things. The above woman's difficult husband had made significant contributions to the world and had enriched his wife's life greatly *and* he had treated her badly. The young woman's abusive father had also helped her to set up a business for herself. Mourners often get locked into these poles of idealization or condemnation. Yet mourning probably cannot be resolved without having a realistic perspective of the full relationship.

In bereavement groups, there are two signs that tell me that healing is occurring. When participants, who have idealized the person who has died, begin to remember some of his or her less attractive qualities, recalling peccadillos and faults, I know that they are moving beyond idealization and into a phase that will take them beyond mourning. Or, in relationships that have left many negative feelings in their wake, I know that the mourner is moving toward healing when he or she begins to recount some of the good qualities of the person who has died.

Exercise 10·1
Moving into the Gray Area

Do you idealize the deceased? Can you tolerate someone else speaking in less than glowing terms about him or her? To break through idealization, write some things about the person who died which made—or which still make—you uncomfortable. These can be trivial or major. They can stem from differences you had with the person, his or her faults or other discomforting qualities, or actions you remember. If the opposite is true and your resentment is what is most felt, see if you can find one or two redeeming qualities to remember about the deceased.

Is it difficult for you to remember or write down things that do other than eulogize the deceased? That is not uncommon. Whatever the reason for this, whether the person you mourn was flawless, whether you are idealizing that person, or whether it is just too painful to think of the relationship, I remind you of the Talmudic instructions regarding funeral orations: They are "to break the heart in order to cause much weeping," and speakers who exaggerate the good qualities of the deceased (and mourners who affirm their words by saying "Amen") will have to answer for these inappropriate expressions. We answer for denying the more troublesome feelings by having them fester inside of us, making it difficult for us to move on with our lives.

If you are unable to remember anything good about the deceased, I urge you to see if you can find something. This is not to absolve the person who died, but to give you something positive to build on, even if what you come up with is a determination to reject a negative role model. As the young woman above said, "I learned from my father's cruelty how fragile and in need of love a child can be. I initially went into education, something I really love, as a way of protecting children from cruel parents like my father."

Exercise 10·2
Letter to the Deceased

This next exercise, in which we will write a letter to the deceased, builds upon the mystical belief that by saying Kaddish the living help redeem the souls of the deceased. We deduce from this that the soul and its relationships remain dynamic and that it is possible for the living to continue to address unfinished issues in the relationship. This concept creates the framework within which we will address unresolved psychological issues between ourselves and the deceased.

This "form-letter" format is designed to stimulate a variety of feelings. Through it you will strive to maintain the intimacy you once shared or create an intimacy that may not have existed before the death. This letter is neither a eulogy nor a memorial. It should address the full range of feelings you have toward the person you mourn: sadness, anger, love, yearning, words that still remain unsaid.

It might be helpful to look at a picture of the deceased before writing the letter. Allow yourself to absorb the image and the feelings the picture generated within you. If you already know what needs to be said, just begin writing. Otherwise, the guided statements below may help you discover what you need to say.

Dear _____ *(fill in the space with the name of the person as you would address him or her in a letter)*

It has been _____ *(length of time since death) since your death, and still the dialogue between us continues. When I feel the need to communicate with you, I usually feel* _____

_____

When I think of you, I remember _____

_____

The last thing I remember that you did was _____

_____

These memories make me feel _____

_____

The biggest change for me, as a result of your death, has been _____

_____

I hadn't expected that _____

_____

Shevirat Kelim *The Breaking of Vessels*

I have learned that _____

_____

During your lifetime, I wish that I could have told you _____

_____

If you were alive, _____

_____

The biggest surprise has been _____

_____

The hardest thing has been _____

_____

The thing I fear the most is _____

_____

I'd like you to know this about who I am now: _____

_____

In losing you I feel that I have lost _____

_____

I wish you could be here to help me with _____

_____

Part Two

I would like to ask you _____

_____

What I always wanted to hear you say was _____

_____

You didn't understand that _____

_____

What I would have liked to know about you is _____

_____

I wish you could have understood _____

_____

What you didn't see about me is _____

_____

The thing I resent the most is _____

_____

I am most grateful for _____

_____

What I have learned about you only since your death is _____

_____

Shevirat Kelim *The Breaking of Vessels*

The thing I feel most guilty about when thinking about you is _____
_____

What I don't miss about you is _____
_____

What I miss the most is _____
_____

What I will emulate about you is _____
_____

What I will do differently in my life from what you did in yours is _____
_____

Despite the things that separate us, the things we share are _____
_____

I hope that you now are _____
_____

   Signed, _____

Part Two

Those were tough questions. Painful feelings may have been stirred up which represent some of the most difficult aspects of your relationship with the deceased or the greatest pain of your loss of that person. Perhaps it is hard to deal with the feelings churned up by these exercises. The impulse is often to run to do something that will squash the feeling, often something compulsive and self-destructive. But try not to deny what you are experiencing. These are the raw feelings of loss, and you must experience them before you can let go of the person who has died.

While writing the letter, one or two specific issues may have come up that clearly need to be addressed. You may want to work on these by continuing to write on any of the questions or on other questions that may have been raised in the process of writing the letter. Perhaps you might discuss what you have written with others who knew the deceased or are familiar with your relationship with him or her.

I hope that you found this process valuable. It is never totally finished because we can always learn more by reflecting upon our experiences. Deep change happens slowly and usually without drama. Saying the Kaddish for the full year after a death lets that kind of change occur, often imperceptibly. Reciting the prayer over and over again, either in reality or symbolically as it was presented by the letter-writing exercise, helps us to sort out our entanglements so that we are free to go on living our lives without being burdened by what was unresolved with the person who has died.

Giving ourselves time to heal and creating space for the process allows the painful memories to be replaced gradually by more pleasant ones. The pain subsides and

> Finishing business means that I open my heart to you, that whatever blocks my heart with resentment or fear, whatever I still want from you is let go of and I just send love. . . . I open to you as you are . . . not as I wish you to be or as I wish me to be . . . no longer looking to be forgiven or to show others how unfair they were. To finish our business we must begin to stop holding back.
> —Stephen Levine

Chapter Ten

one remembers the whole relationship, not just the most recent memories of the illness and the death. We make peace with what was unresolved. The longing becomes less intense. Ultimately, mourning and, especially, reciting the Kaddish help us to reclaim our own lives as much as to redeem the life of the deceased.

> When we mourn, we strain our ears,
> listening for the voice of the deceased—
> until we hear that voice coming from our own hearts.
> Mourners, we yearn to continue the conversation.
> We search for the unsaid words, to resolve the unfinished issues. The Kaddish can take us there. '
>
> Kaddish parts the curtains. It forces open the space between the worlds, breaking open the crevices, where the voices still come through; where all the worlds are one.
>
> For the price of our yearning, our anger and our tears, the Kaddish will carry us beyond the edges of the world we know. It takes us to a place of wholeness— of peace—all polarities dissolve, life and death, black and white, male and female, God and not-God merge— become one. Adonai Ehad.
> The words of the Shema become the reality of the world.
>
> Kaddish ends exile. It suffuses the most profane regions with the holiness of God's name and wrests an Amen from the place it has not yet been forthcoming, the Amen we have been listening for for our entire lives. That Amen sustains the world.
>
> —(Journal Entry, Los Angeles, 1994)

Dreams: Connecting Heaven and Earth

Mourning is intense. Now it may be time to attend to yourself. One of the most nourishing ways to do this is to have a dream that gives you a clear, unmistakable message about what you are struggling with. Since dreams come from our deepest selves, they speak in a language that is uniquely our own. If we can work to decipher their language, they will make the connections for us between the deepest parts of ourselves and the highest places in the universe.

In a curious ritual mentioned in the Talmud, mourners were required during *shiva* to invert the beds in the house of mourning. This practice, abandoned around the time of the destruction of the Temple, suggests the primitive nature of feelings during the early days of mourning. Upside-down beds require one to sleep on the ground, where one is closer to the earth, closer to the place where the dead are buried, and closer to the primitive instincts. These connections are reminiscent of Jacob, who slept on the ground with a stone for his pillow. Close to the earth, we make the primitive connections between our hidden voices and their higher meanings, just as Jacob did when he lay down alone on the first night of his journey from his parent's home. His dream, about angels ascending and descending on a staircase, linked him to the heavens while his body rested on the cold, rocky earth.

Mourners often yearn for a dream about the person that has gone. And while sometimes a dream comes shortly after the death, often it takes a long time before this wish is fulfilled. I would encourage you to attend to your dreams with the hope that it would be another place where heaven and earth could come together to help you to continue the conversation with the person who has died. One woman spoke to me of the way in which her husband, who died many years ago, frequently appears in her dreams and how she has come to treasure her dream world as a time when they can be together. Another, whose son recently died, told me of a conversation that she had with him in a dream. He explained the challenges he had faced in his too short life and the liberation he felt at being relieved of them. Both women were comforted by the presence of their departed loved ones in their dreams.

Exercise 10·3
A Visitation

Have you had a dream of the person who has died? Recount it here as well as your understanding of the significance of the dream. Do you feel that it was actually a visit from the person who has passed on? Is it possible to embrace the images that appear to you in the dream world as a continuing conversation that transcends our understanding of the boundaries between not only our waking life and the dreamworld but also between life and death?

Exercise 10·4
Invoking a Dream

A Kabbalistic practice calls on knowledge to which we do not normally have access for solving our problems. Resembling a process now known as lucid dreaming, it seeks guidance from our unconscious in addressing a problem. To begin, articulate an issue or feeling which keeps you from making peace with the deceased. Formulate this into a question or a request and write it in the margin.

Before going to sleep concentrate on what you have just written. Take ten deep breaths, relaxing more with each one, and then recite this ancient incantation, attributed to Rabbi Joseph Karo, who wrote in the sixteenth century.

I adjure you with the great, mighty and awesome Name of God, that you visit me this night and answer my question and request, whether by dream, by vision, by indicating a verse from Scripture, by automatic speech . . . or writing.

If you had a dream, write it down the following morning and see if there is an aspect of the dream that speaks to the concern you articulated. If you do not remember having a dream, try automatic writing: spend fifteen minutes immediately after awakening writing anything that comes into your head as fast as you can without censoring or second-guessing what you are writing. If neither of these methods is helpful to you, try Karo's third suggestion, "indicating a verse from Scripture." With your eyes closed, take a copy of the Bible and open it randomly. Then, again with your eyes closed, run your finger down the page and stop suddenly. Read the passage at which your finger stops and see if it helps you clarify what you need to do to ease your mourning.

The bond connecting heaven and earth, signified by Jacob's dream, is one we will strive for as we try to connect you both with your deepest self and with the furthest powers in the universe—from your mourner's place on the floor. I know that this place of sleeping on stones is pretty uncomfortable. But as Jacob discovered when he awoke from his dream, "How [awesome] is this place. This is none other that the abode of God, the gateway to Heaven."

We will now stand at the Gateway to Heaven, crying for the gate to open and grant you peace. We will do this by using one of the more elemental and more powerful forms of human expression—prayer.

God was in this place and I, I did not know.
—*Genesis* 28:16

Chapter Ten

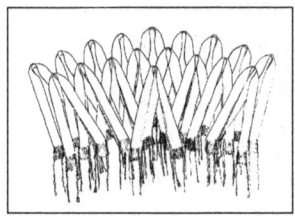

Rend your heart and not your garments; turn back to God.

–Joel 2:13

11

תפילה

Keriah *and Prayer: Speaking Out from the Distress of Your Soul*

IN OUR WORK together, we have taken on almost everyone. We have challenged both the living and the dead. There is only one more target for our intense feelings: God. We will do this through an ancient way of accosting God—prayer.

This section, like the other parts of the book, can be read literally or as metaphor. It addresses prayer as a spiritual process for aligning oneself with the Divine, as well as a means of satisfying the psychological needs that cause one to reach out to something beyond the self. For this reason I don't think one has to believe in God for the exercises of this chapter to be helpful as we move on to confront the Divine.

פ.ל.ל **PLL:** to pray, intercede, judge, plead, entreat, mediate, incriminate oneself

What Is Prayer?

Prayer is one of the most traditional ways of lightening our load and transcending our wounds, and for some, the most potent. Prayer can disturb us, and in doing so, shake us loose from some of our habitual ways of doing things. A genuine act of prayer extends from our deepest feelings and reaches out to petition, confess, assert, give thanks or praise. It seeks to conceive of something beyond the limits of our understanding and our lives. Prayer addresses something that will always be there and is not subject to death. Prayer is also a model for focusing our emotional experiences. Through prayer, we let these experiences transform us, as we reach beyond ourselves and hope to touch that which is eternal.

Prayer Is Not Just for "Believers"

Do not be intimidated by the idea of prayer, even if you are an atheist or an agnostic. Prayer does not have to be predicated on faith. It can also be predicated on need. Prayer is a reaching out in the struggle to open ourselves.

Prayer is often especially hard for mourners. We are angry with God and the way in which the universe delivers its blows. Many people are sustained by their faith during difficult times. But often even those whose belief in God is strong sometimes find that mourning is a time when faith is tested.

The rabbis who formulated the Jewish mourning rituals understood that mourners often feel separated from God. By prohibiting mourners from reciting certain prayers and from certain religious obligations during the periods of *aninut* and *shiva* they recognized that the profound alienation of early mourning extends to the relationship with God.

But mourners are not alone in their feelings of spiritual detachment. Prayer is one of the strongest taboos for educated modern people. Many of us in this post-Holocaust, nuclear age, gravely doubt that there is a Higher Power. The Patriarchal God of the Bible is an especially hard one to believe in, for how could "He" have permitted a creation which began with the Garden of Eden to evolve to the edge of destruction? Or "His" people to die in Auschwitz?

If we have spiritual yearnings, it is hard to identify them as such. These things are seldom named. Often we lack the vocabulary to articulate our spiritual yearnings. Sometimes we are too busy to even notice them. Many who feel a profound existential emptiness that might be alleviated by spirituality pursue distractions to fill that emptiness that is so hard to name. This is acknowledged by treatment programs for substance abuse and other addictions, such as Alcoholics Anonymous, which focus on spirituality.

Indeed, if we can name that emptiness as a spiritual craving, we are often embarrassed, since people who search for the spiritual are often dismissed as naive or aberrant. In fact, given what we know about the condition of the world and our understanding of the God of the Bible, it can be embarrassing to admit that we struggle to encounter something higher and deeper than our familiar, concrete human existence. Our concept of the Divine stifles our need for It. Prayer becomes impossible.

> Prayer . . . is about the tension that we feel at the imperfection of the universe . . . about Exile and alienation and about letting God back in.
> —*Rabbi Abraham Joshua Heschel*

Chapter Eleven

Confronting Your Doubts to Explore the Possibility of Prayer

All these doubts are my own doubts. Throughout my life I have struggled to obtain a concept of the Divine that could account for the variety in our universe. But the word "God" did not work for me. It throws me back to my childhood experiences of counting the light bulbs in the dome of my synagogue rather than connecting with the words of the prayerbook.

In the early drafts of this book, I avoided the word "God" completely. When a participant in a workshop I led on prayer asked why I never spoke of God, I had to question myself. I responded by saying that I wanted to make it easier for people who do not believe in God to find the healing that I believe is present in the universe. "Healing," I thought, perhaps that's my concept of God. For in conceiving of healing, I feel a connection to something greater than myself, something that I feel I can tap into in the process of working to heal myself and to heal the world.

Still, I realized that I am uncomfortable saying the name of God. It may be the inhibitions I wrote about earlier, but it is not just that. When we have a name for this infinite mystery that is the source of it all, we begin to limit it. By naming it so often, we wear it out; it becomes familiar. We think we know it. It diminishes the mystery, the way electric lights can dim the stars. By having such an immutable name for The Source, we fix that which is holy and beyond definition; in trying to quantify the ineffable, we deny the flow of mystery. Perhaps that is why the Hebrew name for God—יהוה—is never pronounced, or why many observant Jews put a hyphen in place of the "o" when writing the word "God."

יהוה **YHWH** was—is—will be—the central, unarticulated name of God.

I struggle with the word "God," but I can experience the Holy Presence. And I do believe in prayer as a way of aligning myself with that Presence and basking in Its light. I learned that the Biblical word for prayer means to intercede or intervene and that there is even an ancient Arabic word that may be related that means to cut oneself with the notched edge of a sword. I feel that I can intercede in Divinity. I can place myself in the midst of Holiness. I don't believe that I need to wait for some power far away to take responsibility for my life, but that I am empowered to open up to the Divine and bask in its holiness. Sometimes in order to let the Divine enter, I must cut myself open, find my wounds, and let them speak.

פ.ל.ל PLL: . . . from Arabic . . . notched edge (of sword, etc.); to cut oneself in worship.
—Brown, Driver & Briggs

Examine your idea of what it is that runs the universe. Is faith in God a central part of your life? Or is it totally irrelevant? Perhaps you don't think God is directly involved in everyday life, but you have another concept of what created and animates the universe. What have been your experiences with prayer and meditation? If possible, address the following questions regarding your belief system: Do you believe in God? Can you describe your God-concept? Do you believe that God might intervene in your life or hear your prayers? How has the loss affected your belief in God or your belief system about the universe?

Exercise 11·1
Believer, Agnostic, Atheist, or . . . ?

If what I have said regarding God or the spiritual is alien to you, do not be concerned. We are working here with a process. That process addresses healing wherever it can be found. My concern is to help you find a source of your healing, not to put you into a category or convince you to believe a particular dogma. No matter what you may feel about God or prayer, I invite you to join me on this part of the mourner's path to explore the meaning of prayer and seek to transform your loss. As I have said before, Judaism requires actions, not beliefs, and the process created by prayer may give you an opportunity to express yourself and conceive your healing whether or not it brings you to God.

Avodah: *Prayer and Sacrifice—The "Work" of Worship*

Before there was a prayer service, there were sacrificial rites. Originally, the Jewish prayer service was centered around ritual sacrifice in the Temple. Individuals gave animals or agricultural products to the priests in the Temple. These donations were considered restitution for sins committed or infractions of rules, or to mark occasions, celebrate transitions or communal events, or to honor or thank God. They were incinerated by the *esh tamid*, the eternal fire, which burned at all times on the Temple's altar.

Korban, the Hebrew word for sacrifice, has the same root as the words for closeness, relatedness and unite. In the Temple that nearness and relatedness was experienced as nearness to God. All watched as the flame changed these offerings from matter to smoke. As the smoke gradually became invisible, the sacrifice was believed to have been transmuted from matter to spirit. As the ancients watched their material sacrifices

ק.ר.ב. **KRV:** to unite, bring near, be related; closeness, relatives; *Korbanot*: sacrifices go up in smoke, they too made the transition from matter to spirit, and connected with the invisible and omnipotent God.

If the Jewish people were to remain an entity after the destruction of the Temple, it was necessary to create rituals that did not require the Temple or the sacrificial rites performed there. To achieve this, what eventually became the modern prayer service began to take form. Its liturgy was structured along the same lines as the sacrificial rituals in the Temple, and many of its words and prayers are substitutes for these rites. Now, centuries after the destruction of the Temple, the reasons that people brought sacrifices to the Temple—absolution, celebration, propitiation, petition, thanksgiving—are still the reasons that people pray.

This image of sacrifice is an icon for the work of mourning. We begin by mourning the death of a physical being, and ultimately redefine our connection to that being in non-physical terms. That this is "work" is validated by the fact that the sacrificial ritual was called the *Avodah* (or "work") service.

Recognizing prayer's roots in sacrifice can help us understand what is lost and what is gained by praying. The process of transformation begins by giving up something. In the case of the mourner, some level of sacrifice is self-evident: The mourner has given up a relationship with a living being, and must now make profound changes in his or her life in order to transform the loss into an ongoing relationship with the deceased.

ע.ב.ד. **AVD:** to work, toil, worship; liturgy, worship, labor, Divine Service; *Avodah*: the sacrificial worship service in the ancient Temple

Prayer is not a substitute for sacrifice.... Prayer is sacrifice.... Offer our sacrifices, satisfy our needs, wage our battles, bring us close to God.
—*Rabbi Abraham Joshua Heschel*

Chapter Eleven

Exercise 11·2
Sacrifice: Connecting with What Does Not Die

Can you conceive of something that is eternal? Describe it and the extent to which you are aware of it in your daily life. Does it nourish you? Is it benevolent or evil? Are there parts of you and parts of the deceased that are eternal? Do you feel a connection between them?

Keriah unites the concepts of prayer and of sacrifice. It calls for sacrificing something of personal value. When we personalize the act of *keriah* by symbolically ripping ourselves open to expose our deepest feelings, we are in the midst of an act of prayer. In an effort to transform your pain and bring you closer to that which is eternal, just as the *esh tamid* transformed the Temple sacrifices into the smoke that reached toward God, I remind you again of Job. It was Job who, while "speak[ing] out in the distress of [his] soul," confronted all—including God—challenging them with his assertion of injustice in the universe.

Spontaneous Prayer: From Dreams to Prayer

Prayer can be individual or communal. Some prayers are spontaneous and others were written millennia ago. We will first explore spontaneous individual prayer.

Finding the deep voice of emotions that link a person with spirituality is one of the purposes of prayer. But being able to spontaneously express our deepest feelings, especially without censoring them, can be a tremendous challenge.

What have I done to You, Vigilant God? Why make me Your target?

—*Job* 7:20

Imagine that you stand at the Gates of Heaven, face-to-face with the power that metes out judgment and justice. From the depths of your soul, cry out about the way the universe works. Remember Job, who refused to be censored. Remember Hannah, who spoke from a place of such uncommon depth that she was mistaken as drunk. Letting Job and Hannah be your models; do not restrain yourself.

Exercise 11·3
Crying Out in the Distress of My Soul

That crying out (that sacrifice) is the beginning of prayer. Did you feel that your pain was heard or did you feel that you were alone in the universe? After crying out, did you detect any change in your feelings? Take a few minutes to reflect on the effect of crying out. When you are finished, you might want to go to your Shabbat list and choose something you can do to nurture yourself.

The Sound of Prayer

That cry of the heart is where prayer begins. We reach out in anger or need for something which we feel is beyond our power. While prayer can amplify our feelings, it can also calm or soothe them. It has been found that repeating simple prayers creates what is known as the "relaxation response," which reduces stress and produces calm. We can assume, then, that prayer's soothing effect is one of the reasons people pray. This can be true whether or not one believes or, even, understands the words of the prayers. In fact, as has been said, Kaddish is not chanted in Hebrew, but in Aramaic, the language spoken in the land of Israel when rabbinic Judaism was first evolving.

> God: In their distress, they sought you: Your chastisement reduced them to anguished, whispered prayer, like a woman with child, approaching childbirth.
> —Isaiah 26:16-17

There may be certain advantages to saying a prayer in a language which is not familiar to you. When you don't know what the words really mean, they may resonate in a deeper, more primitive way than if the words had meaning. They may affect you on preverbal and sensory levels. You may be so moved by their sound, tune, and rhythm that you rock or sway to them as you intone them. This motion, which is often seen among Jews in deep prayer, has been the cadence for one generation after another around the globe. The power of that connection is greater than words.

Exercise 11·4
Sound and Motion

Stand and breathe quietly and rhythmically. As you breathe out, find a sound that reflects where you presently are in handling this transformative and sacrificial process of mourning. It may be a deep sigh or an angry snarl. If necessary, see if you can change the sound to give it a comforting quality. Repeat this sound for about five minutes, allowing whatever motion spontaneously arises to move your body in cadence with it. Write about your experience.

Prayer as Alignment

In the previous exercise, we looked at something akin to the biological nature of prayer. We also explored prayer as the wounded cry of our preverbal selves. It gives voice to our primordial rages and desperations and soothes us by sounds and rhythms. We have experienced prayer as a solitary cry of the moment and as an ongoing tribal dance.

We will now use a more structured form of prayer to harness the primitive universal voice which you found. This will connect you with greater strengths and powers than you might feel are available to you, and summon the power to heal.

The petitional prayer is perhaps the most common form of prayer. A petition is sent out whenever a person asks God for something. People turn to God throughout the day when they ask for help with mundane matters: "Dear God . . . let me find that paper . . . find a parking place . . . find my keys." When a person is in crisis, petitioning is more intense: "Dear God . . . heal my child . . . end this pain."

Many of Judaism's prayers are petitional prayers. Through the formal liturgy, we ask for rain, healing, redemption, health, peace, loving kindness, mercy. The list goes on and on, appealing to God on behalf of every sort of human need.

A petitional prayer begins with a need. It also assumes some willingness to believe in the possibility that the need can be met. For our purposes, absolute belief that God will answer your prayer is not a prerequisite. But if you are willing to believe in the possibility that there may be a force that can help you—whether or not that force is called God—then there is also a possibility that your petition can bring you healing. This is about hope—even if hope is held by a very slim thread.

In the next few exercises, we will take apart the process of prayer. Then we will piece it together, bit by bit, starting with this simple sliver of hope. We will follow that hope, through different experiences and see if it can lead to a statement of faith. Faith is an evolutionary process, one that is likely to be in transition in the

> Sometimes the bird turns away. Sometimes it does not open its mouth to sing. Sometimes it is afraid. Sometimes it is afraid of the dark. But when it forgets it is afraid and opens its mouth to sing, it fills with light.
>
> —Deena Metzger

Chapter Eleven

time of mourning. If you do not now have this hope, do the exercises that follow as if you do. Then see what the exercises yield for you.

A midrash says that the manna which God provided the Israelites as they wandered in the desert tasted different to each person. Each found in the manna the specific nourishment he or she required. To a baby, it was mother's milk; to the old, it brought youth; to the tired, it was invigorating. The same phenomenon occurred when God spoke from Sinai: Each person heard God as if he or she were the only one for whom God's message was intended.

These midrashim illustrate the rabbinic belief in God's ability to satisfy each person's needs and explain the many descriptions of God in the Bible and prayer books. They portray a God who can speak to each of us.

Jewish tradition tells us that there is one ultimate name for God. As I said earlier, that name cannot be said aloud. We are not permitted to say it. Nor should we try. In the time of the Temple, this name was pronounced once a year by the High Priest. All the other words used as names for God are closer to descriptions, titles, or epithets. They describe how humans perceive God. They are garments to clothe that which would otherwise be impossible to visualize. And they are conceived in the human image.

We are told that the human being was created in the image of God. The converse is also true. We perceive of God in the human image, projecting from human need a conception of the nature of the power that moves the universe. Prayer—and your own yearning—will help you connect with the image of God that can bring you the help you specifically need.

The Amidah: Standing Before God

At the center of the Jewish prayer service, following the Shema, is the Amidah, the standing prayer, which is often recited silently. On weekdays it consists of nineteen blessings. The first three welcome the Divine Presence, celebrate Its achievements and attest to Its role in the lives of those who had faith in God in the past. The next thirteen benedictions make various requests of God. The Amidah ends with three prayers of thanksgiving. On Shabbat and Holy Days the Amidah is somewhat different.

We will follow the structure of the weekday Amidah, to help you summon your own healing, invoking the quality of Divinity that can most directly soothe your pain. We will address the "Face of God" that represents that healing and connect you with those who have called for help in this way in the past. Then you will ask for help. Finally you will praise that quality of Divinity to which the prayer was addressed.

You might want to examine the prayer, used in High Holy Day liturgy, and taken from the book of Exodus, which lists God's attributes. This will give you an idea of how others, in moments of distress, have imagined the Divine healing power.

> Adonai! Adonai! God compassionate and gracious, slow to anger, abounding in kindness and faithfulness, extending kindness to the thousandth generation, forgiving iniquity, transgression, and sin.
>
> —Exodus 34:6–7
> *High Holy Day liturgy*

Part 1: Salutation: Welcoming the Divine

We begin with a salutation. In the last exercises, your rage and desperation—as well as your comfort—found their voices. Think about the wounds they described. What pain blocks your ability to go forward

Exercise 11·5
Learning How to Pray

with your life? It is also the key to the quality of God that you must invoke for healing.

Imagine an energy or force, what we will call a "face of God," that has the powers and qualities necessary to heal your wounds.

If you are so overwhelmed that you can barely get through a day, you might want to imagine healing as the power to focus. If your anxiety is so fierce that you are living on the edge of panic attacks, your "face of God" might be a soothing one. Now invoke that "face of God" and address it as you would a friend in a letter.

Dear God: Source of _____

I call upon you and your power of _____

_____

Part 2: Ancestors—Where the Energy Has Worked in the Past

The second phrase of our prayers looks to one of the opening prayers of the Amidah which mentions the ancestors who put their faith in God. It usually calls upon the "God of Abraham, God of Isaac and God of Jacob." Many congregations also invoke the "God of Sarah, Rebecca, Leah, and Rachel." Invoking God in this way helps remind the person who is uttering the prayer that this type of healing has worked in the past and could work again.

It also reminds God of the merit of those before us. We invoke z'chut avot, *the merit of our ancestors,* when asking for favors, hoping that we will be able to benefit from their faith and goodness.

> In performing [established prayers] one continues a conversation with God which was begun by their ancestors centuries ago.
> —Rabbi Jakob Petuchowski

Now recall another time when you were in despair. Remembering that we have survived great pain in the past can assure us that there is a precedent for healing. By recalling patriarchs and matriarchs—and ourselves—we are saying: "As it worked for our ancestors, let it work for us. . . . As it worked for me in the past, let it help me now."

In the exercise below, you will remind that power (and yourself) of your past connection. You will first identify healing in your life or in the lives of others, then align yourself with that healing power. Introduce yourself as you might in a letter to someone you know but haven't seen for awhile or create a letter of introduction for yourself, referring to someone else for whom you know God has worked in this way in the past. Here is an example of the first kind of introduction:

> I called on you years ago while coping with the breakup of my first marriage. I thought I'd never be part of life again, but you somehow got me through that pain. You got me interested again in my garden and then my work, slowly drawing me back into routines and activities until I realized that I was again alive in the world. You made it possible for me to love again and eventually remarry, knowing a trust and companionship far richer than I had known before. And now I mourn the loss of that partner.

Complete the following:

You remember me. I am (Or you could give the name of a role model): _____

_____

_____

Chapter Eleven

Shevirat Kelim *The Breaking of Vessels*

> Prayer is either exceedingly urgent, exceedingly relevant or . . . useless. . . . God is ensconced in mystery, hidden in the depths. Prayer is pleading with God to come out of the depths.
> —Rabbi Abraham Joshua Heschel

This is who I am today: _____

_____

_____

Part 3: Benediction: The Actual Petition

Having given your background, now plead your case. Say exactly what you need and why you need it. Accost whatever you believe is the Source of Power in the Universe. Open your heart and appeal on your own behalf. It is said that only where the hearts are broken does God hear the prayers. Let your prayer be heard so that The Holy One will know you are open and ready to bring the Healing Presence into your life.

Part 4: Praise: Closing

Now further align yourself with the Divine and affirm Its existence. Praise It, state your gratitude that It is available, and express your appreciation for the greatness of Its power by opening yourself to receive what you have asked for.

Mutual Yearning

You have articulated your need, approached a power that could meet it, acknowledged ways that power has worked in the past, and praised what you perceive as Divine. Now shift your focus from articulating your need and your hope for its fulfillment to experiencing the healing this process may have brought you. This meditative exercise melds the need of healing with the hope for healing. It addresses the alienation we often feel from the Source of our healing and our own healing resources. It brings together the need for healing with healing itself.

Judaism teaches that God and each human together engage in *tikkun olam*, or healing the world. God and God's human partner both yearn for the other so the work can be done, and even the universe yearns to be healed.

Exercise 11•6
The Yearning To Be Healed

Part 1: Reaching Out for Healing

Position yourself comfortably, either standing or sitting with your feet touching the ground. Focus on the "face of God" you have been seeking and on your yearning for the healing this can bring. Now imagine that you are a triangle, balanced on one point, attempting to stand tall. Raise your arms above you, as if they were sides of the triangle, reaching for the healing which you seek. In the balancing effort, reach out to the Holy Place of Healing, reiterating your plea to the source of healing which you seek for the energy required to stay balanced and focused upon that for which you yearn. You might want to imagine that your arms are the sides of the triangle. Raise them as they reach out. Feel the yearning—your longing to be healed. Imagine what life would be like if your yearning were fulfilled. Feel that you are open to receive the healing.

Part 2: Healing Reaches Out

Now imagine a second triangle, representing the Healing Power, anchored wherever your healing has its source. The intensity of your desire to be healed is equaled by the desire of this Healing Power to heal you.

182   Shevirat Kelim *The Breaking of Vessels*

> What is below is like that which is above and what is above is like that which is below.... Ascend with the greatest sagacity from the earth to heaven and then again descend to earth. And unite together the powers of things superior and inferior. Thus you will obtain the glory of the whole world and obscurity will fly away from you.
> —E. J. Holmyard

Just as you struggled to stay balanced and focused on your yearning, so this Healing Power longs to give you exactly what you need. Feel the second triangle joining you so that the desire to heal and the desire to be healed cannot be distinguished. The healing energy that was once beyond you is now within you.

Part 3: Wholeness and Healing

You may have noticed that as the two triangles intersected, they formed a Star of David. To a Kabbalist, the Magen David reveals the mutual interaction between what is above and what is below and the universe's yearning for wholeness. Meditate for five minutes on the Magen David and on the healing present in your heart and in the universe. Visualize yourself as being bathed in it from every direction.

Prayer as Praise

The previous experience was intended to help you identify healing power as being both outside and within you, as something not bound by time or space, or by life or death, and to which you have access at all times. The connection to this eternal healing power is something that can be nurtured over time and invoked whenever you feel a need for it. With this in mind, we move to the final exercise of *keriah*.

> The light is far away. The only way to see it is to close your eyes.
> —Rabbi Jonathan Omer-Man

Actually, we are ending where *keriah* is technically supposed to begin. When ripping cloth, upon hearing of the death or at the funeral, a mourner recites the following blessing: "Barukh Attah Adonai Eloheinu Melekh Haolam Dayan Haemet," "Blessed are You, God, Ruler of the universe, the true Judge." It may be difficult to

א.מ.ת **Amet:** truth, faith, firmness, reliability, faithfulness imagine praising God's wisdom at such a moment. Perhaps this is intended to remind us of a wisdom we cannot understand. Perhaps in ancient times the act of *keriah* was so intense that it took the mourner through all the emotional release that we have covered in the last three chapters. But here we are at the end of them. And while you still have to fully integrate your healing, by now there has probably been a shift in your feelings toward the deceased, toward God, and toward yourself.

ברוך אתה, יי אלהינו, מלך העולם, דין האמת.

Barukh Attah Adonai Eloheinu Melekh Haolam Dayan Haemet.
"Blessed are You, God, Ruler of the universe, the true Judge."

Chapter Eleven

PART III

12 Immortality in HaOlam Hazeh:
Living On in the World of the Living

13 Olam Haneshamot (*Immortality in the Next World*):
A Walk through the World of Souls

14 Matzevah (*The Unveiling*):
Raising the Curtain on the Rest of Your Life

15 Yizkor, Yahrzeit, *and the Cycle of Seasons*

16 Shalom:
Hello, Goodbye, and Peace

17 Those Who Say "Amen":
How to Comfort the Bereaved

תיקון
Tikkun
Healing

The final phase of the creation process, as seen by the Jewish mystics, is *Tikkun,* or healing.

Here the holy sparks which were inaccessible during earlier phases are redeemed, reorganization takes place, and that which has been damaged is restored. In this section we will attend to your own healing by creating vessels to transform your loss into a living memorial and address your ongoing healing process.

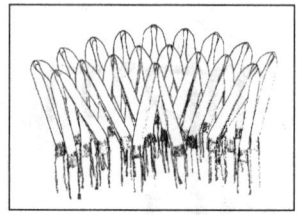

But the spirit is mightier than the grave.

–Rabbi Maurice Lamm

12

העולם הזה

Immortality in HaOlam Hazeh: Living On in the World of the Living

IN EXPLORING PRAYER, I hope you were able to identify something that exists both inside and outside of you and is not subject to time. We sought to help you align yourself with a spiritual essence defined by the Quality of Divinity that you felt could bring you healing. I hope that in the process you had a sense of touching some eternal, ever-present source of strength and could bask in its presence.

What Transcends Our Separation from Those We Have Lost?

As we build a relationship with the ineffable entities we cultivate an identification with things that transcend the separation of life and death. Within this spiritual identification exists the seeds of your continuing relationship with the deceased. This leads us to the subject of immortality.

We begin by identifying what is immortal about the person who has died—that which is ever-present and not subject to time. This begins the crucial work of healing through which we explore ways in which your ongoing relationship with the deceased can continue to be vital and satisfying.

In the preceding chapter, we learned that prayer is rooted in the ancient sacrifices that turned the material into the spiritual. While the parallel is not exact between your great sacrifice and the sacrifices of the ancient Temple, which were usually offered willingly, it is in this transition between physical and spiritual that an ongoing relationship is created and healing and transformation become real.

Judaism and Immortality

עולם **olam:** the world, the universe, outer space, eternity

Let's begin by exploring the meanings and possibilities of immortality and by exploring how immortality can be expressed in things that continue on Earth, the *olam hazeh* (this world) after one has died. In the process, we will help you to connect with the immortal qualities you continue to share with the deceased.

Immortality in HaOlam Hazeh: Living On in the World of the Living

A common misunderstanding of Judaism is that it is entirely focused on life on earth and is not concerned with the afterlife. This perception is understandable. The world so needs healing that our obligation to that task and the demands it places upon us can distract us from concerns about the world to come. Yet Judaism, particularly Jewish mysticism, has always been concerned with what becomes of the soul after death, and many theories about that question have developed.

Healing the world—*tikkun olam*—and being concerned with the afterlife are intertwined. Healing the world, one of the strongest injunctions in Judaism, actually mirrors the ultimate Jewish hope for the afterlife. To understand this, let's look again at the Kaddish. This time we will focus on the literal meaning of its words.

The Kaddish asks for the hastening of the day when the earth reflects Godliness. It describes a world in which God's perfection and the praises of God's name are so evident that God's world and the world on which human history unfolds become the same. It affirms the possibility of healing the world and calls for the peace of "God's high place" to be known here on Earth. The goal of the Kaddish is to bring together the two worlds of *olam hazeh* (this world) and *olam haba* (the world to come).

So when we consider Judaism's various concepts of afterlife, we must consider that which is earthbound and material as well as that which is spiritual and part of the world to come. In this chapter and the next, we will explore both views of immortality: the way in which we and the world continue to be affected by those who have died, as well as the fate of the soul of the deceased in the spiritual realms of the afterlife.

Chapter Twelve

Immortality in Olam Hazeh

How can we relate to the immortality of the person who has died? Jewish tradition tells us that those who have died live on in the acts of goodness they performed and the way they touched the lives of those who remain on earth. By identifying the qualities that made your relationship worthwhile, you can realize which of the deceased person's qualities and deeds live on and continue to be useful. It is also important to determine which qualities you can do without. This helps in the separation process, or, in the Kabbalistic sense, in the possibility of your soul and the soul of the deceased being allowed to live out their individual and unique destinies.

In addition, when we do something that reflects our continued relationship with the deceased, we bring merit to the soul of that person. Mystics believe this helps further cleanse the deceased's soul. This also helps to continue the mystical work of cleansing the soul, which we began with the *Viddui, taharah,* and *Kaddish*. I hope that in this work of cleansing and transforming your own soul will find some relief from the pain of mourning.

> So long as the children live, so long does the parent live.
> —*Rabbi Simeon bar Yohai*

Exercise 12·1
Biological and Physical Immortality

Identify some traits of the deceased that continue after death. They may be physical, emotional, or intellectual qualities that you associate with that person. What do you see in yourself or in others whose lives he or she touched? Is there a gesture that you make, a phrase you use, or a way that you react to something

Part Three

that reminds you of the deceased? When you look at a family member—a child, an aunt, a grandfather—do you see an expression or a physical resemblance which reminds you of the person who died?

Exercise 12•2
The Immortality of Influence

Now consider any of your character traits, interests, and beliefs which have originated with the deceased. What are these? These may be positive or negative legacies. If they are positive, how nice to identify their source and affirm that they still live on. If they are negative, identifying them as such can help free you from the continuing burdens of the relationship. Just as we said the Kaddish to purge evil from the soul of the person who died, we also said it to clear away your persistent negative entanglements.

Describe how these legacies continue to manifest themselves, for good or bad.

Memorializing with Actions

Biology and influence are naturally occurring forms of immortality. Jewish tradition also offers creative ways to memorialize the dead. We perform mitzvot in their memory. We connect their name with a project that continues their values. We donate money or effort as a righteous act of *tzedakah* in their memory. We name children after them.

A Kabbalistic understanding tells that just as the Kaddish helps to elevate the souls of the departed, these memorial acts also help to further the ascent of their souls. When an act is performed in memory of a person

They who leave worthy children do not die in spirit. Their mortal remains are interred in the earth, but their teachings remain among men.
—*Rabbi Maurice Lamm*

who died, it is equivalent to that person performing the mitzvah. The merit accrued becomes an asset attached to their soul. By performing the mitzvah on someone's behalf, we become that person's feet on earth. While it is common for people to make donations in memory of someone soon after a death, many people are not aware of the mystical significance of this gesture. That is a shame, since knowing its spiritual significance might make it even more meaningful to the person who performs it.

Exercise 12·3
Counting Mitzvot

Were acts of tzedakah *performed in memory of your lost one? Write some down. Did they seem appropriate? How did they affect you?*

The Ethical Will: Preserving the Values of the Deceased

We should consciously determine which mitzvah to perform on behalf of someone who has died. It can be a very creative way to continue your relationship with the deceased. It can also mark a point for the transition of responsibilities between you and the one who has died. These acts are concrete evidence that you have truly accepted the new role that is assumed when one says the Kaddish. When saying the Kaddish, you affirm not only the values of the deceased, but also the values of all the people for whom that person said the Kaddish, and on and on beyond them. Kaddish is the chain which links generations and through which values are transferred.

Reciting the Kaddish and performing mitzvot and acts of *tzedakah* in memory of someone who has died not only encourages us to keep the values of the deceased alive, but these acts also help anchor us in the reality of life on earth. This helps us to separate from the deceased and to move on to the concerns of our own lives.

One way to determine the appropriate acts of memorial is to write an Ethical Will. This is a document that parents prepare to summarize their paramount values and concerns, hoping it will continue to influence their descendants' behavior. Unlike the familiar Last Will and Testament, which transfers possessions, the Ethical Will is designed to pass on wisdom, which is spiritual wealth.

Ethical Wills have their antecedents in Jacob's parting words to his children from his deathbed, in David's instructions to Solomon about his behavior after David's death, and in Moses' farewell address to his people. They were commonly written in medieval times when Jewish life was precarious and parents weren't certain that they would be alive to influence their children's moral development. But examples exist from all eras, documenting parents' attempts to influence their children and future generations.

> David to Solomon: I am going the way of all the earth. Be strong and show yourself a man. Keep the charge of . . . God; walking in (God's) ways and following God's commandments . . . rules and . . . admonition as recorded in the Teaching of Moses, in order that you may succeed in whatever you undertake and wherever you turn.
>
> — 1 Kings 2:2-12

If the deceased wrote an Ethical Will or made a verbal statement equivalent to one before dying, you have a real treasure from which you can draw inspiration. If not, you now have the opportunity to write an Ethical Will in memory of that person. What was important to him or her? What would (s)he hope his/her

Exercise 12•4
Writing an Ethical Will

life represented? What would (s)he like to have done by those who survived him or her? Write the Ethical Will as if it were a letter from the deceased to you. (For inspiration and assistance in writing an Ethical Will you will find help in *So That Your Values Live On: Ethical Wills and How to Prepare Them*, edited by Rabbi Jack Riemer and Professor Nathaniel Stampfer, Jewish Lights Publishing, Woodstock, VT 05091.)

Dear _____
(insert your name above)

Exercise 12·5
A Joint Ethical Will

Now consider your relationship with the deceased. What values did you share? What projects did you work on together? What might you have done together had death not occurred? Address any conflict in your values so you can determine what you can do in the memory of the deceased that would be consistent with your values as well as his or hers.

Creating an Action Plan for Commemorating the Deceased

The next step is to decide on an appropriate act of *tzedakah* to honor the memory of the deceased. In English, *tzedakah* is often translated as "an act of charity," but the Hebrew root, *tzedek,* is found in words that mean "justice" or "righteousness." A *tzadik* is a pious person. That these words share the same root make it clear that Judaism places a high value on each act of *tzedakah*.

Immortality in HaOlam Hazeh: Living On in the World of the Living

There are many ways for you to determine the *tzedakah* you will do. One way is to find something that the person did in his or her life and commit yourself to doing it. A woman in one of my groups spoke of her husband as a generous and caring landlord. Despite some difficulty continuing to do things as he had done them, his widow was determined to continue serving her tenants with the thoughtfulness they had expected from her husband.

Another woman took up gardening, one of her husband's favorite hobbies, even though she formerly had no interest in it. To her, this felt like continuing to care for her husband, and also as if she was continuing her relationship with him. She carefully tended his roses. The first Purim after his death, she gave away jam she had made from a plum tree that her husband had planted. Gardening had started as an act of remembrance for her husband, but it soon took on a life of its own and became her stepping stone to a new life.

> Memorials can be joyous: After my father dies, I will be telling his jokes and his laughter will continue. My Aunt Sarah's recipe for mayonnaise deserves immortality. She recited it into my tape recorder when she was living at the Jewish Home for the Aged. Her memory was failing, but she still knew how to make the mayonnaise which we spread on the Challah (egg bread) every Friday night: "Take one egg, the juice of one and a half lemons and add salt and pepper and a teaspoon of dry mustard. Then you take the oil, and beat it in a little bit at a time. The importance is to beat it slowly, adding a little more and a little more. I use up to two full cups, depending on the size of the egg and the amount of lemon juice." (Journal Entry, New Orleans, 1992)

An impressive memorial project was the AIDS Quilt, created to commemorate individuals who have died of AIDS. The act of creating a panel for the quilt, in

---

צ.ד.ק **TzDK:** to be right or correct; justice; *tzadik*: a righteous person; *tzedakah*: a charitable act, alms

No matter how exalted is the place in Heaven, it lacks the opportunity for doing mitzvot . . . survivors offer *tzedakah* in the name of the dead . . . [and] invite the soul to come and share in . . . the observance of a mitzvah.

—Rabbi Zalman Schachter-Shalomi

Chapter Twelve

memory of a loved one, has been powerful in helping people focus and transform their pain. In the process each person makes a public statement about the individual who has died and about the disease. The Quilt Project has created a vast healing community with both spiritual and political dimensions.

Common acts of *tzedakah* include projects undertaken, volunteer time committed, books donated, financial contributions made to projects and organizations which the deceased supported in life. These are worthwhile and important projects. The main thing is to feel that your *tzedakah* reflects the values of the deceased, continues your relationship with him or her and is consistent with your own values.

Of course your values and those of the deceased may sometimes conflict. Resolving the disparity between these and finding an act that you can comfortably perform in his or her memory can be an important way to resolve tensions between you. Your *tzedakah* can help you find a connection no matter what other differences you might have had. One man, for example, contributed to a Big Brothers program in the name of his recently deceased alcoholic father. This act acknowledged his wounds, while seeking to achieve a symbolic (though partial) compensation for his father's cruelty.

Your memorial act picks up the deceased's mantle, weaving it into your own fabric. Many prayers begin with the phrase "God of Abraham, God of Isaac, God of Jacob," to which many egalitarian communities have added "God of Sarah, God of Rebecca, God of Leah, God of Rachel," reminding us that each generation draws on the experience which preceded it, while finding its own way within the context of its own times. So it should be with your act of *tzedakah*. Draw upon the values of the one who preceded you and articulate a plan in your own language of action.

In many ways I feel that this book, which I hope will help others overcome some of the obstacles that were insurmountable in my mother's troubled life, is a way of making restitution for her suicide. My mother was intelligent and studious. She valued Judaism and studied psychology, but was unable to connect with sustaining spiritual values. I feel that I have taken the learning which was her positive legacy and added to it the understanding gleaned from my own experience. In the process I feel I have resolved our difficult issues and reclaimed my life. Hopefully this has also helped to compensate for her mistakes and, in the mystical sense, to elevate her soul.

As we have discussed, regrets and guilt almost inevitably accompany a loss. *Tzedakah* can be an act of restitution which makes amends to the deceased. A woman who felt guilty about not being present at her husband's death because she had gone out to lunch with her sister who had come from out of town to give her support, volunteered at the hospital where her husband had spent his last days.

Sometimes one consciously chooses something out of character for the mourner that would have been meaningful to the deceased. A young man, whose alienation from Judaism had created much tension between him and his father, said the Kaddish for his father each day for eleven months after the death. He had not suddenly become religious, nor did he feel that he had wrongly chosen a path which was unacceptable to his father. But he felt that some ways in which he had

Chapter Twelve

expressed those differences had been deliberately hurtful. By saying the Kaddish for his father, he was making amends for some of his harsh words.

Exercise 12·6
Finding Your Deed: The Obligations without Measure

If a particular act of tzedakah *is not immediately evident to you, this exercise may help you find one. This exercise draws on a passage from the Talmud, as it is included in the prayer book. These lines, which detail the valued actions of Jewish life, are recited daily as part of the morning prayer service. Scanning this list might inspire you to come up with an act to memorialize the person you mourn. In the space provided, jot down things you might do that would reflect values that you shared or that seem like a fitting memorial to the deceased.*

These are the obligations without measure, whose reward, too, is without measure.

To honor father and mother:

_____

_____

To perform acts of love and kindness:

_____

_____

To welcome the stranger:

_____

_____

To visit the sick:

_____

_____

To rejoice with bride and groom:

_____

_____

To accompany the dead and console the bereaved:

_____

_____

To pray with sincerity:

_____

_____

To make peace when there is strife:

_____

_____

Chapter Twelve

And the study of Torah is equal to them all, because it leads to them all.

_____

_____

Now make a commitment to an act in memory of the person you are mourning.

_____

_____

This act is an affirmation of your continued partnership.

You have committed yourself to an act which continues your relationship and insures the earthly immortality of the person you have lost. It is now time to explore the immortality of the soul.

> Many a tzadik would have exchanged all the treasures and rewards of Heaven for the possibility of doing one mitzvah here on earth.
> —*Rabbi Zalman Schachter-Shalomi*

Part Three

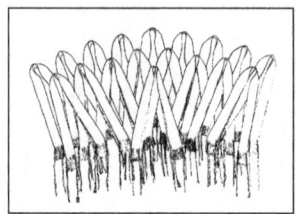

**In each incarnation
we weave or unravel a few
more stitches in the garment
of light. At a certain point
one has finished
and can go home.**

–Rabbi Jonathan Omer-Man

13

עולם הנשמות

Olam Haneshamot:

Immortality in the Next World—A Walk through the World of Souls

THE KADDISH INVOKES the great transition that will occur when *olam haba* (the world to come) and *olam hazeh* (the earthly world) become one. We look to the Kaddish as we make the transition from our concern with earthbound expressions of immortality to our focus on the fate of the soul once it has lost its earthly connection. The Kaddish alludes to one of the visions of *olam haba* at the End of Days: The final Day of Judgment in which all souls stand together, righteous and pure, cleaving to God.

The World of Souls

But what happens to the soul in the period between the end of earthly life and the End of Days?

Through the ages there have been many different concepts of what might happen to the soul after death and the end of its ultimate journey. In this chapter we will accompany the soul of the deceased as it encounters the various stages of postmortem life, taking a walk through *olam haneshamot*, the world of souls, as it is described in certain mystical Jewish sources that are an important part of Jewish tradition going all the way back, according to some scholars, to the Prophets.

As in previous work, it is not necessary for you to share the spiritual assumptions of Jewish mysticism for these metaphors to be effective in facilitating the separation process. These teachings of Jewish mysticism regarding the afterlife are compelling to me because they address the psychological process of separation. As with our work using the Kaddish to frame the need for continued communication with those who have died, I feel that the concepts presented by the world of souls brilliantly facilitate our letting go of the person we mourn. Do I believe in this "world of souls"? I do not know. But exploring it has brought me insight and peace as I applied its visions to my own life as well as the lives of the people I have lost.

Judaism and Afterlife

Despite Judaism's emphasis on the world of the living, the afterlife is, in fact, quite present in Jewish thought. Traditionally it is thought that the soul's punishment or reward in the afterlife is based upon its righteousness

> Rabbi Jacob: This world is like an anteroom before the world-to-come; prepare yourself in the anteroom that you may enter into the banquet hall.
> —*Pirke* Avot 4:21

during life itself. The more righteous the soul, the shorter the purification process in *gehinnom* (hell or purgatory) and the sooner its ascent to the higher celestial realms. Those who have performed good deeds throughout their lives are said to experience the joys of the heavenly Garden of Eden (*Gan Eden*) shortly after death. The desire for a pleasant postmortem fate and the fear of divine retribution for misdeeds have motivated good deeds for generations.

According to Jewish mystics, the soul's ultimate goal is to be united with God. So with that in mind, we will now begin an imaginary "walk" with the deceased through *olam haneshamot* (the world of souls) to help him or her progress to the final goal. Bear in mind that even for the righteous, this ultimate goal is unlikely to be the reward for just one lifetime. Some mystics believe that the soul may be reincarnated many times before this goal is achieved. Jewish mysticism teaches that one of the purposes of earthly life is to construct the spiritual body necessary to achieve ultimate unity with God. It notes that there are 248 limbs of the body and 248 positive commandments ("thou shalts") and 365 blood vessels and 365 negative commandments ("thou shalt nots"). The sum total of these—613—correlates with the total number of commandments. With the satisfactory performance of each mitzvah a corresponding spiritual limb or organ is created until the full 613 has been constructed. At that point, we are told, the soul can be joined with God. Since this process is presumed to take many lifetimes, the afterlife journey of the soul is through several purifying realms. This prepares it to once again enter a body and experience a new earthly life with new opportunities for righteous deeds.

> In Jewish tradition there is no death since both body and soul continue on, that is, return to their source.... Death is neither a decree nor a punishment but is a part of creation.
> —Kenneth Kramer

Chapter Thirteen

Each soul has its own history and destiny, the mystics tell us. As sad as it may be to contemplate separating from the soul of the deceased, the fact that we must do it teaches us an important lesson about the need to concentrate on our own destiny. It might help to imagine your soul and the soul of the deceased as two magnetized bubbles, attracted to each other during life. These two souls shared parts of the same magnetic field, yet retained their individual destinies which will, according to the mystics, take many lifetimes to actualize. As we separate, obligations that we have to the dead begin to be supplanted by the obligations we have to ourselves and to living our own destinies. This is essential for moving on with our lives.

Our concern, as we do this work, is to cultivate insight and compassion. Judgment, reward, and retribution occur in *olam haneshamot*. They are not our concerns here. Without infinite understanding we have neither the knowledge, the understanding nor the power to pronounce Divine judgment. So we do not walk through the world of souls to judge the deceased, but in pursuit of forgiveness, separation, and acceptance.

What Do We Mean by **Soul**?

The mystics tell us that the soul is independent of the body and separate from the personality, actions, and relationships of the deceased. The body and the soul are connected only from the moment that the soul enters the body with the first breath to the moment of death. As mentioned earlier, a Hebrew word for soul, *neshama*, also means "breath." It is believed that God breathes a soul into the body at the moment of birth.

נ.ש.מ **NShM:** *neshama*: the soul, a breath, living creature, the spirit

That breath of life transmits the individual's uniqueness, destiny, and potential. The Talmud speaks of the paradox that despite the fact that all humans are created in the image of God and made human by the breath of God, each individual is completely different. This is another testament to the infinite variety of God's faces.

When a soul enters a body it is pure. It has an unsullied potential for actualizing its unique embodiment of God. It is not yet encrusted with the layers of personality and other factors that define how a person behaves in the world. It is as if that electromagnetic current, which is switched on at birth, also draws to the soul the various elements that make up an individual's personality. Upon death, when the "magnet" is turned off, the qualities and attachments that the soul attracted during its lifetime begin to drop away. Souls that were once connected begin to separate, and the soul of the deceased slowly returns to the purity with which its life began.

Yet, according to the mystics, death does not automatically restore the purity of the soul. This is done by various postmortem cleansing experiences which occur as the soul travels through the world of souls. And these are augmented by the collateral action of those of us on earth who act in memory of that soul, such as reciting the Kaddish and performing acts of *tzedakah*.

This process of purification begins with the work of the *Chevra Kaddisha*, described earlier. This escorts the soul of the deceased to the threshold between the worlds. Then the soul takes off, on its post mortem journey.

> The Body, that marvelous instrument on which the Soul plays life for God . . .
>
> —Rabbi Zalman Schachter-Shalomi

Chapter Thirteen

Exercise 13·1
The Soul Is "Gathered to [its] Ancestors"

(*Genesis* 49:29)

The Zohar, Jewish mysticism's commentary on the Torah, as well as other mystical traditions and accounts of near-death experiences, say that upon death, a person is reunited with previously deceased relatives and friends. They guide the departing soul along the first part of the postmortem journey and help ease the transition from life to death. Their presence was alluded to in the earliest Biblical reference to death, in which departed individuals were said to be "sleeping with their [ancestors]." (1 Kings 11:43) For example, Jacob called his children to his deathbed and said he was about to be "gathered to my kin." (Genesis 49:29)

List those whose death preceded that of the person you mourn and who might welcome him or her into the world of souls. Describe what that reunion might be like.

Much of the journey in the afterlife evaluates the life that has just ended and determines the appropriate reward or retribution. Retribution is not just punishment. It is an opportunity for purification. Because it is believed that the soul yearns to be reunited with its source, the time spent in atonement, purgation, and cleansing makes the agony of alienation from the Divine quite painful.

Exercise 13·2
The Pangs of the Grave

The soul is said to leave the body with an ease equivalent to "taking a hair out of a bowl of milk"(Talmud: Moed Katan 28a). Yet, it is believed that many people experience hibut hakever, *"the pain and anguish of the grave" (Zalman Schachter-Shalomi), in which they struggle to hold onto life. This is said to be experienced by those who had a great fear of death and had difficulty severing their concerns with earthly matters. What do you think was the hardest part of life for the soul of the deceased to give up?*

According to the mystics, the process of cleansing the soul begins once the "silver cord" (Ecclesiastes 12:6) which connects the soul to the body is cut. The story is told that two angels stand at each end of the world and toss the soul back and forth with a *kaf hakela* (catapult) from one end of the universe to another. This rids the soul of the "dust" that represents the accumulated emotional debris of a lifetime. Slowly, over an entire lifetime, the dust builds up and begins to eclipse the radiance of the pure soul. It leaves "marks" that are traces of obstacles encountered by the soul as it works its way through life. These become calcified and produce defense mechanisms, emotional wounds, and personality problems—all of the dust of personality that distracts us from the pure radiance of the birth soul. Recognizing the wounds and obstacles which the pure soul encountered in life is especially important if there were unresolved, difficult issues between you and the deceased. Remember that people's souls are believed to be pure at birth and that it is the "dust" that blinds their perceptions and makes them perform misdeeds.

> There is a grief which has no earthly counterpart, though they say, here, this place, Earth, is the only place death exists.
> —Deena Metzger

What were some of the personal obstacles that clouded the vision and obscured the pure radiance of the soul of the deceased? Describe how the "dust" that accumulated on his or her soul may have been

Exercise 13.3
The Kaf Hakela: Shaking Free of Dust

Chapter Thirteen

responsible for actions taken during the lifetime which may have been hurtful to others or to him or herself. Describe the layers of dust that might be shaken off the soul of the deceased in what Rabbi Zalman Schachter-Shalomi calls the "cosmic centrifuge" of the kaf hakela. What does this understanding help you recognize about the limitations of the person you mourn?

The scars that we wear as a result of the pains we encounter do much to alter our relationship to life and to the people in our world. To picture the soul of the deceased free of those scars makes it possible to imagine a better relationship when the bond was troubled. And it provides the relief of imagining that the person who has died is truly at peace, This allows the mourner to feel more compassion toward the deceased.

The fact that we pray to *El Malai Rakhamim* (God Full of Compassion) as the body is about to be buried indicates that compassion is a quality that most helps in saying goodbye.

> At death he has already entered the harbor—the haven of rest in the world-to-come.
> —Midrash: *Shemot Rabbah* 48, 1.

Exercise 13·4
A Swim in the River of Light

Following the experience with the "cosmic catapult," the soul is said to encounter a river of light that has been created from the perspiration of angels singing praises to God. A dip in this river cleanses the soul of the dust that has already been shaken loose.

Imagine the soul with all the dust washed away, and stripped of personality. Envision a pure light cleansing the soul. This dip in the river of light assures that the soul maintains its cleanliness and is restored to the radiance with which it entered the world.

Part Three

Purgatory and Paradise

The mystical tradition tells us that the soul next journeys to *Gehinnom*, where it suffers in atonement for any misdeeds during its life on earth. This is where mystics say that the soul resides during the period that the Kaddish is said. The length of a soul's stay in *Gehinnom* depends on its righteousness while on earth. No one remains in *Gehinnom* longer than twelve months, which, as we have discussed earlier, is the maximum time that mourners recite daily Kaddish for deceased parents (and the reason the Kaddish is more often recited for no more than eleven months rather than imply that the deceased needs to serve the maximum term in purgatory).

From your knowledge of the deceased, what qualities would need to be transformed in Gehinnom? *What were the sins or misdeeds for which atonement might be necessary? You might want to review the letter you wrote in Chapter 9 or your memory of any of the wrongdoings of the deceased. Were there flaws that would need to be confronted? What were the transgressions for which he or she would have to repent or atone as part of the purgation process in* Gehinnom?

Exercise 13·5
The Purification of *Gehinnom*

A second dip in the river of light completes the purification process and the soul progresses to the celestial *Gan Eden* (Garden of Eden), where it resides for an unspecified amount of time, moving to higher and higher rungs—closer to God—at each *yahrzeit* (anniversary of the death). *Gan Eden* is a place of bliss in which souls savor the joy of paradise, delight in worship and experience the emotional, intellectual or spiritual bliss appropriate to the level to which they have risen. All postmortem work concerned with release from the pains and concerns of earthly living is completed.

On the lower rungs of *Gan Eden*, fulfillment is emotional and associated with the joy of being close to God's radiance. The higher rungs of *Gan Eden* bring spiritual fulfillment and ecstasy.

> Happy are the righteous for their days are pure and extend to the world that is coming. When they leave this world, all their days are sewn together . . . radiant garments . . . to wear . . . to the world that is coming, to enjoy its pleasures.
> —Zohar 1:224a-b

Exercise 13·6
"The Righteous in Prayer"

Souls residing in Gan Eden *are very powerful. Because of their prayers, the earthly world continues to exist. As the Zohar says, "If not for the righteous in prayer on the other side, the world would not exist for one hour." Do you ever experience moments when you feel you are protected by the deceased or that he or she somehow inspires or guides you? If so, describe moments when you have felt this.*

Ibbur *and* Dybbuk

Many who follow the mystical tradition believe that the souls of the living and the souls of the dead remain in contact, continuing to influence each other's lives. Two of the lingering connections are the *ibbur* and the *dybbuk*. An *ibbur* is a soul whose purity is almost regained. In a form of benign possession, it attaches itself to the soul of a living person. Through that person, the deceased soul performs a mitzvah that has not previously been completed. *Ibbur* actually translates as "impregnated" and can be viewed as a form of continued positive communication with the person who has died.

Conceiving of an ibbur *gives us an opportunity to imagine how the deceased might continue to be helping you from the world of souls. How do you continue to be open to the presence of or pregnant with the spirit of the person who has died? What good is inside of you that names the deceased as its source? How do you feel that you continue to communicate in a positive way with the person who died? Write about the ways in which you feel positively imbued or guided by the soul of the person, or ways in which you feel that they continue to communicate their inspiration.*

Exercise 13·7
Acknowledging the *Ibbur*

On the other hand, a dybbuk *is not a welcome guest. The word* dybbuk *means "stuck." This adhering spirit can be a frightful appendage. It is a form of demonic possession wherein an evil spirit invades the body of a living person. The* dybbuk *takes hold of a person in a terrifying way. It appears to be glued to the soul of the survivor. We will interpret it as the very uncomfortable way in which one experiences the continued influence of the person who has died. What are the damaging and painful connections or the negative judgments that just won't go away? Write about the ways in which you feel that the negative influence of the deceased continues to be glued onto you. What are the ongoing issues that still encumber you? Write about them.*

Exercise 13·8
Encountering the *Dybbuk*

Chapter Thirteen

ד.ב.ק **DBK:** to be stuck, to cleave; gum; *dybbuk*: an adhering spirit, demon

The mystics tell us that sometimes these troubled souls are desperately seeking to perform the mitzvah that is needed to release them from a very tortuous experience in *Gehinnom*. Is there an act that you could perform that might bring that release? Is there a way that you can make peace with this adhering spirit? Perhaps your work in the previous chapter to find appropriate acts of *tzedakah* might give you some ideas for actions you could take to make peace with your *dybbuk*. If there does not seem to be a way of satisfying and expelling this spirit, it might be wise to consult a rabbi or a psychotherapist for help in working though what still remains unfinished.

Gilgul: Reincarnation

As joyous as *Gan Eden* may be, it is still one step from the ultimate joy of being united with God. Mystics tell us that once the soul has completed the formation of its spiritual body, it resides in *Gan Eden* forever and becomes one with God. Until such perfection has been attained, the mystics teach that the soul continues to return to Earth, and take on human life to fulfill mitzvot that have not been completed or to make restitution for wrongs that were committed. Each imperfect soul thus has the opportunity to experience reincarnation, or *gilgul*. Few souls do not require *gilgul*.

ג.ל **GL:** a wheel, a wave; *gilgul*: reincarnation

Exercise 13•9
Gilgul

In this final exercise of intimacy with the soul of the deceased, speculate on what the deceased might be seeking if his or her soul were to return to earth. Should

the soul of the deceased require gilgul, *what task might it seek? What deeds might need to be performed? What unfinished business might it have on earth? What might be left to be learned?*

We will now leave the soul of the departed to *gilgul*, and bring you back into your own life cycle, as you prepare to leave the world of the mourner.

No Righteous Person dies until a similar one is created, as the Biblical verse shows, "The sun rises, and the sun sets."
—*Talmud: Kiddushin 72b*

Chapter Thirteen

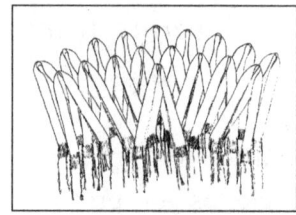

. . . Rachel died [and] was buried. . . . Over her grave Jacob set up a pillar; it is the pillar at Rachel's grave to this day.

–Genesis 35:19–20

14

מצבה

Matzevah

The Unveiling: Raising the Curtain on the Rest of Your Life

TIME PASSES. As the soul of the deceased finds its place in the afterworld, the souls of the living must find their place on the earth. Near the end of the first year after a death, those who have mourned an individual meet again at the grave to dedicate the tombstone. This monument not only is a marker for the resting place of the body, but also signifies the beginning of the end of mourning. Therefore, the unveiling is a dual "coming out." It lifts a veil on the tombstone and on the mourner's new life.

צ.ב.ה **TzVH:** to bear witness, make a stand, stand upright on the earth; *matzevah*: tombstone, altar, or pillar

Leaving a Marker

The Hebrew word for tombstone is *matzevah*. This word's layers of meaning reveal much about the unveiling. In the Bible, *matzevot* were erected to commemorate oaths that had been taken and to delineate boundaries. Jacob and his conniving father-in-law, Laban, erected such a pillar for both purposes: to witness their truce and to mark the boundary between their lands (Genesis 31: 43–47). *Matzevot* were also built to mark moments of great awe and triumph; for example, Jacob built a pillar of stones on the place where he wrestled with God's messenger.

Matzevah is also a word for altar. Throughout the Bible, it refers to the altars at which pagans worshipped. Jews considered these rites to be evil and swore to destroy the places where they took place. We can bring these sensibilities to the unveiling. The tombstone symbolizes our commitment to the deceased and our oath that he or she will be remembered. The fact that we place the tombstone at the end of the mourning period rather than immediately after the death seems to indicate that it marks not just the grave of the person who died, but also our struggle to integrate and transform the loss. This monument to our struggle is reminiscent of the monument that Jacob built after his struggle with God's messenger. In this way, placing the tombstone becomes a memorial to the journey as well as to the individual who died. Also like Laban and Jacob, the stone creates a boundary between that struggle and the rest of our lives. It puts a border around our grief-work and begins to declare an end to it.

Matzevah: *Raising the Curtain on the Rest of Your Life*

At the unveiling, we also commit ourselves to the responsibility of being on this earth. All this does not mean that mourning has been completed. It does, however, acknowledge that our status as mourner will soon change.

The association of *matzevah* with primitive practices is also significant. Following a loss, we need continued communication with those who have gone. We need to experience their presence. This treads upon another boundary: what is and is not acceptable in Judaism, a religion which forbids worshipping ancestors. We worship only the one God. Yet, the need to stay in touch with the dead is so strong that it elicits primitive impulses. Building a *matzevah*—a kind of altar to the dead—acknowledges needs that are often expressed through superstitious beliefs about the place where the body of someone who was once close to us lies.

> To speak to the deceased in the form of prayer is outlawed by the Bible and borders on blasphemy (Deuteronomy 18:11).
> —*Rabbi Maurice Lamm*

As you set the gravestone, is there a promise or commitment you want to make to the deceased? Write a letter to him or her, stating your commitment and promising to stand by it.

Exercise 14·1
Making an Oath

If the soul's ultimate goal is to join the Holy Presence (or whatever that eternal spiritual essence may be for you), then another way to connect with the deceased is for you to connect with Hamakom—*the Place that defines the spiritual essence which is now the abode of the person who has died. Can you find*

Exercise 14·2
Connecting with the Eternal

comfort through a spiritual connection? Have your feelings about what is eternal changed during your mourning? Do you tap into that connection through prayer, meditation, etc? Could these also connect you with the deceased?

The Unveiling as a Reenactment of the Funeral

> The self is more than the self.
> —Rabbi Abraham Joshua Heschel

While there is no formal liturgy for the unveiling, the service which accompanies the setting of the tombstone usually includes three elements essential to the funeral: words similar to the *hesped* are said about the deceased, and the *El Malai Rakhamim* and Kaddish are usually recited. In fact, the funeral, with its wrenching sense of separation, can be considered a dress rehearsal for the unveiling. Ironically, the unveiling is sometimes more painful than the funeral. Having worked through grief's early protected phases, the unveiling can be like a funeral without the numbness.

Exercise 14•3
Contrasting the Funeral and the Unveiling

If the unveiling has already occurred, compare that experience to the funeral. If it has not yet taken place, how will you prepare yourself for what is likely to happen? Think of the people who will be there as well as where you feel you are in your mourning process. What can you do to make sure that your needs are addressed? How can you nurture yourself before, during, and after the ceremony?

Part Three

While for some people the unveiling is more painful than the funeral, others consider the unveiling to mark the end of their mourning. But the truth is that few people ever feel completely finished with mourning. Some feelings and issues may always remain. This is probably not reassuring to a mourner who expects that the formal end of bereavement means the complete absence of pain. But that kind of healing is likely also to mean the absence of memory and would ultimately negate the relationship that a mourner had with the deceased. To lose our capacity to be moved, touched, and to remember would betray the person who died and the significance of our relationship with him or her. Ultimately, it would betray ourselves.

The hesped summed up the life of the deceased, often in many words. The epitaph on the tombstone summarizes in very few words that same life. Have you achieved some clarity about your relationship with the deceased and about his or her life? Based on that understanding, write an epitaph for a tombstone. Sum up the life of the deceased in a few words. Write this for yourself and not necessarily for anyone else to see.

Exercise 14·4
The Epitaph

Returning to the El Malai Rakhamim: Releasing Your Soul

The experience of the *El Malai Rakhamim* at the unveiling is quite different from the experience at the funeral. This prayer, which was first recited at the funeral shortly before the body was actually lowered into the grave, marked a moment of separation, when the soul was released to God's compassion. When the *El Malai Rakhamim* is recited at the unveiling, it is the soul of the mourner that is being released.

The themes of the *El Malai Rakhamim* have been the themes of our work together: separation, compassion, and connecting with something eternal. Let's return to that prayer to see what understanding your mourning has brought you.

Since the funeral, we have worked to help you experience the sense of being separate from the deceased, as we have explored the extraordinary uniqueness of each soul. Undergirding all our work has been the word *rakhamim*, or "compassion." Compassion guided our work to redeem the soul. It guided us as we accompanied the soul through the realms of the afterlife. It helped us view the soul of the deceased more and more as its most radiant self, as we thought less of the frailties and defenses that might have defined the deceased while he or she was alive. We sought compassion toward ourselves, as we explored our own failings in the relationship and our difficulties with healing. And when this prayer spoke of the compassion of God, we began to explore our connection with something spiritual and eternal that could nurture us.

> No one can claim to be wise about life whose wisdom does not include a relationship to death.
>
> —Rabbi Jack Riemer

Exercise 14·5
Where Are You Now?

The unveiling represents the passage of time since the death. It is an opportunity to reflect on what you have learned since the death, or how you are feeling about time passing and getting on with your own life. Whether or not it has been a year since you began your grief-work, how are you feeling at this point about yourself and your relationship with the person who died? Have you changed since you began your grief-work? How do you feel about those changes?

> God cares for every [person], . . . and suffers in the loss of every one of [God's] creatures.
> —Rabbi Maurice Lamm

Exercise 14·6
Compassion for the Power that Runs the Universe

How far does your compassion extend? In Chapter 10, we spoke about rage at God and the universe—rage which is central to the experience of mourning. In removing the obstacles to expressing those feelings, we sought a spiritual connection. Does your compassion extend to the Ineffable? Does it reach toward God and the universe? Can you forgive the universe for what it has done?

One more reason we say the Kaddish is to comfort God on the loss of a holy creature: one of God's partner's in healing the world. Can you look out at this mysterious galaxy, which appears to mete out joy and pain randomly and without compassion, and embrace the unbearable truths of this cruel and beautiful universe, extending your compassion and condolence to God, Creator of it All?

Return to the Kaddish

Throughout this book, we have explored Kaddish from several perspectives. We started at the funeral using the Kaddish as a way of anchoring ourselves to the earth. Then, we looked at Kaddish as a way to mark transitions and to connect with others. Later, we moved into the mystical use of Kaddish to raise the status of departed souls and to heal relationships. Finally, we used Kaddish as a way to comfort God on the loss of the life of the deceased. We now will return to the deceptively mundane view of the Kaddish, the one encountered at the funeral.

In a sense, the Kaddish is the coordinate of our position on earth. As Rabbi Maurice Lamm has said, it is a "horizontal" connection, creating a community of mourners from minyanim (prayer groups) across the planet who gather to recite the prayer in memory of departed souls. It is also a "vertical" connection. It aligns us with those for whom we say Kaddish and those for whom those persons said Kaddish, reaching back into Jewish history and ahead into the future, connecting us to those who will say Kaddish for us and all who will say Kaddish for them.

Exercise 14·7
Making a Stand

Here we are at the center of this time/space, affirming our connection to all others past and present who share these values. The words of Kaddish help hallow the earth, and make it a place suffused with God's holiness. After the travails of bereavement, restate your commitment to life. List what you hope to do for yourself and for the world as you lift the veil to enter the next phase of your life.

Exercise 14·8
Leaving a Pebble at the Grave

It is customary to place a pebble on a gravestone after visiting it. Some say this pebble is simply a marker to commemorate the visit. If so, then it is similar to the Biblical matzevot, *which were, in fact, piles of stones.*

Part Three

Others say this practice originated in the superstition that the pebble will so weigh down spirits that they cease interfering in the lives of the living. This recognition of the need to separate from the spirits affirms our move to focus on the future.

Put a metaphorical pebble on the grave as a way to say that it is time to separate and move on with your life. Write one last letter to the deceased, this time telling him or her that you are shifting your concerns to those of your own life and your own destiny. Assure the deceased that throughout the year, you will remember his or her soul and your relationship, by observing such days as yahrzeit *and* yizkor *(memorial prayer recited four times a year). But state emphatically and compassionately that you will no longer walk the path of the mourner.*

And now, cross the boundary. Step out of mourning. Lift the veil on your new life.

Chapter Fourteen

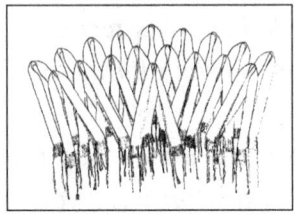

> ... Judgment will be turned into mercy, and the mourning into joy. ... "Thou didst turn for me my mourning into dancing." (Psalm 30:12)

–Kitzer Shulkhan Arukh

15

יזכור

Yizkor, Yahrzeit, *and the Cycle of Seasons*

THE PHRASE "time heals all wounds" can be very misleading. For those who hold their breath and hope that the steady procession of the calendar will end their pain, the promise of this phrase may eventually bring great disappointment. But for those who have learned to use time as a tool, the progression of the seasons provides many opportunities for healing.

This understanding is embedded not only in Jewish mourning rituals, but also in the Jewish calendar. As we have seen, the legislated season of mourning lasts up to a year, beginning with the death itself and ending with the last recitation of the Kaddish. This progression acknowledges the varying needs of the

> Eternal cyclical time bellows out in cycles into the visible world from the great inner room.
> —*Ernest Becker*

mourner and the way in which those needs change over time. This understanding is beautifully recognized in *Yizkor* and *Yahrzeit*. These are five days of memorial, four of which (the days of *Yizkor*) are observed communally and one (*Yahrzeit*) that is observed by those remembering an individual on the anniversary of his or her death.

Healthy Mourning Has Ongoing Needs

These five days of memorial create a framework for acknowledging the need for continued grief-work after the end of the year of the formal mourning period. They affirm the life-long need to stay connected with the people and the worlds we have lost. They provide markers of our progress as we grow and change, in a world where those we have lost are no longer physically present. They provide tools for assessing our own growth as individuals in a world without those we mourn, allowing us to reevaluate past relationships in light of that growth. *Yizkor* and *Yahrzeit* provide spaces of ongoing support for grief's task, which mourners so resist: surrendering to the reality of loss in order to turn the physical connection into a spiritual connection.

Yizkor and *Yahrzeit* can compress remaining issues of mourning into five days so that during the rest of the year you can go on with your life without the preoccupation of intense mourning. Each of the days of *Yizkor* provides a unique window on the nature of grief, encouraging us to approach healing from different perspectives as we address the different tasks, or seasons, of mourning. Since each of these days comes in a different season, these days of memorial can provide us with times earmarked for specific kinds of feelings and help to focus and intensify those emotions. Providing specific days for revisiting grief's emotions, may make it easier to explore those feelings. Time will pass and we will enter a new season. We can feel safe to give way to our tears or our rage, knowing that celebration and affirmation are also part of the cycle of remembrance.

This chapter will acquaint you with the days through the year on which there are rituals for remembering the dead. It contains exercises that explore the use of the seasons to help you in your continuing grief-work. In addition to the exercises specific to this chapter, you will want to review your work throughout the book to find other exercises relevant to where you are in the healing process. We will explore the nature of each of these memorial days. We will use the particular characteristics of the individual days to address persistent issues of grief. Focusing on these days of remembrance rewards us with a context for continuing relationships with those who no longer live in our world.

The *Yizkor* Prayer

Yizkor is a prayer that is said four times during the year on four specific Holy Days: Yom Kippur, Shemini Atzeret, Pesach, and Shavuot. The *Yizkor* prayer asks God to remember the soul of the deceased. *Yahrzeit* is a Yiddish word referring to the anniversary of the death of that person, according to the Jewish calendar (Sephardic Jews refer to this as Anos).

Yizkor Prayers
(for a male)

יזכור אלהים נשמת. . . שהלך לעולמו. בעבור שאני
נודר צדקה בעדו, בשכר זה, תהא נפשו צרורה בצרור
החיים עם נשמות אברהם, יצחק ויעקב, שרה, רבקה,
רחל ולאה, ועם שאר צדיקים וצדקניות שבגן עדן. אמן.

Yizkor elohim nishmat . . . she'halach l'olamo. Ba'avur she'ani nodeir tz'daka ba'ado, b'shachar ze, t'hei nafsho tzrura bitz'ror hachayim im nishmot avraham, yitzchak v'ya'akov, sara, rivka, rachel, v'le'ah, v'im sh'ar tzadikim v'tzadkaniot she'b'gan eden. Amen.

May God remember the soul of . . . who has gone to his world. As I swear righteousness for him, because of this, may God bind his soul in the bond of life with the souls of Abraham, Isaac, and Jacob, Sarah, Rebecca, Rachel and Leah, and with the rest of the righteous whose piety is in the Garden of Eden. Amen.

(for a female)

יזכור אלהים נשמת. . . שהלכה לעולמה. בעבור שאני
נודר צדקה בעדה, בשכר זה, תהא נפשה צרורה בצרור
החיים עם נשמות אברהם, יצחק ויעקב, שרה, רבקה,
רחל ולאה, ועם שאר צדיקים וצדקניות שבגן עדן. אמן.

Yizkor elohim nishmat . . . she'halcha l'olama. Ba'avur she'ani nodeir tz'daka ba'ada, b'shachar ze, t'hei nafsha tzrura bitz'ror hachayim im nishmot avraham, yitzchak v'ya'akov, sara, rivka, rachel, v'le'ah, v'im sh'ar tzadikim v'tzadkaniot she'b'gan eden. Amen.

May God remember the soul of . . . who has gone to her world. As I swear righteousness for her, because of this, may God bind her soul in the bond of life with the souls of Abraham, Isaac, and Jacob, Sarah, Rebecca, Rachel and Leah, and with the rest of the righteous whose piety is in the Garden of Eden. Amen.

God brings everything to pass precisely at its time and puts eternity in our mind.
—Ecclesiastes 3:11

The annual cycle of four *Yizkor* services provides a context for creative grief-work. The themes of the four holy days on which the prayer is recited correspond to major phases in the mourning cycle and encompass the full range of mourning. Each day provides an opportunity to explore a different aspect of mourning through which we assess our growth and define the challenges which lie ahead.

Part Three

Yizkor: *A Time for You to Remember and to Heal*

In the midst of the joys of celebration, holidays may also bring up feelings and memories about people who have died, reminding us of their absence and recalling unresolved issues. *Yizkor* services come at these times of the year, when we are particularly vulnerable to the loss, regret, despair, and yearning that accompany grief. This is likely to be true even if the death happened long ago.

In the *Yizkor* service we remember those who have died, but the word *Yizkor* is actually a request that we make of God to remember the deceased. Remembrance, then, is something that we do in partnership with God. Rabbi Richard Levy teaches that *Yizkor* can be understood to mean "to make present." We engage memory as a way of inviting those we have lost into our lives again, so that we can continue the essential conversations that are the bone structure of our emotional life.

Engaging memory as a tool for healing is our concern. Ironically, through remembering, the yoke of the past is loosened, the pain of our history becomes less of a burden, and the words of one of the blessings given to mourners becomes a reality: memory becomes a blessing.

ז.כ.ר **ZCR:** to remember; a memory, trace; *Yizkor*: memorial service or prayer

Yom Kippur

Yom Kippur, the Day of Atonement, is a time to settle accounts with other people and with God. During the Days of Awe, we go from person to person, asking for forgiveness and making an effort to heal what is amiss in our relationships. With regard to mourning, it is an opportunity to put right our relationships with the

כ.פ.ר. **CPR:** forgiveness, probation, ransom, expiation; *Yom Kippur*: the Day of Atonement

people who are gone, to ask them for forgiveness, and to focus on unresolved issues and feelings and guilt that we may still carry.

The intensity of these themes of Yom Kippur gives us a framework to review some of the most difficult work of this book: the work to absolve our own guilt, resolve resentments, and work through lingering issues with the person who died.

In addition, the spirit of Yom Kippur acknowledges the need for reciprocal healing. This is evident in the fact that it is not only a day to deal with our own regrets. Yom Kippur is also a day to forgive those we mourn. Also called *Yom Hakippurim* ("the Day of Atonements"), this plural form signifies that it is a day when we atone not only for our own sins, but also for those of others. This is reminiscent of our mystical work with the Kaddish and the efforts made by the living to cancel any evil that might have adhered to the soul of the deceased. In addition to the exercises below, you might want to look back to Exercise 9-2: Letter to the Deceased to see what other issues you might want to address regarding resentments you still carry.

Kol Nidre: *Releasing Vows*

Yom Kippur begins with *Kol Nidre*. This haunting chant is recited to start the liturgy of the Yom Kippur evening service. *Kol Nidre* (All Vows) is not a prayer, but a legal formula. A *beit din* (religious court) made up of three of the community's leaders stands before the congregation, holding the scrolls of the Torah. The Aramaic words of *Kol Nidre* are recited in a dramatic musical setting intended to legally annul all vows that might be made in the year to come. This perplexing intent is understood to have risen out of times when Jews were violently persecuted and forced, at the point of a sword, to forsake Judaism and convert to other religions. Viewed in this context, *Kol Nidre* can be seen as an acknowledgment that during the year to come members of the community might be compelled to swear allegiance to other spiritual paths. The chant's formula preemptively dissolved any such vows they might be forced to make.

What Are Vows with Respect to Mourning?

A vow is an oath, and the oaths that mourners make are often set into action by guilt, fear, or regret. For example, sometimes deathbed promises are made to dying people. These promises are often impossible to fulfill. People may blame themselves for the breakup of a marriage or torture themselves over an all too human mistake.

Mourners continually second-guess themselves with these painful thoughts. They tell themselves that they should have or could have done things differently, suggesting that omniscience and omnipotence were available in the difficult moments (or years) before the death. More often than not, it is likely that they did the best that they could at the time.

Over and over, I have seen people torturing themselves with elaborately constructed phrases that begin with the words "if only." They begin as speculative thoughts. But with each repetition, the wistful thoughts become more and more solid. Mourners come to believe that they are true, committing themselves to these beliefs. They become like vows, freezing time and making it harder to move forward in their lives.

Chapter Fifteen

This is a defense mechanism—a message of denial. If we can argue with the past, we may still have some power over it. Also, it is often easier to blame ourselves than to come face-to-face with the overwhelming reality of our powerlessness over the great mysteries of life and death. In making these vows, we convince ourselves that we could have made a difference, as if it were possible to know to what end these roads not taken might lead. What began as thoughts or feelings become castles in the minds of mourners. They take residence in these constructions, as they continue to torment themselves.

Exercise 15•1
Annulling Your Vow

Conceiving of these speculative "truths" as vows, can you identify any ideas that you have come to believe about how you might have done things differently that may not be true? Are you holding onto an idea about how things should have unfolded that is detrimental to your ability to move on in your life? In the literal meaning of the word Kippur, *identify some punishing part of yourself that needs to be ransomed, that might be understood as a vow that needs to be annulled.*

Teshuva: *Changing Your Bad Deeds into Good*

To further facilitate your ability to forgive yourself for any of the things you may wish you had done differently, we turn to *Teshuva*.

Teshuva, as described in an earlier chapter, is a positive healing process. It is the theme of Yom Kippur and the period leading up to it. It involves confession, contrition, and restitution. According to Maimonides, the great twelfth-century Jewish philosopher whose contributions have shaped Jewish thought, there are three major steps in the process of repentance: First, we recognize and confess our wrongdoing; then we genuinely express our regret at the misdeed, rejecting it in future actions; finally, we make a commitment not to repeat our wrongdoing.

In its tractate on vows, *Nedarim*, the Talmud says that *Teshuvah* was created before the world, on the eve preceding the first day of creation. Like gravity, *Teshuvah* is embedded into the universe, invisible yet assured. It promises that if we are willing to make amends for our deviation from the prescribed path, and if we are sincere in our desire to realign with our highest intentions, we can begin again. We can find our way back to God's house.

Teshuvah's process of refinement culminates with the fast of *Yom Kippur*. While *Teshuvah* is often translated as "repentance," it actually describes the ability to return, free of shame, to our original intentions. It is a guarantee of forgiveness and renewal vocalized each morning, throughout the year, in two of my favorite phrases in the morning liturgy: *"b'kol yom tamid, ma'aseh bereshit*/each day, always, the work of creation begins again" and *"lo navosh l'olam va'ed*/ never, ever, feel shame." These snippets of text are daily reminders of *Teshuvah*'s assurance of the continual opportunity to return to the Garden of Eden and start over.

The process of *Teshuvah* should not lead to *atzvut* or depression. One way to avoid this is to focus on specific acts for which it is possible to actively express regret. Then we can commit ourselves to change.

Chapter Fifteen

Exercise 15·2
Dealing with Regrets: "Averting the Severe Decree"

Repentance, prayer, and generous acts avert the severe decree.

—High Holy Day Liturgy

After all this work to release you from regrets you may have regarding your relationship with the person who has died, do you still have lingering issues? If your answer is yes, then we can engage Yom Kippur's focus on teshuva *to help you make restitution for what you wish had been different. On Yom Kippur we are told that the severity of the decree of judgment against our sins can be averted and an act of repentance can be sustained by three methods:* Teshuva, Tefilla *(prayer), and* Tzedaka. *If you continue to harbor regrets concerning some aspect of your relationship with the deceased, use this as a worksheet by which you can detail specific acts that you might undertake in your process of repentance.*

Teshuva—*penitent turning away from wrongdoing with earnest efforts to make good our mistakes by acting differently in the future*

_____

_____

Tefilla—*committment to serious prayer—such as reciting the Kaddish*

_____

_____

Tzedaka—*acts of generosity and good deeds*

_____

_____

Yizkor, Yahrzeit, and the Cycle of the Seasons

Settling the Accounts of the Deceased

As was said earlier, the fact that this day is also called *Yom HaKippurim* provides an opportunity for the person who has died to also do *teshuvah*. By allowing them to do this work, we assert that souls can be redeemed, even after death. Just as our relationship with the deceased has the potential for growth and change, so does their relationship with us. We continue this work so that both your soul and that of the person who died can be free from the difficult entanglements that leave dust on our souls, preventing us from "making memory into a blessing." So we work to close their accounts on earth so that their souls, can rise, in the spirit of the *El Maley Rachamim*, which is recited at *Yizkor,* to join the other departed souls under the wings of the Shekhinah.

> There is not one person on earth who does what is best and doesn't err.
> —*Ecclesiastes* 3:11

In Chapter 5, we used the Viddui *that is said at the deathbed to give voice to the concerns of the person who has died. Since another version of the* Viddui *is recited by the congregation on Yom Kippur, we will return to that prayer, as we explored it earlier in Exercise 5:2. Without looking at your earlier writing on the* Viddui, *visualize him or her doing another life review. How would you imagine the deceased might feel after having gone through the cleansing processes described in the chapter on the World of Souls and with passage of time? Are there regrets? Feelings of pride? How would he or she feel about the relationships with those left behind? Might the beliefs about God and the Universe have*

Exercise 15• 3
Viddui from the World of Souls

changed? When you have finished, go back and review the earlier exercise. Has the story changed?

Still, even after all this work, there may be issues that remain unresolved. Guilt and resentment can really take hold of the psyche. Some people spend lifetimes flagellating themselves, or the ones they remember, with these tough emotions. But the wisdom of the *Yizkor* cycle can protect us from such obsession. The seasons change and so does the theme associated with remembrance. Perhaps by the next year's Yom Kippur, the feelings explored during the other days of *Yizkor* will have softened some of Yom Kippur's tough concerns. This begins with, Shemini Atzeret, the next time *Yizkor* is recited. It is a day which encourages us to put a fence around these feelings and move on.

Shemini Atzeret

ע.צ.ר ATzR: to stop, detain, or brake; an assembly; *Shemini Atzeret*: the Eighth Day of Assembly

Shemini Atzeret means "eighth day of assembly." The root of *Atzeret* is found in words that mean "curfew," "to brake," "detention," or "containment." The concept is of a container, a holding environment. It puts a stop to things.

Shemini Atzeret is a less well-known holiday, that ushers in the winter season. It takes place on the day between two days of joyous celebration: the last day of *Sukkot*, the fall harvest festival, and *Simkhat Torah*, when the annual Torah reading cycle ends and the scroll is rewound to begin the cycle again.

Shemini Atzeret is a quiet holiday. It ushers in the winter season with a slight change in the daily liturgy. Instead of praying for dew, we begin to pray for rain. On *Shemini Atzeret* we hold on a little bit to the season that is just closing. Trying not to let go of the festive spirit of *Sukkot*, we resist the need to move from the celebration of harvest to the dreariness of winter. We pray for rain, even as we remain in the open-roofed sukkah (where we'd be uncomfortable if our prayer was answered!). Just as our tears must fall, the winter rains must come. The seasons must change. The communal joys of *Sukkot*'s abundance must be surrendered to the more inward-turning, contemplative, and bleak winter.

On *Shemini Atzeret* we pray for rain and prepare for winter. Reciting the *Yizkor* prayer on this day brings us closer to the cold and brittle part of mourning. This time of the broken heart is as necessary to healing as the time when the earth lies fallow, absorbing moisture necessary to bring forth the buds of spring and the harvests that follow. We connect our tears to the rain, recognizing the necessity of enduring a winter that will prepare us for the reawakening of spring. We acknowledge that winter must come and yield to the wisdom of the seasons and the passage of time.

A legend is told about the observance of *Shemini Atzeret* in the ancient Temple in Jerusalem, which was a place known, according to the Book of Isaiah, as "a house of prayer for all peoples." Indeed, the Temple's rituals of healing and attunement drew people from the corners of the ancient world. The joyous festival of *Sukkot* especially brought visitors from great distances. When the festivities were over, they would head for their home communities. It is said that once the others left, God spoke longingly to the people of Judea and Israel, pleading for another day of assembly: "Don't go!" God beseeched, "Stay an extra day."

> Praise to God, who makes the wind to blow and the rain to fall.
> —*Prayer on Shemini Atzeret*

Chapter Fifteen

That feeling is familiar to mourners. We yearn for one more day with the people we have lost. *Shemini Atzeret* and its poignant connection with that longing is well suited to the nature of bereavement. Filled with the memory of that which is gone, we are likely to be unwilling to let go and welcome the tears that can transform our pain.

Exercise 15•4
Resistance to Moving On

One of the first exercises of the book compared the impulse toward moving on and the impulse to resist change. What have you learned about the parts of you that do not want to do the grief-work prescribed in this book? How have you shown respect for your resistance? How have you learned to counter it?

Our *Yizkor* work for *Shemini Atzeret* is to focus on the feelings of winter and let them carry us to the next season. It calls for honesty, once more reminding us of the difference between the words "eulogy" and *hesped*. But praying for rain, while remaining in the sukkah, embodies a truth about mourning: filled with the memory of the person who has died, we are often unwilling to move on. We do not welcome the tears that can transform our pain. We do not want to make the sacrifice and give ourselves over to the rain. We resist the change of seasons, despite the knowledge that without rain, the cycle cannot continue and the world cannot be in its proper order. But this flow—the rain and the tears—will move us through the cycle of our emotional seasons into another time of harvest. All we have to do is make it through one day of tears to dance with the Torah the next day—*Simkhat Torah*.

There are genuine tragedies, sadnesses, and injustices that one cannot deny or rationalize away when taking the measure of a life. What makes you saddest when thinking about the life and death of the person you are remembering? Write about it and then let yourself take some time to quietly feel that sadness, without holding back any feelings that come.

Exercise 15•5
The Tears of Winter

Remembering that there will be other seasons makes it easier to yield to the tears of Winter, and ask, through this *Yizkor,* for the strength to surrender to the seasons, letting the tears come like rain, so that we can release ourselves to whatever comes next. In addition, when we allow ourselves the tears of winter, we begin to yearn for spring.

Pesach/Passover

Pesach is the spring festival when we commemorate the Exodus of the Hebrew slaves from Egypt, as well as our release from the grip of winter and its tears. Both aspects of the holiday are powerful metaphors for mourning. Passover's *Yizkor* can focus us on the mourner's special insight into bondage, as we move, with this season's *Yizkor* prayer, from concern about the person who died to concern with our own healing.

For now the winter is past, the rains are over and gone. The blossoms have appeared in the land.
—*Song of Songs* 2:11

The Hebrew word for Egypt, *Mitzriyim,* means "narrow" or "tight places." Our effort here is to find the passage from the tight places that remain in your mourning process, restricting your peace of mind and enjoyment of life. The hope is to deliver you to the freedom to live your own life.

צ.ר.ר **TzRR:** a rock, trouble, distress, a narrow place, enemy, or foe; *Mitzrayim:* Egypt

We persist in our work to find where you are in the conversation with the deceased. Auspiciously, the literal translation of the Hebrew word for Passover prescribes this effort: *Pe* means *"mouth."* And *sach* means *"conversation"*! When we tell the Passover story, we open our mouths and are obliged to have a conversation about the liberation from Egypt as if we personally experienced the bitterness of slavery and the sweetness of freedom. The *Yizkor* recited on the eighth day of Pesach provides a template for exploring that contrast between the suffering and the release. This struggle is illuminated by the Torah reading for that day, which describes the ambivalence of a slave who wishes to remain with a longtime master.

Exercise 15•6
Of Mourners' Bondage

The ties that keep us from freedom can be rooted in any number of emotions—positive or negative. Mourners experience bondage in many ways. They may be tied to something fulfilling of which they are unable to let go or they may be bound by unresolved issues. They may be bound to do the work of people who have died, living the agenda of those deceased and not their own. Mourners may have the sense that they're living in someone else's house or someone else's land. Do you feel that you're still in bondage to the deceased? How does it manifest itself?

Exercise 15•7
Passing Through Egypt: A Guided Relaxation

In order to determine the places where your constricted muscles reveal that you are still in bondage, we will explore the difference between slavery and freedom as you experience it in your own body. Through progressively tensing and relaxing your muscles, we will pass through, not over, your personal Egypts: the tight, narrow places in your body. Lie down on a mat. Loosen any tight articles of clothing that you're wearing. Start with your toes and move slowly up your body to the top of your head, alternately tensing and relaxing individual muscles. Breathe in as you tense and out as you relax, feeling the difference between freedom and bondage in your own body. Are there tight spaces that will not allow the relaxation to enter? Can you identify them with any emotions connected to your grief? What are those places where you're unable to experience freedom? Recognize that in deciding to tense and then to relax, you're exercising a choice between the two. Can you choose to let go of your personal Egypt?

During the Seder, the story is told of four children. Each comes to the Passover table with a different attitude. Their attitudes might help you to assess where you are, this year, in the journey toward freedom. The Simple Child *represents the primitive yearning that can make mourning so unbearable. The* Angry Child *is the one enraged at being trapped in the wilderness with no sense of home. The* Mute Child *is the one who is stunned, unable to feel what is happening in its life. The* Wise Child *is the one that has made peace with the loss and found an ongoing connection with both the deceased and with a universe where death is part of life. This Passover, which of the four children is closer to your current experience of mourning? As you revisit this exercise each year, you may find that you identify with a different child than in the past.*

Exercise 15•8
The Four Children

Exercise 15•9
Inflation and *Hummutz*

On Passover we eat matzoh or unleavened bread. To prepare for the holiday, homes are purged of any foods that contain Hummutz. These leavening agents, which cause bread to rise, are the great taboo of the holiday. Throughout the week, no foods are eaten that contain them. Hummutz, which puffs things up, can be equated with the inflation and idealization of the deceased, which can be a danger to the mourner, making it difficult to find an honest connection with the person who has gone. How bound are you to an idealized version of the person who has died? Are you able to see that person as human and imperfect? Share some of his or her limitations as a way of allowing yourself to move from an idealizing relationship to an authentic one.

Exercise 15•10
Questions in the Key of Passover

PHARAOH: *How has your loss become a tyrant in your life, holding you in bondage? How is it your taskmaster, as you continue to do its bidding and not that of your higher self?*

_____

_____

THE PLAGUES: *What punishments have you endured because of this bondage?*

_____

_____

MATZOH: *What have you failed to give proper time, attention, and nurture due to mourning?*

_____

_____

THE SEA OF REEDS: *What obstacles must you pass through to get to freedom?*

_____

_____

MANNA: *What has sustained you during your journey?*

_____

_____

THE GOLDEN CALF: *What has distracted you from the tasks of healing?*

_____

_____

MOSES AND MIRIAM: *Who have been your role models and teachers in this wilderness?*

_____

_____

THE PROMISED LAND: *Describe the life you hope for in the future.*

_____

_____

GOD: *Envision a healing power or energy to carry you to freedom and the Promised Land.*

_____

_____

Exercise 15•11
Retelling the Story

Each year we are commanded to retell the Passover story, through the medium of the Seder meal. Because we are constantly changing, the story and our interpretation of it is at least a little different each time it is told. When you review your relationship with the person you're remembering, what are the differences in the way that you tell the story this year and the way you have told it in the past? With each telling we bring new insight to the story. What new aspect of freedom and liberation are you now experiencing?

As with the work of liberation, grief is an evolving process. As we move from Egypt, we prepare to accept the teaching of a newly defined way of life on our way to experiencing the memory of the deceased as a blessing.

Shavuot

Shavuot is the harvest festival that comes at the beginning of summer, seven weeks after Pesach. It is a time when nature's richness is in evidence and one is moved to celebrate and give thanks. Shavuot is also the festival that commemorates the giving of the Torah. It marks that moment in our history when all the Jewish

ש.ב.ע **ShVA:** a week, seven, an oath; *Shavuot*: harvest festival commemorating the giving of the Torah souls that have ever been and will ever be are said to have stood at the foot of Mount Sinai to receive the gift of the Torah and to affirm our part in the Covenant. Before Sinai, we were a band of people with a shared history. After Sinai, we had a collective destiny—a role in history. We were given a detailed way of ethical living and we made a promise in exchange for this gift: We accepted the responsibility of being God's partner on earth by performing mitzvot and working in a mutually dependent relationship with the Creator to heal the world.

During Shavuot we gather together to affirm what we have been given and express our gratitude. In the time of the Temple, people brought sacrifices from their harvest, to show their thanks and affirm their commitment. With regard to mourning, Shavuot's *Yizkor* is a time to make a positive statement about what has been gained in our association with the deceased. It is also a time for rededication to actions in memory of the deceased to affirm what has been learned from them in life and from the process of mourning them and to give thanks for those lessons. In doing this, we assure their immortality and follow through in our commitment to *tikkun olam*, healing the world.

> Restore our fortunes, Adonai, like watercourses in the Negev. They who sow in tears shall reap with songs of joy. Though they go along weeping carrying the seed-bag. They shall come back with songs of joy, carrying their sheaves.
>
> —Psalm 126:4-6

On Shavuot we celebrate the knowledge that became ours with the giving of the law on Mount Sinai. What knowledge have you received as a result of your relationship? What are the things that you have learned from the person who died, or from the process of mourning that person?

Exercise 15•12
The Teachings of Your Relationship

Exercise 15•13
Acts of Thanksgiving

How would you like to commemorate the life of the deceased and give thanks for what you have learned? (You might want to review your work in Chapter Eleven with the Ethical Will and the exercises following it.)

Exercise 15•14
First Fruits:
The Thanksgiving Offering

Before we go forward, we acknowledge what came first. Write a note of gratitude to the person for whom you are reciting Yizkor.

Exercise 15•15
Seven Praises

The first fruits Shavuot offering included portions of the seven species for which the land of Israeli is praised in Deuteronomy 8:8—wheat, barley, grapes, figs, pomegranates, olives, and dates. List seven praises for what has been lost.

1. _____
2. _____
3. _____
4. _____

Part Three

5. _____

6. _____

7. _____

What have you learned from whom or what you mourn?

Exercise 15•16
Affirming the Harvest—
The Torah of What Is Gone

What memorial act will you perform to commemorate what has past?

Exercise 15•17
Acts of Thanksgiving

Accepting Your Life—Its Seasons and Their Lessons

We have now completed the cycle of seasons, as marked by the four recitations of the *Yizkor* prayer. In the process, I hope you have gained tools for continued healing, as well as help in understanding how the relationship has a continuing potential to help you grow—a potential that transcends death.

Chapter Fifteen

> A season is set for everything, a time for every experience under heaven.
> —*Ecclesiastes* 3:1

ש.נ.ה **ShNH:** to change, repeat; study; different; *shana*: year

Emotional growth often requires that we return to some issues over and over again. When faced with what seems to be a repetition of old emotional material, we can be hard on ourselves. But with each new pass, we come at a familiar truth from a different perspective and gain new insights. We must learn to measure our growth by our deepening familiarity with the truth of our emotional life. In the process, the grip of these truths becomes less incapacitating.

The wisdom embedded in the calendar guides us in focusing on the lingering issues of mourning and enables us to approach our loss in every season. It encourages us to give full expression to our feelings on the days that are marked, giving us clearly marked containers for our feelings and protecting us, so that we are free not to mourn on other days. It also makes it safer to express our various feelings in all their intensity, as each recitation of *Yizkor* occurs on only one day. It is safe to explore the guilts and rage which might be felt on Yom Kippur, when we know that there will also be Shavuot, with its opportunity to celebrate and give thanks.

Anticipating Yahrzeit

The fifth day of memorial, *Yahrzeit,* begins privately, by lighting a memorial candle at sunset. Thus we have the opportunity to spend some private time remembering the deceased, before joining others at the synagogue to say Kaddish.

Yahrzeit is probably the day when the early experience of mourning is most often felt over again. Sometimes people who do not realize that the anniversary of the death is coming find themselves overwhelmed by grief only to look at the calendar and realize that it is the time of the *Yahrzeit*. Psychotherapists call this unconscious anticipation of the date of death "an anniversary reaction." It underscores the necessity of preparing for *Yahrzeit* every year.

How Can You Prepare for Yahrzeit?

There are things you can do to help you go into this difficult day with awareness, ready to learn from it what you can. You might buy a candle, arrange to attend synagogue, or bring together a minyan with which you can say Kaddish. You might want to spend some time talking with someone about the deceased or about how you anticipate the *Yahrzeit* to feel. You also might want to review this book to find exercises most relevant to the grief-work you need to do now. Preparing for *Yahrzeit* can protect you from the onset of a surprise grief reaction.

In addition to attending a minyan and lighting memorial candles, *Yahrzeit* is also observed by visiting the cemetery and performing acts of *tzedakah*. Mystics tell us that on the *Yahrzeit*, the soul rises closer to God. As we have learned, this process is aided when survivors remember the deceased by saying the Kaddish or performing acts of *tzedakah* in his or her name.

> It is a meritorious practice to fast on the anniversary of the death of one's father or mother, as an incentive to repentance, and to self-introspection. By doing this, one obtains Divine Grace for one's father and mother in heaven.
> —Kitzer Shulkhan Arukh 221:1

Other Days When Your Mourning May Return

Each year we have an opportunity to build on the work that went before it, to continue our healing, our acceptance of the death of the person we mourn and the advancement of the soul of that person in its rise toward God. In addition to the five days of the year specifically set aside for those purposes, on other days you may be drawn back to the feelings of mourning, as well. Birthdays, anniversaries and other holidays that were shared are times when we are vulnerable, a date that commerates a diagnosis is a milestone in the illness of one who died might also cause a renewed grief reaction.

Any change in our lives—illness, a move, a joyous event, or the death of someone else to whom we were close—may trigger feelings about the ones who have died. Perhaps we would want them to share in the celebration of a particular rite of passage, or we might wish we had their support. We might feel guilty that we are getting something that they did not. Or we might simply be reminded of them and begin to miss them in a difficult way. Mourning reactions triggered by these experiences may be fleeting or they may take hold of us for a period of time. They sometimes make people doubt the usefulness of the grief-work they have done in the past, and they become annoyed with themselves for "not getting over it." But these are normal, predictable reactions, best addressed by lovingly giving them attention. They will pass.

Remember that the Exodus from Egypt took place in a day, but it took forty years in the desert to get the slavery out of the Jewish People. Remember, as well, to be patient with yourself as you pass through the seasons of mourning. Go forward with your life, and use the tools of the seasons to heal you. As each season passes, you will gain new strength.

Part Three

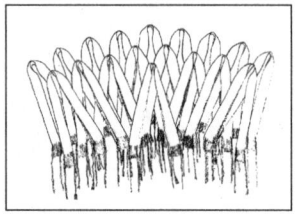

**And so long as you haven't experienced this:
to die and so to grow,
You are only a troubled guest on the dark earth.**

—Goethe (translated by Robert Bly)

16

שלום

Shalom:

Hello, Goodbye, and Peace

SHALOM WELCOMES THE SEASONS, says farewell to the past and makes peace with what life has brought. It indicates a sense of benign balance and the harmony which follows when both partners to a contract have fulfilled their obligations. You have discharged your obligations of mourning. I hope that this work has helped you progress toward shalom.

    Here is a story from the Dubner Magid, the confidant and advisor of one of eighteenth-century Judaism's great teachers, the Vilna Gaon. Once there was a king who had a beautiful diamond. But this

ש.ל.מ **ShLM:** to fulfill an obligation, to complete; wholeness, to be intact, profitable, rewarded, in balance; *shalom*: peace beautiful diamond had a flaw—a scratch in the middle. The king sent word throughout his kingdom that great riches would come to anyone who could rid the diamond of its flaw. Gem cutters, jewelry makers, and artisans from around the kingdom came to the castle, but no one could erase the diamond's scratch. Finally, a young man came and announced that he could make the diamond more beautiful than ever before. Everyone scoffed as he disappeared into the king's treasury, but they gasped with awe when he came out—and presented the king with the stone. The scratch was still in the diamond but it was—indeed—more beautiful than ever before. For in the center of the diamond the young man had carved a beautiful rose, using the scratch for the stem.

I hope that our work together has given you tools for transforming the tear caused by the death into something that is beautiful, despite the loss.

> The universe says loss demands birth and the two are lovers.
> —Deena Metzger

"Acceptance" and the End of Your Grief-Work

How do we know that our grief-work is finished? There are always likely to be issues connected with our losses, but there is also a point when the active work of mourning can be set aside and our psyches are free to move into the future.

We have been told that "acceptance" is the final stage of mourning. But what does that mean? Does acceptance mean that you are no longer troubled by your loss, that you move forward gladly in a world without the presence of the person who has died? I think that such expectations are unrealistic.

Acceptance is more an ability to make peace with a situation. It means coming to a place of shalom, perhaps not every day, but more and more frequently. It means being able to look forward to the future after integrating some of the reality and the repercussions of the loss. It means approaching a sense of completeness with issues that were unresolved when the person died. Acceptance means finding a way to feel some harmony and continued sense of partnership with the deceased, as well as a renewed harmony with a universe that permits loss. When you reach this stage of mourning, you are likely to feel that your life is again your own.

Each of us has issues that won't go away. When people come to me for therapy, one of the first things that I tell them is that I cannot cure them of being themselves. The facts of their lives and the stories that they have lived don't change. What can change is the way they feel about their history. In our work together, they can come to understand and love the person they are and the life they have lived. By eventually embracing themselves, they come to know their own stories with compassion.

In Hebrew, the word for wound, *petzah,* is closely related to another word which is used to describe the break of day, *miftziah hashachar,* the moment when the sun breaks from behind the clouds. This transformation, which comes through the opening initially caused by a wound, can be the foundation of a bright future.

פ.צ.ע **PTzA:** to wound, break, cut, burst forth; *miftziah hashachar*: break of day

Seeking Growth—Not Miracles

In this book, we have not sought the miraculous. We have not tried to erase your wound. Instead we have focused on it in order to support the growth of an

Chapter Sixteen

exquisite rose. Your wound was the scratch in the diamond that helped you grow a rose.

What better example of the transformation of a wound do we have than in Jacob's confrontation with God's messenger on the night before he was to cross the Yabbok River to meet his brother, Esau? Jacob had not seen his brother, whose birthright he had stolen, since the theft had occurred several decades earlier. He anticipated the reunion with great anxiety.

Jacob wrestled all night with the mysterious being and received an injury, which thereafter caused him to walk with a limp. The struggle ended at daybreak. Jacob realized that he was victorious, and demanded a blessing from his foe.

Jacob knew that he had struggled face-to-face with the deepest force that a person can confront. And because of this struggle, he was transformed. He changed the name of the site of this struggle to Peniel, which means "face of God." He changed his own name as well. He became "Israel," a name which means "One who struggles with God," the name by which his descendants would thereafter be called. And Jacob crossed the Yabbok to confront his destiny (Genesis 32:23–33).

The Day of Atonement ends with driving a nail to build the sukkah, the temporary hut in which we live during the autumn harvest festival of Sukkot. Moving from the intensity of the calendar's most difficult day to prepare for the joyous harvest celebration, we are reminded that all things are transitory. On Sukkot from these temporary dwellings, decorated with fronds and fruits, we celebrate life's ebb and flow.

> What preparations have you made to open to an inner life so full that whatever happens can be used as a means of enriching your focus.
>
> —*Stephen Levine*

Part Three

Go Forward with Strength

I hope that our work together has brought you to a point of harvest, a time of fullness which you can celebrate with a joyous heart, looking forward to what comes next. I hope you have learned to treasure not only that which comes and that which goes, but the process of changing, as well, and that you now have tools to help your transitions. With the awareness that much is temporary, but some things are eternal, I again offer you my hand, as was done in the time of the Temple, and beckon you to join those of us who have been empowered by the wisdom and transformation that comes with the walk on the mourner's path.

Shalom.

שלום

Chapter Sixteen

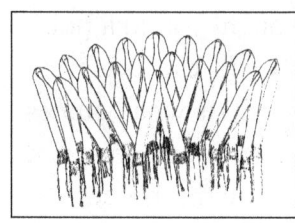

Why are peas the proper food for mourners? As the pea rolls, so does mourning roll from one person to the other. Today's mourner is tomorrow's comforter and today's comforter is tomorrow's mourner.

–Talmud: Baba Batra 16

17

Those Who Say "Amen":
How to Comfort the Bereaved

THE MOVE FROM THE MOURNER'S PATH back into the community, from being one who says Kaddish in the wake of a loss to one who says "Amen" to the Kaddish of another, is a profound shift. It underscores the Talmudic reasoning for serving round foods in the house of *shiva*. When we comfort, whether or not we have recently been mourners, we are not dispassionate others who reach into a strange and alien world to condescendingly offer cheer to the pitiful. We are sibling human beings who are reminded of our common vulnerability. At the same time that we acknowledge the essential uniqueness of each loss, we also perceive an awareness of the common and inescapable human

> May HaMakom (God) comfort you among the mourners of Zion and Jerusalem.
> —The Mourners' Blessing

condition. If we, ourselves, have faced a profound loss, it is with us as we reach out in comfort. Present in our condolence is both the wisdom of what we have learned from our suffering as well as its unresolved issues. In the unlikely event that we have not suffered, we comfort with the understanding that this is a part of life we will have to face. Without these sober perspectives, our words of comfort may lack credibility. Our condolence may be superficial and possibly condescending. We may be likely to distance ourselves from the mourner and offer hollow comfort. This will bring no consolation and may bring pain instead of solace.

This chapter will give you some practical tips on bringing comfort. Cross-referencing pages earlier in the book where each topic is covered in more detail, this chapter will also push you to apply the work described earlier in the book to your own life experience so that you can become the kind of person who truly brings blessing and embodies the invocation of what we wish for mourners: That they may find *HaMakom*: a Place of Comfort.

HaMakom

Perhaps the greatest teaching on how to comfort comes in the name of God that is invoked in the blessing on behalf of mourners (see page 15). There are many names for God in the Jewish tradition and many of them describe divinity through qualities or attributes associated with The Divine. We speak of *HaRachaman* (God, the Compassionate One), *El Emunah* (God, the Faithful One), or *Dayan HaEmet* (God, the True Judge). These are only three of many on the long list naming God through descriptive epithets.

But *HaMakom* is different. *HaMakom,* the name of God that is used in the Mourners' Blessing, is a name that is not descriptive. *HaMakom* literally means "The Place." *HaMakom* embraces without defining the nature of the embrace. It provides a context without a prescription for behavior. It describes neither the face of Holiness whose presence is invoked nor the behavior of the one who is being encouraged to find Its presence. By invoking this face of God, the Mourners' Blessing embraces the mourner without intruding. This non-intrusive embrace is exactly the kind of safe attention that mourners need in order to find their voice of healing. It countenances the array of feelings that mourners may experience without prescribing what mourners are to feel. Invoking *HaMakom* reminds us that what mourners most require are Holy Places of Comfort. These Holy Places are safe caldrons where individual needs are respected and the mourner is given the space in which he or she can summon personal resources and evolve a new life.

When we create a place for healing and name that place "God," we acknowledge the mysterious nature of healing. We assert that healing comes from some place of soul which is beyond our understanding or control. Such a place is not served by the well-meaning and urgent intrusion of those who wish to help.

What Helps?

Mourners often complain that they have to take care of the people who come to comfort them. They gripe about having to teach inept and intrusive people how to help them. (This is beyond the need to feed their visitors (and then wash the dishes), which is absolutely a violation of both Jewish law and common decency (see pages 98–104).) They describe well-meaning people who come with urgent good intentions. These would-be comforters want to make things better. They want to do the right thing or to find just the right phrase that will transform mourning. Their need for reassurance often requires the mourner to step outside of the needed cocoon of mourning to reassure the comforter that he or she is making things better.

Guess what? You can't make it better. You can't take away the pain of loss. You can't bring the person who has died back. Coming to terms with our powerlessness is one of the first steps in learning to comfort the bereaved. Struggling with this very difficult understanding gives us access to the paradoxically profound and simple skill of comfort. Understanding that we can't do the impossible takes away some of the urgency, so that we can focus not on changing what can't be changed, but on being present and nurturing in the midst of grief.

The tools to help others cope with major turning points in their lives are not privileged information. They are taught to all of us through our own life experiences and needs. The heart that is both caring and helpful is born of a marriage of self-knowledge and the ability to attend to others. Because—like the pea—sorrow rolls; when we seek to provide comfort we look into our own lives for guidance. The most important thing you can offer as comfort is your own comfort. This comes from the work you do long *before* you arrive, through which you come to terms with the profound themes in your own life. To help you identify this wisdom, I encourage you to do the exercises in the book. If you are personally fluent in the issues that mourners face and respectful of their sensitive boundaries, you will be helpful. I will guide you to some of the relevant pages.

What you *can* do is communicate to the mourner that you are present and unafraid. You can let the mourner know that you can be there without judgment or shock amid his or her ricocheting emotions. You can remind him or her that all the strange behaviors—the anger, the forgetfulness, and the fatigue—are textbook descriptions of what mourning looks like. You can create an empty space in which there is room for the mourner to explore these feelings.

The Skills of Comfort

To reiterate: The concept of *HaMakom* as a place of healing reminds those who seek to comfort the mourner that there are limits to what one person can do to help another. We cannot return what has been lost. We cannot take the pain away. We can affirm the difficult steps on the mourner's path and create a safe place for someone who has been devastated by loss.

Knowing that we don't have to rescue people in crisis can make it easier to help them. Knowing that what can be done as a caregiver has limits can make it less threatening for those who want to be of help. We are off the hook with regard to performing magic tricks of healing. All we can really do to help them is to affirm *HaMakom*; we can create a place where they feel heard and protected. We can help to give them a sense that they are free to find their own resources for healing. We can let them know that it is all right to progress at the pace that is uniquely their own.

Chapter Seventeen

The irony is that you become capable of serving in this way, by taking care of yourself. You do this by cultivating your own soul, exploring your own relationship to loss, perhaps by doing the exercises in the previous chapters with respect to the issues of your own life. By plumbing your own depths, you create a holy space inside yourself that is spacious enough to hold the mourner and create a place of safety for the shifts of emotion that mourners feel and the existential questions that they ask.

Think back on your own difficult challenges (see page 54). What helped you get through them? What did not help? Was there anything that someone said that made it easier for you to get on with your grief-work and begin to heal? Over and over I hear from people that what helped was not a cogent *bon mot* or profound piece of advice that summed up the experience and set the person on the path of healing. It was the gift of empathetic attention with which someone validated the mourner's experience and provided presence, attention, and lack of judgment. This was offered without intruding in the mourner's private world or forcing the mourner to move beyond his or her comfort zone. It may have come as a light touch, or as the subtle communication that the comforter understood some of what the mourner was going through. Above all, the feeling was conveyed that the mourner had permission to be exactly as he or she needed to be, be it tearful, angry, silent, or confused. Rarely were these reassurances expressed verbally.

This kind of presence says more about who the comforter is than about what he or she says or does when offering solace. It reflects his or her own work on the deep issues of his or her own life, work which makes it possible to comfortably reach out to others move beyond his or her comfort zone when a response is solicited. It reassures the mourner that the confusion and the ricocheting feelings are normal feelings of mourning. It communicates to the mourner that he or she is not crazy, that this is what mourning looks like. It might let them know what they might expect (i.e; "You may be angry at people for no apparent reason;" "You may think you are going crazy;" "You might wake up at night with a wet pillow.") It gives mourners permission to feel exactly the way they feel, and lets them know that this relationship will be a safe place in which to mourn.

Before the Burial

The mitzvot during this period of time are designed to give honor to the deceased. Judaism is very specific on how this is to be done. Care for the body. Perform the mitzvot of the *Chevra Kaddisha* and *Shomrim* (see pages 74–77). Take turns sitting with the body. Read it psalms and other words of comfort. The mourners will be grateful this exquisite care has been given to the deceased at a time when they may be overcome with shock.

Shiva

Encourage people to observe the full week (see pages 86–111) or at least a few days of *shiva*. This will allow them to begin to process their grief and the changes it will make in their lives without the intrusion of normal daily life. During that time, attend to their physical needs, but don't talk too much. The formulaic and ritual

> True comforters are present in a precise and limited way.... They are walk-on players in a minor role.
> —Jonathan Omer-Man

responses (including providing food for the mourners) are designed to carry the mourner through this time of numbness or unreality without too much intrusion. The comforter is supposed to walk past the mourner and wait for a cue from the mourner that says it is all right to speak. We are encouraged to be brief and to speak about the deceased. But mostly the comforter is charged with creating a safe container in which mourning can unfold: a place of nurturing silence in which the physical needs of mourners are taken care of (see pages 90 and 98).

The Meal of Comfort

Bring food to a house of mourning on beautiful plates and bowls (see pages 106–107). This brings grace/*hidor mitzvah* to the obligation of feeding the bereaved. It also requires the mourner to reach out in the days to come, asking friends to come and get their dishes ... a tricky antidote to mourners' tendency to isolation. **Make sure the burden of preparing food (and cleaning up) for the shiva minyan does not fall upon the family of the deceased and that the mood is one that takes its cues from the mourners. Avoid a cocktail party atmosphere.**

When the Funeral Is Not in the City in Which the Mourner Lives

If the funeral occurs in a city other than the one in which the mourner lives, encourage him or her to observe at least one more day of *shiva* in his or her home community. Part of the *shiva* minyan service should include the opportunity for the mourner or someone else to talk about the deceased (perhaps reading the *hesped* that was delivered elsewhere). This will give the mourner a sense that his or her grief is visible in the place in which he or she lives. It ensures that members of the mourner's home community have a sense that they are acquainted with the person who died. Having members of the mourner's daily world hold an image of the deceased can be very comforting.

Saying Kaddish

Allow the mourner the special acknowledgment that comes from standing alone to say Kaddish and receiving the embrace of the community through their "Amen." If your community is committed to everyone standing for the prayer, allow the mourner to stand first or in front of the other worshippers. It is a way of affirming the uniqueness of this time of grief. Help those who say Kaddish to feel comfortable with the words of the prayer. At first, recite it along with them. Say it slowly, lowering your voice as they begin to find their own voice and pace. Share with the mourner some of the deeper reasons for saying Kaddish (see pages 146–163). You might explain the Kaddish as a way of continuing the dynamic relationship with the deceased, or mention some of the mystical understandings of why we say Kaddish (see pages 149 and 151). As always, take your cues from the mourner on how much to share.

Shloshim

Observe the end of the first thirty days of mourning with a ceremony. This is an opportunity for the community, which has been enjoined to comfort in silence during the time of *shiva*, to voice what the loss means for it. So

> Whosoever sees a mourner within thirty days should comfort him, but not ask him how he is feeling. After thirty days, but within twelve months, he should ask how he is and then comfort him. After twelve months, he should comfort him and then ask how he is feeling.
> —Semahot

Chapter Seventeen

many mourners complain, after about a month has gone by, "no one talks about him/her anymore." *Don't be afraid to talk about the deceased.*

Remain Available to Help

Mourners may not find their voices until long after the death has occurred. Be there when they are ready to talk. In addition, it may be many months before a mourner is ready to deal with some of the physical aspects of grieving, such as going through the possessions of the person who has died. Gently remind him or her that there is no time limit on your availability for helping. Be forgiving if your offer of help is not accepted. Let the mourner know that you will continue to be available even if your offers are not acknowledged. Learn to be graceful as you remind them of your availability while at the same time remaining non-intrusive.

Yahrzeit *and* Yizkor

One of the greatest gifts you can give someone who has suffered a loss is the reassurance that the person who has died continues to live in the memories of others. Years, even decades, after someone has died, let those survivors know that you remember. Make a phone call or send a card on significant days. You can't imagine how much it will be appreciated!

Wonder about the Afterlife

Know about Jewish attitudes toward the afterlife, as well as those of other traditions. People want to know that the people who have died are okay, and while we can't exactly assure that, we can speculate with them about what might have happened to the soul of the deceased. By being open to discussion of the possibility of the existence of life after death, you suggest that death may not be the dark and final monolith that so many believe it to be. You don't have to believe; you just have to be willing to explore. This willingness to admit that we don't know the answers can open the door for conversations that can bring hope and spiritual transformation. (See pages 202–215.)

Take Care of Yourself

As you enter a house of mourning, you will often find a bowl of water by the door. This is placed there for people who have come from the cemetery for the purpose of ritual hand washing. This is because it is believed that those who have come in contact with a dead body are *tamai* (see pages 142–145), in need of some ritual cleansing. This understanding of *tamai* needs to be extended to the experience of the comforters. Our tradition tells us that those who visit the sick (and I think we can extend that to include visits to all people who are suffering), take away one-sixtieth of their illness. The question that always rises for me is: Where does it go?

As was said earlier, when we comfort from the wisdom of our own experience, several things happen: the first is that we communicate credible empathy. This can bring comfort. The second is that in confronting the pain of others, the issues of our own lives rise to the surface. This makes it likely that making a condolence call will leave a mark on you. Comforters must have tools to enable them to empty the pain that accumulates.

Chapter Seventeen

This helps them to keep their hearts open and guards against their becoming unconscious with regard to their own soul's journey as they harden their hearts to protect themselves from the deep feelings that are generated by witnessing the pain of another. It is important self-care to debrief about what has been stimulated in your own inner world by what you have witnessed. However it is imperative that the processing you do regarding your own response to a loss be done with someone outside of the circle of mourners. And it should never take place in the house of *shiva*!

There are many tools for caring for yourself. You might exercise, meditate, write in a journal, or do some of the relevant exercises in this book. Most likely you will want to talk to someone else. Friends or professionals can help identify the emotional milestones and unfinished business that may have been re-stimulated by the current grief to which you are witness. If we open our hearts as comforters and do not recoil from the personal issues that are raised, the mitzvah of comforting the bereaved becomes a double mitzvah. Not only do we reach out to others, but also we seize the opportunity for personal growth that will enable us to "open our hearts to [God's] wisdom and treasure each day" (Psalm 91).

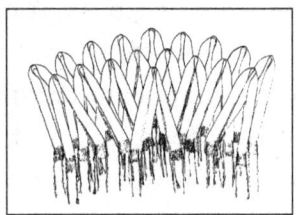

Part Three

Epilogue

The New Mourner's Path—
Navigating the Wilderness of Grief

> A mourner who enters the Temple Mount . . . may enter and walk around to the left. . . . They would then say to him, "May *HaMakom* [the One who dwells in this House] comfort you." Who are they who circle to the left? A mourner, an excommunicant, one who has someone sick at home, and one concerned about a lost object.
> —Talmud: Semachot 6:11

In the twenty-five years since *Mourning & Mitzvah* was first published, my own understanding of grief and its exigencies has continued to grow. With each gleaning, from both my personal work and my work with others, I return, as if on pilgrimage, to the above Talmudic text and its reference to the circular path of healing in the Temple in ancient Jerusalem.

This text began the first chapter when the book was initially published in 1993. In the 2001 second edition, an added chapter explored *HaMakom*, which literally means "the Place," and is the name of God invoked in the blessing bestowed upon those who trod the Temple's healing walkway. I return to this passage once more for this twenty-fifth anniversary edition, to revisit the ancient Temple's Mourner's Path, and to share another view of the choreography of grief.

Around the year 2000, when I visited the ruins of the Temple's southern steps for the first time, my ongoing literary pilgrimage to this text received mysterious validation. Standing in the hot sun, I listened as the tour guide pointed out the remnants of the place designated as the mourners' entrance. Suddenly, a pencil fell out of the sky. I kid you not. That there were children playing above who might have dropped the pencil did not lessen the impact of the moment's affirmation that I should continue to write about the mourner's path.

Mourning into Dancing

> You have turned my mourning into dancing.
> —Psalm 30:11

As I prepare again to circle the mourner's path for new insights into the process of grief, these words from Psalm 30 are on my lips. This psalm is attributed to King David. He is said to have written it to be read at the Temple's ceremonial opening. These words tell me that David envisioned the Temple as a place of healing, a place where mourning is turned into dancing. However, in English neither "mourning" nor "dancing" reveals David's vision. "Mourners" in the time of the Temple included people suffering many kinds of loss. And the dance that David envisioned was very different than the celebratory movements that we usually associate with the word "dance."

When David's son Solomon built the Temple, vulnerable people of the ancient world came to this "house of prayer for all peoples" (Isaiah 56:7) and participated in its rituals. Wounded people, mourners and others, climbed the steps on which I stood the day the pencil fell out of the sky. They entered through the special gate to make their way to the

Mourner's Path. Those walking the Mourner's Path of antiquity included those who faced economic reverses, relocation, change in social status, and illness, as well as those who were bereaved. These mourners walked the path together, demonstrating that all loss calls for similar attention. Those who "circle[d] to the left" might have included the majority of the community.

The word David chose for his projected Temple dance was *machol*. You should know that Biblical Hebrew has at least eleven words, each with its own nuance, that are all translated into English with the same word, "dance." David's meaning is lost in translation. *Machol* describes a ritual dance often performed by women. Its Hebrew root emphasizes the circularity of the dance, connecting it to words such as "writhing" or "twisting," as in the motions made by women giving birth. When the Hebrew slaves crossed over the Sea of Reeds, leaving the tight place of Egypt (remember that Mitzrayim, the Hebrew name for Egypt, means "narrow places") to be reborn into freedom, the dance that was done by Miriam and the women was a *machol*. This window on what in English is simply "dancing" describes the often-painful ritual journey toward rebirth that is required when we mourn.

I imagine a beautifully choreographed dance of healing performed by "those who circled to the left" and those who met their gaze with the blessing "*HaMakom Y'nechem* (May God [literally, 'the Place'] comfort you)." There may be an etymological connection between the word *machol* and the word for illness, *machalah*. Might those who brought their wounds to the Temple have been part of a homeopathic ritual as the community performed a *machol* to treat a *machalah*?

Machol's circular motion underscores our earlier discussions of the cycle of Yizkor services, which provide tools for continuing to harvest our grief, as we also continue to grow. Yizkor is recited on days when pilgrims would customarily come to the Temple. This points to another Hebrew word, *chagag*, also a circle dance, performed in sacred procession. The word is a cognate of the Hebrew and Arabic words for pilgrimage festivals, *chag* and *hajj*. Like the Yizkor cycle, these words invite us to revisit the Temple's path on the holy mountain, sacred to all Abrahamic religions, in a dance of pilgrimage.

Mapping the Path

My goal is to align ancient perspectives on the choreography of grief with recent understandings of mourning. I stand on the shoulders of the twentieth-century pioneers in thanatology, such as Dr. Elizabeth Kübler-Ross, who made it possible for us to speak of death and grief in a culture that denied them both. They created a psychotherapeutic mourner's path for modernity, which has brought much healing.

In the twenty-first century, the conversation progresses. The profound revelations harvested from the depths of those willing to face death and its aftermath call for a new mourner's path that explores grief as a spiritual journey. This goes beyond the medical or psychological models and wrests it from those who calcified grief into stages, such as Kübler-Ross's familiar path: denial, bargaining, depression, anger, and acceptance. Trying to tame the messy and unpredictable experience of grief, those who sought to help mourners embraced this model, leading many to expect an orderly, predictable, linear journey with a beginning, a middle, and an end. This is at odds with the chaotic experiences that mourners report, as well as with the circular movements of mourners and comforters along the Temple's path and the understanding embedded in the Yizkor cycle.

Grief is certainly not orderly! It is a *machol* filled with ups and downs and twists and turns. We must return to places on the path, and just when we think we have it nailed, we are blindsided by another emotional experience. Grief is about learning to navigate an unruly wilderness. It is about yielding to the dance.

Sadly, often the five stages have been used to diagnose, rather than humanize, the experience of loss. Portrayed as scripted experiences, they pressure mourners to look outward, to describe their process, rather than inward, to mine their unique emotional experience for growth and wisdom. "What's wrong with me?" a mourner once asked me. "Shouldn't I be in anger by now?" He was using an external measure to judge his unique (and chaotic) journey.

I am also concerned that many of the words used to label the stages frame grief negatively, or as a medical condition. "Depression" is an illness. "Denial" can sound delusional. And "anger" is often seen as an unacceptable breach of behavior. These words ascribe pathology to normal and essential responses to loss, when the emotions of grief are actually healthy and appropriate in the face of profound change.

One more discomfort that has grown, as I have grown over the last quarter century, is the absence of a spiritual dimension on the therapeutic mourner's path. Illness and grief, as I have said throughout *Mourning & Mitzvah*, can provoke spiritual crises. Mourners must transform their physical connection to the deceased into a spiritual one, while every existential assumption is called into doubt. Previous answers to life's profound questions become insufficient. Often there will also be a need to mourn a previously sustaining understanding of God. This earthquake of meaning is an essential part of loss. In order to heal, mourners must write a new contract with the person who has died, as well as with life, God, and the Universe.

My work here is to design places of comfort. I build upon the affirmation given to mourners on the Temple's path, expressing that hope that they will find *HaMakom Y'nechem*, the Place of Comfort. I am creating *mekamot* ("places") to name the stops on the mourner's path. Calling them *mekamot*, the plural of *Makom*, God's name in the Mourner's Blessing, is a declaration that each place is holy. I underscore that sacredness by giving each of these places a holy Hebrew name. Furthermore, I am calling these places *sukkot* (plural of sukkah).

Sukkot are the temporary tent-like shelters in which Jews live for seven days each autumn during the observance of the pilgrimage festival of the same name, Sukkot. These fragile huts, open to the sky, with roofs woven out of fronds and branches and decorated with hanging fruits and vegetables, commemorate the tents of the liberated Hebrew slaves in the forty years they wandered in the desert. This time of vulnerability is also named *Z'man Simchateinu* ("the time of our joy"). This is a profound paradox of spiritual life: We are vulnerable; be happy!

During the Sukkot holiday, living in these tents is both *commanded* and *temporary*. I emphasize the words "commanded" and "temporary" in the hope that mourners will enter these structures with less fear. "Commanded" and "temporary" proclaim these tenancies as required, but offer reassurance that they come with a short-term lease.

Each of these *sukkot* is an essential place where mourners must dwell in order to come to terms with loss. Once more, Hebrew provides guidance. The words for "wilderness" (*midbar*) and "to speak" (*medaber*) come from the same Hebrew root. They evoke the arc of grief's journey through an untamed wilderness in which one must make peace with what it means to be human. Mourners move from the chaos of the wilderness of grief to a literal "coming to terms" with loss, as mourners both find their voice and the language to describe their unique experience of their mourning.

Humbly, I choose words to house the experiences of those who pass through grief's wilderness. I choose these holy Hebrew names to remove any attribution of pathology from these vital human passages. Each word will name a sukkah in which we must dwell if we are to become fluent in being human.

Sukkot of Transformation

Ma tovu, ohalecha Yaakov, mishkanotecha Yisrael!
How good are your tents, Jacob, your holy dwelling places, Israel!
—Numbers 24:5

The above Biblical phrase, used in Jewish liturgy and song, describes my intention for these spaces of transformation. These words, from the Moabite sorcerer Balaam, were meant to curse the newly liberated Hebrews as they traveled from Egypt to the Promised Land. However, when Balaam opened his mouth to curse, out came this blessing. Not only was his intention transformed, but so were his words. By the line's end, both Jacob and his mundane tents are transformed. "Jacob" becomes "*Yisrael*, one who wrestles with God," and his "tent" becomes a *mishkan*, a holy place where God can dwell. Both *miSHKaN* and *YisraEL* contain names of God: *SHeKhiNah* and *EL*. In the *sukkot* that lie ahead, I hope that the Godwrestling that will take place in each of these tents in the wilderness of loss will enable mourners to infuse their journey with holiness, and that they will see each tent become a *mishkan* and find blessing in the midst of what seems to be a curse. In the words of the Mourner's Blessing, I hope they will find *HaMakom Y'nechem*—a holy place of comfort.

In our wilderness of mourning, there will be five *sukkot*. Within them, the mourner will find different emotions and different experiences of Holiness. The names will be explained in full when we visit each tent, but to introduce them I will say that two of these, *Sukkat Kavod* (*sukkat* means "sukkah of") and *Sukkat Kodesh*, have names taken from Biblical terms for God's holiness. Another pair, *Sukkat Yisrael* and *Sukkat Yirah-Yehudah*, are named for Biblical characters who represent different ways of encountering God. An additional name, *Yirah*, is applied to both the first and the last *sukkot*: *Sukkat Yirah-Pakhad* and *Sukkat Yirah-Yehudah*. They describe the two sides of *yirah* (the Hebrew word for "awe"): fear and amazement. In Proverbs, it is said that "the beginning of wisdom is *yirat Adonai*" (Proverbs 9:10), which can be translated as either "fear" or "awe" of God. In both of these *sukkot* of *yirah*, the mourner trembles with awe. However, in the first, *Sukkat Yirah-Pakhad*, the awe is based in fear (*pakhad*). In the final, *Sukkat Yirah-Yehudah*, it is infused with amazement, love, and gratitude.

As we begin to travel through this wilderness of grief, from the narrow place of Egypt to the spacious Promised Land, I remind you of grief's circuitous path. There is no particular order for visiting the tents. The work of each sukkah is to learn the size and shape of your emotions, so that they become allies in the process of change. Each sukkah will need to be visited many times until you become comfortable with the experience it represents and learn to embrace it as an ally in healing. As we explore each sukkah and the prescribed movement within it, I hope that you will gain the tools to fulfill David's promise and turn your mourning into dancing.

THE MOURNER'S PATH:
A Therapeutic Path
Denial----► Bargaining----► Anger----► Depression----► Acceptance

THE PATH OF THE SOUL:
A Holy and Creative Path

Egypt/The Narrow Place   The Promised Land

The Wilderness of Grief

Yirah: Lower Awe   *Yirah*: Higher Awe

Fear and Trembling   Gratitude and Amazement

Sukkot in the Wilderness

Yirah-Pakhad   *Kavod*   *Kodesh*   *Yisrael*   *Yirah-Yehudah*

The First Sukkah: *Sukkat Yirah-Pakhad*

Fear and Trembling at the Edge of the Wilderness

Our souls' grief-work journey begins at the edge of the wilderness. The psyche initially reacts to startling changes by withdrawing. Needing to create protective defenses, it contracts, in disbelief or numbness, to allow us, when confronted with profound change, to slowly assimilate the life-shattering truth.

In 1995, after my father's funeral, I sat in stunned silence on his living room couch. My cousins filed by, as well as members of his community. They held my hand. They kissed my cheeks. They told me stories of my father's generosity. They seemed to be speaking foreign languages. I responded with a forced grin, appreciating their intentions but unable to take in their words. Meanwhile, members of his synagogue came twice a day. They brought meals and joined me in prayer. They said "Amen" as I recited the Kaddish in a faltering voice, despite my previous visits to the wilderness of grief. I watched from behind my eyes, at the back of my skull. My mouth moved as I recited the prayers, but I wasn't sure where my voice was coming from. I did not feel human. I was not "in denial." While my mind knew that my father had died, my cells had not yet taken in that this good man who had always been present was gone. I had been blindsided. I was summoning resources for what was to come.

"Denial" can sound pejorative, perhaps implying willful delusion. Yet, I think what this word attempts to describe is actually healthy resistance. Instinctively, the mourner is incapable of integrating the new paradigm until it feels safe. I name this tent *Sukkat Yirah-Pakhad* to affirm our inability to surrender our basic assumptions when we first enter the wilderness of grief.

As mentioned above, the Jewish mystics speak of two sides of *yirah* ("awe"): lower and higher awe. This is the sukkah of "lower awe." We enter this sukkah of early loss with trepidation or fear (*pakhad*) and dwell in *Sukkat Yirah-Pakhad* during the frightening time when mourners teeter at the edge of grief's wilderness, feeling trapped in the Egypt/mitzryim-like narrow space that is the contraction of early grief. On the other side of the wilderness, there will be an encounter with "higher awe," sometimes described as "radical amazement," in the waiting Promised Land, where the face of awe is graced with love and reverence.

Yirah-Pakhad describes the shock of coming toe-to-toe with life and death's great mysteries, before we can possibly absorb them. *Yirah* communicates the intense, numbed state of the early mourner, when loss is first confronted and mourners must build the defenses needed to filter the blinding light of the unbearable truth. They may feel alienated, from both life and God. Judaism exempts mourners from specific routine spiritual practices in the earliest stages of grief. Mourners, this acknowledges, are in the midst of spiritual crisis.

In this sukkah, dancing, David's prescription for healing, seems impossible. The mourner sits frozen on the couch, body contracted, mouth mute. Slowly, he or she begins to thaw: The hips sway with the words of the Kaddish. The head nods in response to condolences. Small bites of eggs or bagels are taken and slowly swallowed. These slight movements begin the work at the core of David's vision for the Temple of Healing.

In perhaps the most significant movement in *Sukkat Yirah-Pakhad*, suffering eyes look to heaven in puzzled horror. It will require the intense feelings that are waiting in the *sukkot* ahead to make the transition from trembling in the presence of the vast, unfathomable mystery of loss to dancing in the presence of the Sacred in the sukkah of awe and amazement, which is on the far side of the wilderness of grief.

The Second Sukkah: *Sukkat Kavod*

Gravitas: Weight and Glory

> Please, let me see your *Kavod*.
> —Exodus 33:18

Moses begged to see God's presence: "Please, let me see your *Kavod*!" he beseeched, pleading with God for a face-to-face meeting. YHVH (the ineffable name of God) refused this request, saying, "[Humans] cannot see My face . . . and live" (Exodus 33: 20). Like mourners residing in *Sukkat Kavod*, Moses yearned for what he could not have.

We enter the next sukkah as the frozen state of *yirah-pakhad* has begun to thaw. The death is no longer news. The fact of the diagnosis, divorce, or other change is beginning to sink in. The mourner begins to sift through the ashes. He or she may still feel wrapped in gauze, but less numb and more in touch with the feelings that are beginning to emerge. Each labored breath is accompanied by yearning. The mourner is overwhelmed and exhausted. The absence is felt and there is fear of what lies ahead. Used well, *Sukkat Kavod* can provide a time for respite and contemplation.

Mourners merit this contemplative time of the broken heart. Yet, they resist this gift, because it hurts to reside in *Sukkat Kavod*, where tears fall. "Once I begin to cry," they agonize, "the tears will never stop." But they will. As I said earlier in the book:

> Pain has a size and a shape, a beginning and an end. . . . Feelings that find expression change. And *that* change is the process that brings transformation.

In *Sukkat Kavod*, those tears water shattered and contracted hearts, hearts that are like seeds in winter. Tears soften hearts that have been turned to stone, so that they can love life again.

A month after receiving a diagnosis of metastatic breast cancer, Sarah, a mother of three school-age children, came to my office. She sat down on the couch opposite me and sank deep into the fluffy red pillows, almost disappearing. She settled shapelessly and sat for a while, taking short, shallow breaths. Finally, she let out a sigh and began to speak. "I am depressed," she said in an almost inaudible voice. "I feel heavy. I can't move. I cry all the time. I have no desire to go on with my treatment." A slow trickle of tears ran down her cheek. "My children . . ." she continued, without finishing her sentence. With that sigh and those tears, Sarah pulled back the flap to enter one of the most difficult places in which those who face profound loss reside in the wilderness of grief: *Sukkat Kavod*.

As with most of the *sukkot*, the choice of this name is counterintuitive. I chose the holy word *kavod* to emphasize the fact that grief, unlike depression, is not a disease.

With its painful and palpable yearning, burdensome sadness, and frequent despair, a stay in *Sukkat Kavod* can feel like a bout of clinical depression. But why pathologize appropriate sadness? Grief is hard enough. Must mourners also think that they are mentally ill?

Kavod is most often translated as "honor," as in the Biblical commandment to honor mother and father (Exodus 33:18). We congratulate someone who has done a good job by saying, "*Kol haKavod* (all the honor to you)," but *kavod* can also mean "weight," "heaviness," and "glory." It can also mean "presence," as when Moses pleaded to see God's *Kavod*. In this sukkah, mourners long for the presence of what is lost.

Kavod describes the gravitas of grief. Like *yirah*, *kavod* has two poles. Here, the mourner moves from grief's emotional heaviness to the ability to perceive the presence of holiness. It is a move from weight to glory. The glory was described by the prophet Isaiah, who proclaimed, "The whole world is filled with God's glory (*kavod*)." This higher meaning of *kavod* can be understood as a tangible manifestation of God, the physical precipitate of holiness evident in the majesty of the world that is perceptible to the senses. It could be the beauty of nature or the pulsating awareness of the presence of the numinous.

People who dwell in *Sukkat Kavod* are exhausted. The pulse of the life-force is barely detectable. This lack of vitality is the mourner's organism asserting the opposite of what the culture demands. "Get back to normal," everyone encourages. However, the mourner's weary cells know that what was normal is no longer available. They proclaim: "We will not move. We will stop. We will honor what is gone."

> Like a deer yearning for water, my soul yearns for you, God. My soul thirsts for the God that lives. When will I stand in God's presence?
> —Psalm 42:1–2

Sukkat Kavod takes time. Like all of the *sukkot*, it will take more than one visit. Each sojourn empowers us for repeat stays in other *sukkot*, until the emotions represented are no longer terrifying and have become tools for growth.

Here, in a tent of tears, there is the slow dance of longing. It is painful to surrender our physical connection with who or what has been lost. This may be the hardest of human tasks. The mourner struggles to find a bond that can transcend death and to build a bridge like the one I discovered in yoga class, when I felt the curtain between life and death pull away. Meanwhile, the mourner moves to a new understanding of God. The anthropomorphic God (created in our image) begins to fade as the mourner begins to take comfort in *HaMakom Y'nechem* ("the Place of Comfort"), the God of the Mourner's Blessing.

In *Sukkat Kavod* the question is posed: "what does it mean to be human on a planet where living things die?" In tearful contemplation, the mourner is forced to sit and to ponder. With this focus, something lightens and there might come a new connection to that which is holy.

As this sukkah's task—to move from heaviness to glory—progresses, the unbearable experience of grief yields to an ability to feel compassion for the Mysterious Unfolding of the Universe. I capitalize this because it is a translation of YHVH, the name God revealed as "my true name" to Moses at the Burning Bush. *Sukkat Kavod* can also give access to another "true name" of God, revealed to Moses: *HaRachaman*, "Compassion."

When Moses asked to see God's *Kavod*, he was placed in the cleft of a rock to be shielded from the devouring radiance of the Holy One. What Moses saw as God's true face were God's attributes of compassion:

> Adonai, Adonai, the Eternal, is merciful and gracious, slow to anger, abounding in loving kindness and truth, keeping mercy for thousands of generations, forgiving iniquity, transgression, and sin, and wiping clean.
> —Exodus 34:6–7

About six months after the deaths of my mother and sister, I was living in a room in a boarding house in Berkeley. I rarely spoke to anyone. I did yoga and wrote in my journal. I attached a small piece of paper to the wall, on which I had drawn an infinity sign. I wrote one word on each side of the drawing: "Unbearable" and "Compassion." I contemplated the image night and day as I swayed from side to side in imitation of its lines. As my hips swayed to the right, I chanted, "Unbearable." As my hips swayed to the left, I chanted "Compassion." "Unbearable compassion; unbearable compassion," I chanted, as I danced into a holy world in which I could hold the paradox of love and loss in one body.

In *Sukkat Kavod,* the implications of what it means to be human are so stunning that it is as if the mourner has seen God's *Kavod* without any protection from "God's devouring fire" (Babylonian Talmud: Sotah 14a). Mourners may feel burned in the encounter. The mourner may come closer than even Moses was allowed to come to the presence of Holiness. Moses, after all, was protected, in the cleft of a rock.

After dwelling in *Sukkat Kavod,* after enough tears have fallen, the mourner is likely to feel the residue of having come face-to-face with death's great mystery, as if having seen God's *Kavod.* Perhaps it is possible to make a tenuous peace with a world that is beyond our understanding.

The Third Sukkah: *Sukkat Kodesh*

Rekindling the Holy Fire Within

> You shall be holy, for I YHVH your God am holy.
> —Leviticus 19:2

The commandment to be *kodesh* or "holy" was issued in the wilderness as the blueprint for human behavior. What exactly does it mean to be holy?

In the first sukkah, at the edge of the wilderness, *Sukkat Yirah-Pakhad,* mourners fearfully contract when confronted with their own vulnerability. The second, *Sukkat Kavod,* offers the softening effect of exhaustion and tears. Once mourners enter the third, *Sukkat Kodesh,* they have regained some of their energy. Facing a radically changed world, their eyes narrow. Their teeth clench. Their palms tighten into fists, as they summon the strength for the task of getting on with it. The life-force begins to return. Often without grace, the mourner stumbles back into the world, intent on asserting integrity and individuality in the rise from profound trauma. I choose the word *kodesh* to affirm the holiness of the return of life-force and passion that takes place in this sukkah.

This often looks like anger, and *kodesh*—a word most frequently used to describe God—might seem a curious word to name this sukkah. But I make this choice to affirm the power of this often-maligned emotion. There is tremendous creativity, fire, and life-force behind anger, and this sukkah is the place in which the mourner can harness its sacred, transformative passion. Indeed, the intensity of anger may be what is needed to pierce the numbness of *Sukkat Yirah-Pakhad* or overcome the grave inertia of *Sukkat Kavod*.

However, anger often masks its intentions. In the case of mourning, anger can be the life-force returning, often expressed without grace. I want to protect mourners from those who harshly judge their clumsy efforts to reassert that life energy when they lash out at a hurtful universe, sometimes injuring those who mean well.

Kodesh can also mean "set aside" or "separate." Shabbat Kodesh is a day separated out from the other days of the week and made holy. In the Temple, animals were set aside as *kodesh*, to be consecrated for sacrifice and to bring those who offered them closer to God. In a betrothal ceremony, partners are *meKuDeSHet,* set aside and designated as holy for the person who will be their partner.

The dance in *Sukkat Kodesh* engages anger's passionate life-force to help mourners focus their energy as they create new boundaries and new identities. With holy anger, they confront individuals, the universe, or the Deity. They use the fire of anger to draw a line around themselves, as if to assert, "I am here."

The summer after my father's death, I spent a week at a conference in Colorado, where I was asked to facilitate a group for mourners who needed support. Each evening before sunset, about eight of us would sit in a circle on the grass. We took turns sharing stories of the day, focusing on how we were handling our grief in the supercharged environment.

One evening midweek when the group came together, a prickly emotional timbre was palpable. Irritably, members spoke about insensitive remarks by other attendees at the conference, exasperating encounters with conference staff, annoyances with the facilities, and outrage at the overload of offerings that made it hard to take in the richness of the experience. Members interrupted each other as they poured out their frustration. The fiery energy was escalating.

Hearing this outpouring, I pulled on the arm of the person to my right. She stood up and followed me as we formed a circle and began to stomp on the ground. She pulled the arm of the person to her right, and soon, in a chain reaction, the others joined us. Our circle began moving to the left as our feet struck the ground with chaotic, angry motions. Each step pounded the day's frustration, sorrow, and anger into the grass.

At first, grunts and groans punctuated the pounding of our feet hitting the earth. Voices became louder as they amplified the raw and angry sounds of our individual grief. While each of us was lost in our singular emotions, there was camaraderie in the discordant noise. After a while, the uneven cadences of our individual steps began to blend more and more with those of the others in our circle. Soon, steps were synchronized as we stomped and chanted "No! No! No!" in unison. As we moved, we witnessed our anger and despair turn to amusement, as our ragtag group of mourners performed a dance of passion.

Finally, we were exhausted. I shouted, "Ring around the rosie; all fall down!" Everyone landed on the ground, tears in our eyes flowing from the place where laughter and sorrow are one. As we lay sprawled on the grass, we looked up at the vast Colorado summer sky and saw a double rainbow.

Sukkat Kodesh provides a safe space for mourners to separate themselves from the past through the fire of passionate and energetic expression. As with the Temple's sacrificial rites, this transformation is facilitated by fire, as physical offerings become smoke rising heavenward to bring us closer to God.

In *Sukkat Kodesh*, we face being separate. This is infuriating. In the delight and drama that is human relations, we bond with others and hold tightly. We become magnetized, attracted to other souls to such an extent that we may cease to experience ourselves as separate. Instead, we look for definitions of ourselves through others, looking into the eyes of the souls to whom we are bound as if they were mirrors. In death, divorce, or another loss that shakes our sense of self, we are thrown back on our self-reflection to determine our individuality. Finding ourselves separate, we recognize that we are alone. In addition to that outrage, we are forced to separate from the life we knew before, as well as recognize that no one can feel our pain, despite their good intentions. We are forced to marshal our resources in search of the holy fire that is uniquely our own.

As human beings, each of us walks separately, each set apart for our unique holy task. Albert Camus said that no matter how positive a relationship is, it obscures a piece of the sky. When we love, this is a sacrifice that we give willingly. As with the freewill sacrifices, separated out in the Temple to create more intimacy with God, we make these sacrifices to be closer and more intimate with those we love. When there is loss, that obscured piece of the sky is returned to us.

This can be infuriating. After a loss, we don't want our obscured piece of the sky. We don't want to assert our uniqueness. We want our old life back. And so we rage. In *Sukkat Kodesh*, against our will, we reestablish that sense of separateness. Our anger catalyzes passion and delineates a sense of boundaries and of integrity.

When people suffer, their anger can be self-protective. It can also be destructive. Mourners express rage at those who have wronged them, at God, and at the workings of the universe. They are angry with themselves and with others—even with the person who has died. They rage at what they should have done differently. They blame others and are furious at those who seem protected from pain and appear to lead charmed lives. Ultimately, their deepest rant is at the powerlessness that humans feel at not being able to control the universe.

When we express this anger, we dare to assert that we have boundaries. We risk differentiating ourselves from others. We put our need to blend in and to please aside in service of our willingness to assert our limits and our uniqueness. When we do this, we also assert our holiness.

This anger/passion can be a turning point to energize and stimulate the work of healing.

In the Bible, Job's anger helped him confront the mystery of both Divine and human behavior. His words of complaint were directed first to his friends and then to God:

> Job: *[To his friends]* You . . . have turned against me. . . . I refuse to be quiet. I will cry out my bitter despair. . . . *[To God]* What have I done? Why have you made me your target? Let me speak, and answer me. What crime have I committed? How have I sinned against you? Why do you hide your face? —Job 19:13; 7:11; 13:23–24

In *Sukkat Kodesh,* there is a fire. This fire, like the eternal light that burns in each synagogue, is a symbol of the undying light of the Divine. In *Sukkat Kodesh,* the fire is the constant affirmation of the inner holy spark that burns continually inside the human soul. Each day in the liturgy, we are reminded that this soul cannot be contaminated, even in the face of death.

In the tent of *Kodesh,* as the fires burn, we painfully attempt to define, refine, and sanctify the self that remains. Often we do this awkwardly and without grace. Mourners have hot lava inside. They desperately yearn to express the seething of the roiling gut and raging heart. They overreact to the peccadillo of an in-law, the insensitivity of an ex-husband, an awkward remark of a friend, the unavailability of a doctor, a universe that has changed its rules, and an inscrutable Deity. Any of these can be the impetus for a fiery volcanic eruption, out of proportion to its trigger. For, despite the fact that people often do cruel and inappropriate things that merit anger, the rage of those who suffer is often not about the precipitating incident. It was just the hot lava looking for an opening into which it could flow. Certainly, this can be dangerous. Mourners must learn to open the furnace of their rage to find the sparks of life energy they will need as they recover their sense of passion without violating others. They must use their fire to warm and not to burn.

In *Sukkat Kodesh,* the mourner must ignite the fuse that brings the fire to life, not to destroy, but to fuel the passion for living. As the mourner reclaims that spark, tending it with wise boundaries, he or she will have successfully mastered the tasks of *Sukkat Kodesh*.

One of my bereavement clients spent part of her sessions riding an exercise bike, which I kept in my office. While it was initially difficult to energize her ride, she soon picked up speed. As she pedaled, she would shriek at the many people who had wronged her. Riding the bike stoked her furnace. She became invigorated and then focused as she learned to express anger. She found the strength to stand up to the uncle who had abused her as a child, and she went on to start her own business and become an advocate for abused children, and finally, become a mother. Embracing her holy anger, she stood up for herself and for others and took her rightful place in the world.

In *Sukkat Kodesh*, we are purified by our rage. Physical exercise is an important tool in this tent. It gets the furnace going. It relieves stress and focuses passion as it stimulates the metabolism and helps purify, cleanse, and energize the self. It will help us care for physical needs, focus feelings, and stimulate the experience of holiness that comes with a well-tuned body. This contributes to our being able to leave *Sukkat Kodesh* with a sense of boundaries, renewed life energy, and a passion for the sacredness of individual destiny.

The Fourth Sukkah: *Sukkat Yisrael*

Struggling with the Forces of Heaven and Earth

The mourner has confronted grief's existential outrages and in the process has redefined his or her boundaries. As with my circle dancers in Colorado, sprawled on the ground and gazing up at the heavens, eyes filled with tears of joy and sorrow, it is time to look into the unknown to find a redefined partnership with life and with Holiness.

In this sukkah, *Sukkat Yisrael*, the mourner continues to wrestles with the forces at the core of the universe, but now the struggle is fueled not by anger, but by hope. Mourners struggle to try to assert authority over forces they cannot control. There is yearning in this sukkah, but unlike the heart-rent yearning in *Sukkat Kavod*, it is empowered with renewed life energy and the sense of secure boundaries they've harvested in *Sukkat Kodesh*.

Etymological roots connect *Yisrael* with words that mean "to persist," "to exert oneself," and "to persevere." It has cognates that suggest "to strive," "to fight," and "to contend," and also "rule," "authority," and "dominion." Significantly, it is also related to a word meaning "survivor." It is my hope that in this sukkah, the mourner will continue to strive for dominion over the challenges of mourning, and will emerge with the knowledge that he or she is a survivor.

Yisrael is, of course, one of the names of the Jewish people and the name of the Jewish State. It is also popularly defined as "one who wrestles with God." I have named this sukkah *Sukkat Yisrael* in honor of the patriarch Jacob, who received his new name, *Yisrael*, after having wrestled with a mysterious force, the "*ish*," and prevailing.

Who was the *ish* of Jacob's travails? While the word *ish* means simply "man," it is often assumed that Jacob's opponent was God, an angel, or his brother, Esau, whose birthright Jacob had stolen many years earlier. Perhaps Jacob sparred with his own inner *ish* and the guilt and rage he had carried since he fled Beersheba (and his brother's rage) many years before. Jacob's inner struggle on the night he thought might be his last, because his brother was coming to meet him with an army, is reminiscent of the late-night ruminations of one lost in the wilderness of grief.

In this tent, mourners strive to establish a partnership with something outside of themselves. There are two especially difficult things for humans to face. One is the sense that they are powerless over the forces that run the universe. The other is the fact that God's justice is, at best, hard to discern and, at worst, nonexistent. Initially in *Sukkat Yisrael*, the mourner strikes deals in order to stave off these bitter truths as well as the inevitability of the loss he or she is facing. It is here, after the jockeying to find some dominion over these existential questions, that the mourner works out a new relationship to God. "You lose your faith," as the wife of a policeman who died at the World Trade Center on 9/11 said, "but you get a whole new relationship with God."

People will do or believe almost anything to avoid feeling powerless. Katherine came to me shortly after her mother's suicide. She sat across from me with despondent eyes and a tattoo of a rose prominent on her shoulder. "My mother hated my tattoo," she moaned. "If only I hadn't gotten that tattoo, she would probably still be alive."

We've talked about this before: The belief that a tattoo or a haircut, a different doctor or having left the room at a crucial moment (the list is infinite) could have made a difference in averting the "severe decree" is also a kind of deal. As we have discussed, these beliefs, often voiced with the opening phrase "if only," are mere fleeting thoughts that soon become rigid beliefs to which mourners commit and may hold for a lifetime.

Mourners choose to suffer this undeserved guilt because they would much rather feel responsible for the suffering they face than be catapulted back to the terrible powerlessness in the earliest sukkah. It can be preferable to believe that they have some control over the forces that shape their lives—even if they are left with the burden of guilt—rather than to accept that they live in a capricious universe.

The belief that life is absurd is a painful foundation stone. So mourners wrestle. They try to make sense of the world. They appeal to a just God, even when no justice is evident. They seek some role for themselves in the workings of the universe. Like Job, they raise their voices in an effort to call forward a God who will offer, if not justice, at least an explanation. In so doing, they continue to redefine their understanding of that universe and of their relationship with Holiness. Like Job, near the end of his story, they put their hands over their mouths in recognition that the Holy Mystery can never be fully understood.

Humans struggle to find sustenance on this planet where terrible things often happen. Within *Sukkat Yisrael* mourners wrestle to find partnership with Holiness. This striving activates their own growth as they come to accept their responsibility for bringing that Holiness into the world.

Jewish liturgy encourages us to present our struggle to God as we reclaim our place on the earth. The petitional prayers of the weekday Amidah ask God for favors and describe the world as it should be. The Misheberach prayer for healing and other prayers also give us opportunities to bring our deepest needs before God. These prayers help us define the world we seek, as well as our place within it, finishing with the Aleinu, the prayer that comes after the Amidah and before the Kaddish. "Aleinu" means "it's upon us," concluding our prayers of petition with the recognition that if we want that ideal world we just asked for, we are going to have to make it happen. This recognition of our own role in bringing God's Holiness into the world ultimately allows us to transform our understanding of the God to whom we pray.

By conceiving of God in human terms, we dishonor God. Assuming that our words might move the Holy One to change history turns God into a kind of superhuman vending machine. Instead of embracing the part of ourselves that is created in the image of God, God is simplified into something created in *our* image. This does disservice to the Mysterious Unfolding of the Universe, YHVH, God's true name. It abdicates our responsibility to create the world as it should be.

In the years after the deaths of my mother and sister, I became a gardener. I learned about organic soil improvement and made an elaborate chart of companion plants. I planted seedlings close together so they could protect each other against garden pests and diseases. I concocted natural pesticides from mixtures of garlic, vinegar, and Tabasco, which left a residue on my vegetables so strong that I could harvest a salad that was already dressed.

Radishes were among the first seeds I put in the ground. They promised an early reward for my efforts, guaranteed to sprout within the week. I remember the anxiety that followed sowing those seeds. Nervously, I counted the days, with little faith that I would soon see life coming out of the ground.

My friends, native to the rural area to which I had escaped in a vain effort to run away from my history, laughed at my lack of faith. None of us understood then that my anxiety over the birth of these radishes reflected my shattered faith in the life process, as a result of the deaths of my mother and sister. Planting vegetables had been a bold step back into the river of life.

That summer, I harvested much of my menu from my own garden. From that, I learned that life continues. Even in the face of death, it was still possible to find partnership with the forces of life. Like Jacob, I had wrestled with the Great Mystery and had prevailed. I left *Sukkat Yisrael* with a sense of partnership with God, aka the Mysterious Unfolding of the Universe.

This wrestling with God helps us let go of a childish understanding of the way in which Holiness operates in the world. Not only do we embrace this new understanding of Holiness, we come to recognize our role in bringing God's Holiness into the world. This may be one of the most important teachings of the Kaddish.

The Kaddish, as I have mentioned before, is not a prayer about death. Rather, it is an invocation of the desire that God's name, the *Shammai Rabba/*the Great Name, be manifest throughout the world. This again reminds us of the prayer that precedes the Kaddish: the Aleinu. "It's upon [or "up to"] us." We are partners in creation.

In *Sukkot Kavod*, there was water, in the form of the tears that readily fell. In *Sukkot Kodesh*, there was the fire that had to blaze and then be banked in order to warm and not destroy. Here in *Sukkat Yisrael*, the element of creation is earth. When beset by suffering, we struggle to find our place on earth again as we renegotiate spirituality. We wrestle to find partnership with the forces that run the world. When entering the sukkah, we might encounter piles of earth mixed with rocks. The rocks represent obstacles faced as we cope with challenges, and are reminiscent of Jacob's hard pillow during an anxious nocturnal struggle.

Mourners ricochet among these four middle *sukkot*. They are propelled by yearning and heartbreak and also by hope. A dead end in one sukkah may force us to find a gateway to another. Mourners move back and forth and find unexpected comfort and answers, and often more questions. Over time, with attention to this grief-work, those who suffer come to terms with the words of the Kaddish. Creating a world filled with God's name now seems a reasonable goal, despite the fact that we may have been cursing God's name in a previous sukkah. Out of the darkness, in which the old concepts of faith have ceased to serve, a new theology emerges. The words of the Kaddish match the mourner's experience as he or she comes through the crisis of faith to articulate a new lived understanding of what is holy. With this awareness, we move to our last sukkah.

The Final Sukkah: *Sukkat Yirah-Yehudah*

Moments of Grace and Gratitude

> She . . . bore a son, and declared, "Now I will praise YHVH."
> Therefore she named him *Yehudah*.
> —Genesis 29:35

Sukkat Yirah-Yehudah is the remaining sukkah on the new mourner's path, the gateway to the Promised Land at the far edge of the wilderness. This is the place where the mourner dwells with a sense of having come to terms with grief. I could say having come to *peace* with grief, but in looking at the Hebrew word for peace, *shalom*, we see another example where the nuanced meaning of the word is lost in translation.

The meaning of *shalom* is a dance that requires continual attention, as the delicate balance called for by the process of peace is always shifting.

I don't use the word "acceptance" to describe the experience in this sukkah either. "Acceptance" can sound like bleak resignation or hopeless surrender to loss's severe decree. It sounds solid and final as well, implying that mourning comes to an end, as if we close accounts with what is gone forever. The mourner's path is not linear, but is instead a never-ending, ever-changing dance, from tent to tent and back again.

In *Sukkat Yirah-Yehudah*, we make fragile, hallowed peace with the difficult situation. We are no longer overcome with despair, anger, or the need to contest reality. The mourner has learned the steps of the dance of mourning. He or she feels ready to return to the world, knowing "normal" has radically changed, knowing the tents are still there when a need arises. Having learned the dance of each sukkah, the one who has travelled the wilderness of grief is not afraid.

Finding him- or herself in this final tent, the mourner has a stunning experience of *yirah*. It is not the fear of *Yirah-Pakhad,* but the uplifting sense of "radical amazement." This higher awe, touched by reverence and love, sees grief with a wider perspective, one unavailable in the earlier *sukkot*. Before, pain felt localized and personal. Now the mourner recognizes that loss and bereavement are common human experiences and that all humans must find a path through the wilderness of grief. The state of *Mochin de Gadlut,* expanded mind, discussed earlier in the book, has come to fruition.

In this sukkah, I have attached the name of *Yehudah*, or Judah, to the word for awe. One of Jacob/Israel's ten sons, *Yehudah* is also another name given to the descendants of Abraham. *Yehudah* was the ancestor of King David. The words "Judaism" and "Jews" come from Judah's name. The word *Yehudah* is related to words for gratitude or thanksgiving and is a word for praising God. At Judah's birth, his grateful mother, Leah, chose his name, saying, "Now I will praise YHVH, therefore I will call him *Yehudah*" (Genesis 29:35).

Judah, like his father and so many Biblical heroes, was not flawless. He played a major role in his brother Joseph's initial misfortune, initiating Joseph's sale to the Ishmaelites on their way to Egypt (Genesis 37:26–27), which preceded the Israelites' four hundred years of slavery. Judah then joined his brothers in deceiving their father as to the nature of Joseph's disappearance (Genesis 37:32–35).

However, Judah is a model for the possibility of change. In addition to other demonstrations of growth and maturity, he showed high character when he stood up to Joseph in Egypt, offering himself as a prisoner in place of his brother Benjamin (Genesis 44:18–34). Because of his personal growth, he is rewarded as the progenitor of the Davidic line from which, tradition holds, the Messiah will sprout to bring peace and redemption. These reversals of fortune and the accompanying Messianic promise make Judah's name a good one to mark this sukkah in which healing, the fruit of transformation, will be proclaimed. In a hasidic commentary, Judah is seen as one who experiences God's grace. Despite actions that were unscrupulous, good things came to pass with little effort on his part. This is another of the reasons I have chosen his name to mark the sukkah at the far edge of the wilderness of grief in which the mystery of healing begins to reveal itself. For, despite all the hard work of mourning, healing is likely to appear as a mysterious act of grace, as if happened upon by chance.

Here in *Sukkat Yirah-Yehudah*, the mourner moves from grief's intense struggles to a sense of amazement. There is an aura of gratitude, not for the loss, of course, but for the mourner's survival and for the harvest from the struggle to make it through.

Celebration and gratitude are primary modes of prayer. The liturgy is filled with praises of thanksgiving. Most blessings are constructed as blessings of gratitude. At the beginning of the month and on holidays, *Hallel* (Psalms 113–118) is recited, which employs a cognate of Judah's name, *Hodu*, to praise God. In Hebrew wordplay, we see that the spelling of *Yehudah* contains YHVH, the four-letter name of God, and the fourth letter of the alphabet, *dalet*, which can be used as a stand-in for the four-letter name. How appropriate for the sukkah in which God's presence is so palpable!

While they are often overlooked in the opaque view of mourning as continual suffering, it needs to be acknowledged that within the grief process there are little moments of grace when the mourner may feel like bursting out in song. Such moments may be felt the first time the mourner sleeps through the night without awaking in an anxious state, in a pool of perspiration. Often, those who suffer are so steeped in the agony of grief that they are not able to notice anything outside of themselves. All of a sudden, they may be overcome by surprising ecstasy when the sound of a bird unexpectedly makes their heart soar. It may be delight taken in playing with a child or a pet, or perhaps the thrill of a beautiful garden. After feeling that it would be impossible to ever again experience unbridled joy, the mourner is accosted by a moment in which he or she is astonished by that joy.

Initially this "*Yehudah* moment" is likely to be followed by a startled or guilty reaction, as well as the thought, "Oh my goodness, I never thought I would feel that sort of thing again!" And very often that awareness may plunge the mourner into a bout of survivor guilt, with him or her exclaiming, "How dare I feel joy when I have lost . . . !" If there has been a death, there may be a sense that the deceased is being betrayed. If there has been a divorce, the belief that it will be impossible to ever be happy again has been challenged.

I like to think of these astonishing moments of unbidden happiness as moments of grace. Each of them creates a metaphorical pearl. The mourner collects these moments of gratitude and praise and at some point exclaims, "I have a whole necklace!" This is the (surprising) evidence that he or she has moved on from the *sukkot* of the wilderness of grief and has almost reached the Promised Land.

I had such a moment one day several years after the deaths of my mother and sister. I was driving through the mountains, not far from where I was living in rural Northern California. I came to a ridge overlooking a deep valley. It was a beautiful, bright place just beyond the shadows of a dark and sacred redwood grove through which I had just driven. I had never been there before.

I parked my car by the side of the road and stood looking down into the dark forest from which I had just emerged. Feeling the caress of the warm midday sun on my skin, I surveyed the new landscape in which I found myself. My heart soared as I took in the beauty of the place as well as the startling recognition that I was emerging from the wilderness of grief. Standing on that ridge under the high sun, I basked in the mystery that is healing. I began to dance. My mourning had turned into dancing. While in the decades that have followed there have been times when the scabs were rubbed off, when the wounds that had healed were reopened, and I had to return to the other *sukkot* to revisit the losses, having danced on that mountain emboldens me to return for deeper wisdom and greater healing.

The fourth element, air, is found in *Sukkat Yirah-Yehudah*. It represents full-breathed sighs of relief, as the winds seem to blow the suffering into flight. It is also reminiscent of the silver trumpet blown by the Levites in the Temple of David's imagining when the daily psalms of praise were read. The silver wind instrument heralds the triumph and celebration that come when struggle is transcended and there is victory over pain. Slowly, life asserts itself again and again.

On this far edge of the wilderness, with the Promised Land in sight, the mourner who has dwelled in the *sukkot* of grief holds the gleanings of these separate places of healing as if they are one place, enriched by the presence of the four elements of creation—water, fire, earth, and air—representing the wholeness, the *shleimut*, that is at the core of healing.

In the Talmud's discussion of the holiday of Sukkot, those who dwell in the sukkah are commanded to gather the "four species" native to the Land of Israel, which are used to celebrate the holiday. These are the *lulav*, or palm branch; the *etrog*, or citron; the *hadas*, or myrtle; and the *aravah*, or willow. The celebrant takes the four species in hand and shakes them. They are then gathered to the heart, and words of gratitude and praise are recited. Standing in *Sukkat Yirah-Yehudah*, we do the same:

> *Hodu l'Adonai ki tov, li l'olam chasdo.*
> Praise God because God is good.
> God's loving kindness goes on forever.

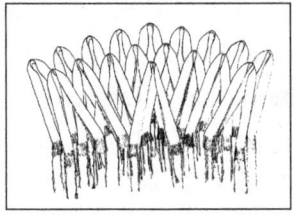

Source Acknowledgments

The sources of the citations throughout the book are listed below with the names of the publishers and authors; they have generously granted permission to print excerpts from the works indicated, for which we are most grateful. Every effort has been made to locate copyright holders of original material.

In most cases, the *Encyclopedia Judaica* has been the source for the spelling of transliterated words. In addition the *American Heritage Dictionary* was consulted regarding the spelling of Hebrew words which are in common English usage; however, the convention used is to transliterate the Hebrew letter ח with the English letters *kh* except when the ח comes at the beginning of the word, as in the word *chevra*, or when the word is commonly spelled with *ch* as in *Pesach*. The Hebrew letter צ has been transliterated with the letters *tz*.

The *Hebrew and English Lexicon of the Old Testament* by Francis Brown, S. R. Driver, and C. A. Briggs was the source of my exploration of Hebrew roots and cognates.

Agnon, S.Y. *The Days of Awe*. New York: Schocken Books, 1948.

Albo, Joseph, Ben Sira, Baal Shem Tov, Bhaya Ibn Pakuda, M.H. Luzzato, Moses Hasid. *A Treasury of Jewish Quotations*. Ed. Joseph L. Baron. New York: Jason Aronson, Inc., 1985.

Becker, Ernest. Class lectures, San Franciso State College, 1968.

Biblical quotes are from *The TANAKH: The New JPS Translation According to the Traditional Hebrew Text*. Copyright 1985 by the Jewish Publication Society.

Used by permission; I have adjusted some passages to include gender-free language.

Bly, Robert. "The Holy Longing." In *News of the Universe.* San Francisco: Sierra Club Books, 1980.

Heschel, Abraham Joshua. *Man's Quest for God.* Reprinted with permission of Charles Scribner's Sons, an imprint of Macmillan Publishing Company. Copyright 1954 Abraham Joshua Heschel; copyright renewed 1982 Hannah Susannah Heschel and Sylvia Heschel.

Holmyard, E. J. Extract from *Alchemy.* London: Penguin Books, 1957. Reprinted by permission of Penguin Books Limited, London.

Karo, Joseph quoted in R. J. Zwi Werblowsky, *Joseph Karo: Lawyer and Mystic.* Used by permission. This quote was originally encountered in Edward Hoffman, *The Way of Splendor: Jewish Mysticism and Modern Psychology.* Boulder: Shambala Publications, 1981; reprinted by Jason Aronson, Northvale, N.J. 1989. p.150.

Keleman, Stanley. *Living Your Dying.* New York: Random House, 1974.

Kitzer Shulkhan Arukh quoted in Solomon Ganzfried, *Kitzer Shulkhan Arukh: Code of Jewish Laws.* Rockaway Beach, N. Y.: Hebrew Publishing Company, 1991.

Kramer, Kenneth. *The Sacred Art of Dying: How World Religions Understand Death.* New York: Paulist Press, 1988.

Lamm, Maurice. *The Jewish Way in Death and Mourning.* New York: Jonathan David, 1969.

Levine, Stephen. *Who Dies? An Investigation of Conscious Living and Conscious Dying.* Garden City, N.J.: Doubleday, Anchor Books, 1982.

Maudsley, Henry. Quoted in Joyce McDougall, *Theaters of the Body: A Psychoanalytic Approach to Psychosomatic Illness.* W.W. Norton, New York, 1989.

Metzger, Deena. *A Sabbath among the Ruins.* Berkeley: Parallax Press, 1992. Excerpts are from the preface and from the poems, "The Bird in the Heart of the Tree" and "The Death of the Wolf."

———. *Looking for the Faces of God.* Berkeley: Parallax Press, 1989. Excerpt from the poem "Under the Sorrow Tree."

———. *Writing for Your Life: A Guide and Companion to the Inner Worlds.* San Francisco: Harper Collins, 1992.

Omer-Man, Jonathan. Lectures and personal discussions.

Petuchowski, Jakob. *Understanding Jewish Prayer*. Hoboken, N.J.: KTAV Publishing, 1972.

Prayers. Most translations and transliterations are adapted from: *The Jewish Mourner's Handbook*. Ed. William Cutter. West Orange, N. J.: Behrman House, 1992. The translation of the *Viddui* was done with Yaffa Weisman and the translation of the Shema is my own.

Rafael, Simcha Paull. *Jewish Attitudes Toward the Afterlife.* Northvale, N.J.: Jason Aronson, forthcoming.

Riemer, Jack. *Jewish Reflections on Death.* New York: Schocken Books, 1976.

Rumi from *Rumi, We Are Three*. Translated by Coleman Barks. Athens, GA: Maypop Books, 1987.

Schachter-Shalomi, Zalman. Workshop at Esalen Institute, January 1990.

Scholem, Gershom. From *Zohar, the Book of Splendor*. New York: Schocken Books, 1977. Reprinted by permission of Schocken Books, published by Pantheon Books, a division of Random House, Inc.

Semahot. From *The Tractate "Mourning: (Semahot) Regulations Related to Death, Burial, and Mourning."* Ed. Eduard Kutscher. New Haven: Yale University Press, 1966.

T.A. From *The Talmudic Anthology*. Ed. Louis I. Newman and Samuel Spitz. New York: Berhrman House, 1945. Other Talmudic quotes, as well as quotes from the *Shulkhan Aruch: Yoreh De'ah*, and some Biblical quotes are my own translations or have been revised to attempt to provide language that is gender-neutral.

Viddui. Translation by Yaffa Weisman.

Zohar. From *Zohar: The Book of Enlightenment*. Trans. Daniel Chanan Matt. Ramsey, N. J.: Paulist Press, 1983.

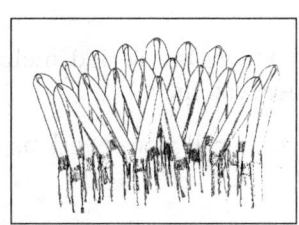

Glossary

Agadah—Recorded stories, legends, folklore, rabbinic homilies; distinguished from Halakhah, which consists of writing about Jewish religious law.

Amidah—"The standing prayer," usually recited silently, except on Shabbat morning when recited communally. It forms the centerpiece of the Jewish prayer service.

Aninut—The period of mourning that takes place between the time of death and the burial.

Avelut—Mourning, the mourning period.

Bikur Cholim—The mitzvah of visiting the sick.

B'tzelem Elohim—In the image of God (Genesis 1:27).

Chevra—A community of friends or like-minded people.

Chevra Kadisha—The "holy society" responsible for the care of the body from the time of death until the burial.

Dayan Haemet—"God the True Judge"; a blessing in praise of "God, the true Judge" is recited upon hearing news of a death.

Day of Atonement—Yom Kippur, day of fasting and repentance, the holiest day of the Jewish year.

Days of Awe—The High Holy Day period including Rosh Hashanah, Yom Kippur, and the ten days between them.

El Malai Rakhamim—A memorial prayer, asking God for compassion for the soul of the deceased.

Gan Eden—The Garden of Eden, paradise.

Gehinnom—Hell or purgatory, the place where souls are cleansed of sins committed during their life.

Gemilut chasaidim—One of the mitzvot, instructing us to engage in acts of loving kindness, good deeds on behalf of others.

Halakha—Jewish law, derived both from the Torah and the Oral Tradition. Derives from the verb *L'lekhet*, which means to walk, as in walking through life.

Hamakom—The Place, a name of God.

Hazkarat Haneshamot—The name of the prayer performed in memory of the deceased; literally, the naming of souls.

Hesped—A eulogy, from the Hebrew word that means "to wail" or "lament."

Hillel—A great sage, living at the time of second Temple, known for the phrase, "What is hateful to you, do not do unto your neighbor."

Job—A Biblical book, telling the story of the righteous man, Job, and his suffering and faith.

Kabbala—The Jewish mystical tradition.

Kaddish—A prayer recited for the deceased, up to a year following the burial, on the anniversary of the death, and at some memorial services. This prayer is said for members of one's immediate family. Versions of the Kaddish are also said at transitions in the prayer service, but are not used as prayers for the deceased. A minyan is required for Kaddish.

Keriah—The ritual of tearing a garment upon hearing of the death of a close relative.

Korbanot—Sacrifices, particularly those offered in the ancient Temple in Jerusalem; literally, closeness or relatedness.

Magen David—The star of David, literally, the shield of David.

Matzevah (pl. **matzevot**)—A monument or tombstone; in the Bible, also referred to altars.

Mekom Hanekhama—A place of comfort.

Mensch—Yiddish word for a decent or proper person.

Midrash—A genre of literature which includes lore, myth, homiletics, law, and investigation into the meaning of the Torah; part of the Oral Tradition.

Mikvah—A pool of water for purposes of ritual immersion in rites of purification.

Minyan—Traditionally, a group of ten men whose attendance is required to recite specific prayers. Today in more egalitarian communities, women are counted in the minyan. A minyan is required to recite the Kaddish.

Mitzvah (pl., **mitzvot**)—Commandment or obligation of Jewish living; colloquially, a good deed.

Neshama—The soul, breath.

Olam Haba—The world to come, to be ushered in by the Messiah.

Olam Haneshamot—The World of Souls, through which the soul travels after death, according to the Jewish mystical tradition.

Olam Hazeh—The material world, the world in which human life takes place; literally, this world.

Onen—An individual mourner during the period of *aninut* (the time between the death and the burial), a period in which many restrictions are placed on the mourner's behavior.

Oral Law—Interpretation of the Written Law, or Torah, traditionally considered to be revealed by God, along with the Written Law, to Moses on Mount Sinai.

Psalms—Biblical book of hymns and poetry; its authorship is ascribed to King David.

Rabban Gamliel—A prominent teacher of first-century Palestinian Jewry, responsible for many reforms including many regarding burial and mourning practices.

Rakhamim—Compassion, derived from the same root as the word *womb*; one of God's significant attributes.

Rekhem—The womb.

Rosh Hashanah—The New Year on the Jewish calendar.

Seudat Havra'ah—The Meal of Consolation, prepared by the community for the mourner after the funeral.

Shabbat—The Seventh day, the day of rest, commemorating God's day of rest after creating the world and all its creatures; the injunction *Zakhor et hashabbat!* ("Remember Shabbat!") is the fourth of the Ten Commandments.

Shaliakh—A messenger, often a legal "agent" in Halakhic transactions.

Shalom—Peace, a salutation used as both "hello" and "goodbye," stemming from the root m.l.w (ShLM), whole.

Shalom Aleikhem—A greeting meaning "peace be with you."

Shamai—A leading teacher of first-century Palestinian Jewry, often involved in controversy with Hillel regarding interpretation of the law.

Shavuot—A festival of thanksgiving commemorating the giving of the Law at Mount Sinai; one of the four days on which the *Yizkor* prayer is recited.

Shekhinah—God's Divine Presence, considered to be the feminine aspect of the Divine.

Sheloshim—The thirty-day period following burial; its close signals the end of the initial mourning period for all close relatives except parents.

Shema—The central statement of Jewish faith and theology, emphasizing God's uniqueness and affirming acceptance of God's sovereignty and oneness; literally, "Listen!"

Shemini Atzeret—The holiday following Sukkot on which the *Yizkor* prayer is recited and a prayer for rain is said.

Shemira—The ritual of sitting with the body from the time of death to the burial, performed by the *shomrim*; literally means "watching" or "guarding."

Shiva—Seven days of mourning period immediately following burial; Sephardic Jews refer to this period as *Siete*, which, like the word *shiva*, literally means "seven."

Shofar—A trumpet made from a ram's horn, blown during the month of Elul and on Rosh Hashanah.

Shomrim—Those who watch the body from death to burial, often reciting psalms.

Siddur—Prayer book.

Taharah—Ritual purification or cleaning of a dead body.

Tallit—A prayer shawl.

Talmud—Commentary based on the discussions and opinions of the rabbis over several centuries (beginning circa 450 C.E.) about the Torah's teachings and their halakhic expression in daily life. It is comprised of the Mishnah's attempts to clarify the Torah and the Gemarah, which is a commentary on the Mishnah. One Talmud was compiled in Palestine and another, which is more authoratative, was compiled in Babylonia.

Teshuva—Repentance and return, an inward spiritual turning.

Tikkun olam—Healing the world.

Torah—The first five books of the Bible (Pentateuch), which are traditionally believed to have been revealed to Moses on Mount Sinai; in addition it is often used as a generic term referring to the complete body of Jewish teaching.

Tumah—Ritually impure, or unable to perform certain practices before having gone through the purification process.

Tzedakah—One of the mitzvot, instructing Jews to engage in righteous acts, often translated as charity, but derives for the Hebrew word for justice. Like all the mitzvot, this is not an option, but a commandment of Jewish life.

Tzimtzum—Kabbalistic notion of Divine contraction.

Tzitzit—Fringes on the four corners of the tallit.

Viddui—A prayer of confession, versions of which are recited on Yom Kippur, as a bedtime prayer, and on the deathbed.

Water of Lustration—A mixture of water and herbs used in the ancient Temple for the purification ritual.

Written Law—Law received by Moses in written form, traditionally the Five Books of Moses (Pentateuch).

Yahrzeit—Yiddish word for the anniversary of the death. The comparable Ladino (Sephardic) term is *Años*.

Yekara de'hayye—Aramaic, "for the good of the living."

Yizkor—Literally, "Remember." Opening word of prayer commemorating the dead, which is recited in memorial services on Yom Kippur, *Shemini Atzeret*, Pesach, and Shavuot.

Yom Kippur—The Day of Atonement.

Zohar—Fundamental work of Jewish mysticism; a mystical commentary on the *Torah*.

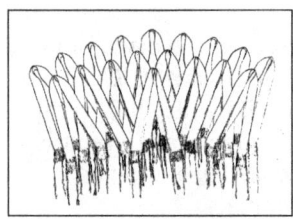

Books to Consult for Further Help

Jewish Texts and Law

Cutter, William, ed. *The Jewish Mourner's Handbook.* West Orange, N.J.: Behrman House, 1992.

Elkins, Dov Peretz. *The Wisdom of Judaism: An Introduction to the Values of the Talmud.* Woodstock, Vt.: Jewish Lights Publishing, 2007.

Epstein, Isadore, trans. *The Babylonian Talmud.* London: Soncino, 1938.

Klein, Isaac. *A Guide to Jewish Religious Practice.* New York: Jewish Theological Seminary of America, 1979.

Lamm, Maurice. *The Jewish Way in Death and Mourning.* New York: Jonathan David, 1969.

Plaut, W. Gunther. *The Torah.* New York: The Union of American Hebrew Congregations, 1981.

Roth, Cecil and Geoffrey Wigoder, ed. *Encyclopedia Judaica.* New York: Macmillan, 1972.

The TANAKH: The New JPS Translation According to the Traditional Hebrew Text. Philadelphia: Jewish Publication Society, 1985.

Weiss, Abner. *Death and Bereavement: A Halakhic Guide.* Hoboken, N.J.: KTAV, 1991.

Commentary on Jewish Text, Law and Living

Breslov Research Institute. *The Empty Chair: Finding Hope and Joy—Timeless Wisdom from a Hasidic Master, Rebbe Nachman of Breslov.* Woodstock, Vt.: Jewish Lights Publishing, 1996.

Broner, E. M. *Mournings and Mourning: A Kaddish Journal.* San Francisco: HarperCollins, 1994.

Cooper, David A. *The Handbook of Jewish Meditation Practices: A Guide for Enriching the Sabbath and Other Days of Your Life.* Woodstock, Vt.: Jewish Lights Publishing, 2000.

Cutter, William, ed. *Healing and the Jewish Imagination: Spiritual and Practical Perspectives on Judaism and Health.* Woodstock, Vt.: Jewish Lights Publishing, 2007.

Friedman, Dayle A, ed. *Jewish Pastoral Care,* 2nd Edition: *A Practical Handbook from Traditional and Contemporary Sources.* Woodstock, Vt.: Jewish Lights Publishing, 2005.

———. *Jewish Visions for Aging: A Professional Guide for Fostering Wholeness.* Woodstock, Vt.: Jewish Lights Publishing, 2008.

Gillman, Neil. *The Death of Death: Resurrection and Immortality in Jewish Thought.* Woodstock, Vt.: Jewish Lights Publishing, 2000.

———. *The Way Into Encountering God in Judaism.* Woodstock, Vt.: Jewish Lights Publishing, 2004.

Heschel, A. J. *Man's Quest for God: Studies in Prayer and Symbolism.* New York: Charles Scribner's Sons, 1954.

———. *The Sabbath: Its Meaning for Modern Man.* Boston: Shambhala, 2003.

Hoffman, Lawrence A. *The Way Into Jewish Prayer.* Woodstock, Vt.: Jewish Lights Publishing, 2004.

Kamenetz, Rodger. *The History of Last Night's Dream: Discovering the Hidden Path to the Soul.* New York: Harper Collins, 2007.

Kaplan, Aryeh. *Jewish Meditation: A Practical Guide.* New York: Schocken Books, 1985.

Levy, Naomi. *To Begin Again: The Journey Toward Comfort, Strength and Faith in Difficult Times.* New York: Ballantine Books, 1999.

Milgram, Goldie. *Reclaiming Judaism as a Spiritual Practice: Holy Days and Shabbat.* Woodstock, Vt.: Jewish Lights Publishing, 2004.

Olitzky, Kerry, and Ronald Isaacs. *A Jewish Mourner's Handbook.* Hoboken, N.J.: KTAV, 1991.

Riemer, Jack. *Jewish Reflections on Death.* New York: Schocken Books, 1976.

———, and Nathaniel Stampfer. *So That Your Values Live On: Ethical Wills and How to Prepare Them.* Woodstock, Vt.: Jewish Lights Publishing, 1993.

———, *Wrestling with the Angel.* New York: Schocken Books, 1995.

Spitz, Elie Kaplan. *Healing from Despair: Choosing Wholeness in a Broken World.* With Erica Shapiro Taylor. Woodstock, Vt.: Jewish Lights Publishing, 2008.

Strassfeld, Michael. *A Book of Life: Embracing Judaism as a Spiritual Practice.* Woodstock, Vt.: Jewish Lights Publishing, 2006.

Siegel, Richard, Michael Strassfeld, and Sharon Strassfeld. *The Jewish Catalog*, Volume I. Philadelphia: Jewish Publication Society, 1973.

Spitz, Elie Kaplan. *Does the Soul Survive? A Jewish Journey to Belief in Afterlife, Past Lives & Living with Purpose.* Woodstock, Vt.: Jewish Lights Publishing, 2001.

Waskow, Arthur. *Seasons of Our Joy.* Boston: Beacon Books, 1991.

Literature of Comfort

Klein, Sandra Jacoby. *Heavenly Hurts: Surviving AIDS-Related Deaths and Losses.* Amityville, N.Y.: Baywood Publishing Co. Inc., 1998.

Kushner, Harold. *When Bad Things Happen to Good People.* New York: Avon Books, 1981.

Levine, Stephen. *Who Dies? An Investigation of Conscious Living and Conscious Dying.* Garden City, N.J.: Anchor Books, 1982. A spiritual approach to healing.

LifeLights. A series of pamphlets offering support and comfort from Jewish tradition; several are on topics of mourning and loss, including "Taking the Time You Need to Mourn Your Loss" by Anne Brener; "Mourning a Miscarriage" by Rabbi Nina Beth Cardin; "Coping with the Death of a Spouse" by Rabbi Rachel Cowan; "When Someone You Love Is Dying" by Rabbi Amy Eilberg; "Bringing Your Sadness to God" by Rabbi Harold M. Schulweis; "From Death through Shiva" by Dr. Ron Wolfson. Woodstock, Vt.: Jewish Lights Publishing.

Liss-Levinson, Nechama. *When a Grandparent Dies: A Kid's Own Remembering Workbook for Dealing with Shiva and the Year Beyond.* Woodstock, Vt.: Jewish Lights Publishing, 1995.

Metzger, Deena. *A Sabbath Among the Ruins.* Berkeley: Parallax Press, 1992. Poetry.

———. *Looking for the Faces of God.* Berkeley: Parallax Press, 1989.

———. *Writing for Your Life: A Guide and Companion to the Inner Worlds.* San Francisco: HarperCollins, 1992.

Moffat, Mary Jane. *In the Midst of Winter: Selections from the Literature of Mourning.* New York: Random House, 1982.

Olitzky, Kerry M. *Grief in Our Seasons: A Mourner's Kaddish Companion.* Woodstock, Vt.: Jewish Lights Publishing, 1998.

Richards, Marty. *Caresharing: A Reciprocal Approach to Caregiving and Care Receiving in the Complexities of Aging, Illness or Disability.* Woodstock, Vt.: SkyLight Paths, 2008.

Weintraub, Simkha Y., ed., and the National Center for Jewish Healing. *Healing of Soul, Healing of Body: Spiritual Leaders Unfold the Strength & Solace in Psalms.* Woodstock, Vt.: Jewish Lights Publishing, 1994.

Wolfson, Ron. *A Time to Mourn, a Time to Comfort,* 2nd Ed.: *A Guide to Jewish Bereavement and Comfort.* Woodstock, Vt.: Jewish Lights Publishing, 2005.

Prayer Books

Central Conference of American Rabbis. *Gates of Prayer: The New Union Prayerbook.* New York, Central Conference of American Rabbis, 1975.

Congregation Beth El of the Sudbury River Valley. *Vetaher Libenu.* Sudbury, Mass.: Congregation Beth El of the Sudbury River Valley, 1980.

Falk, Marcia. *The Book of Blessings.* San Francisco: HarperSanFrancisco, 1996.

Harlow, Jules. *Siddur Sim Shalom: A Prayerbook for Shabbat, Festivals, and Weekdays.* New York: The Rabbinical Assembly, The United Synagogue of America, 1985.

Hoffman, Lawrence A., ed. *My People's Prayer Book: Traditional Prayers, Modern Commentaries.* Multi-volume series. Woodstock, Vt.: Jewish Lights Publishing, 1997–.

Kol Haneshamah. Wyncote, Pa.: The Reconstructionist Press, 1989.

P'nai Or. *Or Chadash: A New Light.* Philadelphia: P'nai Or Religious Fellowship, 1989.

Western Approaches to Death and Bereavement

Becker, Ernest. *The Denial of Death*. New York: The Free Press, 1973.

Frankl, Viktor. *Man's Search for Meaning*. New York: Simon and Schuster, 1959.

Kübler-Ross, Elisabeth. *Death: The Final Stage of Growth*. Englewood Cliffs, N.J.: Prentice-Hall, 1975.

———. *On Death and Dying*. New York: MacMillan, 1969.

———. *The Wheel of Life: A Memoir of Living and Dying*. New York: Touchstone, 1997.

Staudacher, Carol. *Beyond Grief*. Oakland, Calif.: New Harbinger Publications, 1987.

Tatelbaum, Judy. *The Courage to Grieve*. New York: Harper and Row, 1980.

Worden, J. William. *Grief Counseling & Grief Therapy: A Handbook for the Mental Health Practitioner*. New York: Springer Publishing Company, 1991.

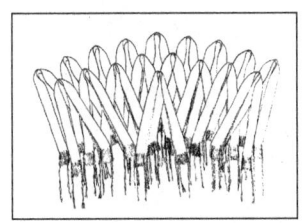

CPSIA information can be obtained
at www.ICGtesting.com
Printed in the USA
BVHW011651060520
579237BV00013B/301